DAUGHTER OF HEAVEN

Also by Leslie Li

Bittersweet: A Novel

DAUGHTER OF HEAVEN

—— A MEMOIR WITH EARTHLY RECIPES ——

LESLIE LI

ARCADE PUBLISHING • NEW YORK

Arcade Publishing books may be purchased in bulk at special discounts for sales promotion, corporate gifts, fund-raising, or educational purposes. Special editions can also be created to specifications. For details, contact the Special Sales Department, Arcade Publishing, 307 West 36th Street, 11th Floor, New York, NY 10018 or arcade@skyhorsepublishing.com.

Arcade Publishing® is a registered trademark of Skyhorse Publishing, Inc.®, a Delaware corporation.

Visit our website at www.arcadepub.com.

10 9 8 7 6 5 4 3 2 1

Library of Congress Cataloging-in-Publication Data is available on file.

ISBN: 978-1-61145-695-0

Printed in the United States of America

To Anton

Contents

Recipes

PREFACE
SUCKING ON A STONE

W hen we were little, my mother thought of a uniquely devious way of getting my sisters and me to eat our dinner. It was usual at that time (the 1950s) for mothers of small children who were dilatory at the table to employ the classic admonition, "Just think of the starving children in China." Or India. Or Africa.

My mother told us a story instead.

The story was based on an incident that occurred in the late 1940s, when my family was living in China and my sisters and I were too young to recall. My father, freshly graduated from the University of Chicago, had been summoned back to China by his father, Li Zongren, who had decided to run for the vice presidency of Nationalist China. He felt that his son's knowledge of communications and technology would benefit his campaign, headquartered in polyglot Shanghai. He also wanted to meet his American daughter-in-law, Genevieve — truncated to a more pronounceable Jenée for his benefit — and his two American granddaughters: Marcy, three years old, and me, half that age. Two more granddaughters would follow in fairly rapid succession: Wendye, born in Shanghai, and Gerrie, in Hong Kong.

My parents set up house in Shanghai's French Concession, where one evening, as they were returning home from a night out with friends, my mother noticed three beggars dressed in rags squatting by the roadside. They were poking at the contents of two tin cans — one in its original shape, the other flattened out into a serviceable pan — cooking on a small brazier. Inside the taller receptacle was freshly boiled rice with a blanket of cabbage leaves, wilted from the steam. In the ersatz frying pan, several stones sizzled in a dollop of oil. The men paid no attention to my mother, or to anyone or anything else for that matter. They filled their bowls with the rice and cabbage, placed a stone or two on top, and began, lustily, to eat.

"They were so poor," my mother told us, her voice betraying both sympathy for the men and gentle reproof toward her daughters, "they had only a bowl of rice and a few cabbage leaves for dinner. Instead of meat they had to fry stones for something savory to eat. They sucked on that hot, oily, salty stone, spat it out into their bowl, ate another mouthful of rice, then picked up the stone again with their chopsticks and sucked on it some more, until all the rice and cabbage were gone. Imagine! Sucking on stones!"

Now, I was old enough to know what plain stones tasted like: bland, perhaps only slightly bitter, and, no matter how well you rinsed them, gritty. And I was young enough that frying stones in oil — peanut, of course, with some shredded scallion, slivered gingerroot, and minced

fresh garlic — was outside the range of my experience or
abilities. My mother's rationale in telling us that story was
to make us appreciate the bounty before us, to shame us
into finishing the food that lingered on our plate. But, my
not being an adult and never having sucked on fried stones,
the anecdote worked somewhat differently in my child's
mind. I did indeed imagine it: a mound, a heap, an enormous quantity of rice and vegetables . . . and a single stone
capable of flavoring it all. That story, recounted with an altogether different purpose in mind, had touched my imagination, which in turn stimulated my senses: my olfactory
nerves, my taste buds, my salivary glands. Instead of feeling sorry for the three ravenous men, or scooping up the
last few forkfuls of mashed potatoes or string beans or
whatever was getting cold and congealing on my plate, I
sucked hard on the virtual stone my mother had conjured
and found it — just like the beggars must have found their
actual ones — delicious.

A spiritual aphorism states that there are sermons in
stones. But as this is a memoir, there are only stories in
mine. Some of the stones contained herein may be considered the heart of the meal, as in my mother's cautionary
tale. Some serve as a condiment or a table setting or the
proper lighting, and come in all shapes and sizes. Massive,
like the soaring limestone cliffs above my grandmother's
outdoor kitchen in Guilin, China. Infinitesimal, like the
grains of sand in the backyard sandbox of our suburban
New York home that she usurped from its rightful owners
to plant her first Chinese vegetable garden in America.
Man-made, like the flagstone patio of our house against
whose smooth steps she sharpened her trusty cleaver, a

female Jupiter wielding her mighty thunderbolt. Symbolic, like the finger game of rock-scissors-paper that my sisters and I played with our grandfather before the cooks Regina and Aiying called us to the dinner table. Solemn, like the feng shui gravestones in front of which my father and I set out platters of pork, chicken, and fish and lit red candles and strings of red firecrackers to frighten away the hungry ghosts. Ghosts not tempted to eat stones.

Food, of course — the growing of it, the cooking of it, the people who prepared it, the people who ate it, the rituals surrounding it, the events which required it in splendid abundance — is the foundation of this book, as surely as rice and vegetables are the foundation of any Chinese meal. As for the savory stone which, if it is worth its salt, should flavor the repast from start to finish, from soup to nuts — that must be supplied by the stories themselves.

"Dessert" follows some tales in the form of a recipe or two. A caveat: these recipes will not (necessarily) help you lose weight, lower your cholesterol, or make you fit for life. They are not for people who push the food around on their plates and peck at the edges, for devotees of *cuisine minceur,* or for the delicate or the over-refined palate. The dragon's share of the dishes I've chosen to include draws upon the vast repertoire of Chinese home cooking — daily fare, to be eaten with gusto. Most of them were prepared by my Chinese paternal grandmother, Nai-nai, or by her cooks Dashao, First Cook, and Jiunyang, in the kitchens of her various homes: those scattered across China where she ran from pillar to post to evade war and revolution; the penthouse apartment overlooking Hong Kong's racetrack; the house in Havana, Cuba, where she lived in exile for eight years while awaiting her American visa; the Dutch-Tudor house in Riverdale where she lived with my family for fifteen years; and finally the house in Guilin that she had built in 1941 as a wedding present for my parents (who, due to the Japanese occupation, never did live in it) and where I was reunited with her in 1986 and again in 1990, the year she celebrated her hundredth birthday.

A second caveat. At first sight, my mother's scant appearance in these pages might be likened to an *amuse-bouche*, the meal's precursor, a promise of things to come, from which she is inconspicuously absent, having served her purpose. On a deeper level, she is the executive chef of the kitchen, the power behind the scenes. She is the theater director of the noisier episodes of the drama (or human comedy), which she quiets with a minimal gesture, a simple glance. She may also be considered a deus ex machina who descends from on high in her golden chariot only when absolutely needed on earth: for the solution of intractable problems, for the smoothing of ruffled feathers, for the restoration of peace and harmony. Outwardly, she is like the most proper of Chinese children: seen (just barely) and not heard (unless rarely). Actually, she is the Taoist absence or vacuum through which everything-that-is comes into being and manifests itself as a presence. When my mother does appear in these pages, she fills them, you may be sure, but quietly, unobtrusively.

Again let me forewarn any reader expecting a traditional cookbook in these pages that the stories that precede the recipes are the meat of the meal. I also confess that a culinary memoir is an odd attempt for a novelist who has for a long time recoiled from the kitchen and everything it represents. There was a time when my revulsion to cooking went uninterrupted for years, on the verge of becoming permanent. Nai-nai, who lived to cook even more than she loved to eat, had an unwitting hand in my aversion to the culinary arts and, many years later, a similar hand in reversing that condition. But more about that later. I now hate cooking — not cooking per se, but carving out the time necessary to make a satisfying meal — only when I am writing or reading or engaged in an activity to such an extent that I loathe tearing myself away to perform something so mundane, so essential, as preparing good food to eat.

Perhaps part of my aversion, or reluctance, is that I came late to cooking, and even later to Chinese cooking. I was not one of those fortunate people who learned to cook at their mothers' — or grandmothers' or aunts' or family chefs' — knees and Garland stoves, who have since gone on to have their own syndicated food columns or open their own four-star restaurants or gourmet cooking schools. I am not mesmerized by the dizzying array of cooking techniques, nor do I wax rhapsodic over a perfect meringue or molded pudding. I can find better things to do with my time than sleuth around the astounding proliferation of fancy food shops for the impossible-to-find (and afford) ingredient or gadget that will allow me to create the menu of the millennium or confer upon me instant dinner-party-legend status. Let others concoct "Babette's Feast" — and clean up after it. Let them eat cake. As for me, I'll take plain boiled rice any day. And now, often, I do.

It wasn't always so. I was a meat-and-potatoes girl once my family left China and settled in suburban New York

City. One of my favorite meals in those pre-calorie-and-cholesterol-counting days was fried chicken, mashed potatoes oozing creamery butter, and corn on the cob, with gobs more butter. This sublimely soporific repast, with nary a green leaf in sight, was prepared by my mother, whose one-half Chinese heritage was nowhere evident in this meal. Nor was that fifty percent apparent in any of the others she cooked for us, like her spaghetti and meat sauce, where the ground round was at least half the sauce. Or her double whammy of fried chicken *and* spaghetti — leftovers which, mitigated only by frozen string beans slathered in butter, produced a heart-stopping meal. Literally. It's only fair to say that my mother did not (and does not) like to cook. I should also add that, at eightysomething, her bones are those of a healthy woman of thirty and her cholesterol level is well within the normal range.

No, my mother's talents lay elsewhere, far from the kitchen range and the Dutch oven, and, in an era when not many women worked outside the home, she was able to practice them from a very early age. At four years old, she was singing and tap-dancing together with her three sisters in kiddie revues in their hometown of Minneapolis. Of the quartet, she was the sole acrobat, performer of anatomical magic. In their late teens, they appeared in vaudeville theaters all over the United States as the Kim Loo Sisters and were dubbed "the Chinese version of the Andrews Sisters." They shared marquees with Jackie Gleason, the Three Stooges, and Ann Miller. The largest was a billboard that graced Atlantic City's boardwalk: a huge blow-up of a publicity photo for George White's Scandals taken on that same boardwalk in 1939. My mother and her sisters are pictured standing in the first row wearing identical hair-styles and identical dresses, with hat, bag, and shoes to match. Besides managing their career, their Polish mother, Lena née Wojcik Louie, also made all their clothes, onstage and off-.

After all her daughters had traded two peripatetic decades in show business for sedate domesticity, my maternal grandmother opened a dressmaker shop — Kim Loo Originals — in New York's theater district. Here Nana created her signature hand-beaded gowns, cut on the bias Jean Harlow–style, for clients who were mostly singers and dancers. The suave Chinese-American dance team Wing and Toy were steady customers. Otherwise, Nana's cramped, crowded shop was anything but suave. But for my sisters and me, it was a splendiferous Ali Baba's cave that we loved to visit once we were old enough to travel downtown by subway with our mother. Behind a glass and oak counter, she ran the hat bar, where she sold chic chapeaux of her own design under the label Kim Loo Creations, while we plowed into the shopping bags and cardboard boxes that overflowed with faux diamonds, emeralds, rubies, and pearls, and secretly imagined that our lives would be just as languid and glamorous as those of the mannequins whose photos filled the issues of *L'Officiel* and *Vogue* that lay about.

When my modiste mother grew too prolific for Nana's tiny shop, her hat-making spread to our dining room table. Soon the entire room became an outpost for balsa wood heads crowned with her works-in-progress and smelled of a potent glue she used, the fumes of which could induce delirium. The dining room was her territory, but not for eating purposes. Meals were relegated to the kitchen, of which she had no wish to be queen.

In 1958 her wish was answered. Nana closed Kim Loo Originals, my mother made her last Kim Loo Creation, and Nai-nai came from China, via Havana, to live with us. My mother, who had just begun working in Saks Fifth Avenue's millinery department, gladly relinquished the reins of the kitchen and the dining room. Nai-nai was only too happy to pick them up. Our familiar dinners of fried chicken or spaghetti and meat sauce or a combination thereof came to an abrupt halt. Life with Nai-nai was about to begin. It started in our sandbox, innocuously enough.

ACKNOWLEDGMENTS

*M*any people were involved in the creation of this book, either directly or indirectly.

I would like to express my heartfelt thanks to Joanne Wang, my exceptional literary agent, to Casey Ebro for her thoughtful and earnest editing, to Stacey Barney for an enthusiastic first read, and to Anton Li for his gift of the laptop on which *Daughter of Heaven* was written.

I owe a debt of gratitude to friends and family members who either served by example, offered inspiration, or contributed support of various kinds — often all three. I would like to mention several of them by name: Solange Ferré, Pamela Frasca, Hilary Blake, Kathryn Kass, Maurice de Vallière, Douglas Manfredi, Julia Zanes, Marian East, Monica Pejic, and Sophie Kandaouroff.

Finally, I would like to express my appreciation to the Fondation Ledig-Rowohlt for the gift of refuge and respite at Château de Lavigny, where much of the gestation of this book took place.

Daughter of Heaven

A WALK IN NAI-NAI'S GARDEN

Into no department of life should indifference be allowed to creep — into none less than into the domain of cookery.

—Yuan Mei, Qing dynasty scholar

When Nai-nai came to live with us, she hadn't learned a single word of Spanish in the eight years that she lived in pre-Castro Cuba. Nor would she learn a word of English in the fifteen years she would live with us. My sisters and I, who spoke only English, learned a few words of Chinese — most notably, and frequently, *Bu dong* (I don't understand) — in a feeble effort to communicate with Nai-nai. Or rather, in order not to. We held our Chinese heritage at arm's length, only to have it thrust upon us in the form of our very odd Chinese grandmother. Nai-nai was not adverse to her new American environment but simply impervious to it. Contemporary suburban American life might have jostled her composure a bit, but her core — solid peasant stock and pre-1949 agrarian Chinese culture — was rock-solid and unshakable. Immune to change, she was nevertheless its agent par excellence, transforming our home and our lives to correspond to the rustic domesticity she had always known.

Food was at the heart of Nai-nai's existence. Not so much the eating of it as the cooking of it. As with a good argument (in which she seldom engaged, yet at which she excelled, if the subsequent crestfallen or bewildered look on my father's face was any indication), she relished good food. She revered its two basic premises: the freshest ingredients (homegrown if possible) and diligent preparation. The first premise should have forewarned us. That, and how scrupulously Nai-nai surveyed our backyard sandbox when she first arrived. It came as no surprise, then, that soon thereafter the swing, seesaw, and slide on which my sisters and I had played for years were dismantled and removed. Nai-nai wanted to plant a vegetable garden and needed our sandbox, minus our toys, to do it in. No matter that we chafed at the desecration of our once sacred space and the expulsion of the rusting remnants of our lost childhood so that Nai-nai could water her tomato and bok choy plants in the same soil where we'd made our mud pies and sand castles. This she did daily in late spring and summer, in the early morning or evening, or sometimes both, when the sun was not particularly hot. Her habits were guided by the sun and just as regular: up at six and out of the house after a light breakfast of *juk,* a thin rice gruel, or *gee ma wot mein,* a light noodle dish, to tend to her sandbox garden.

But her botanical sights did not stop there. They rose to the "ledge," as we called it, a plateau covered in brambles, tall grasses, and a few scraggly blackberry bushes and separated from the sandbox by a swath of lawn and a seven-foot rock wall. The ledge led to our various woodland hideouts: Flat Rock, Teepee, and Old Baldy. Single-handedly, Nai-nai cleared it of weeds, turned over the soil, broke up the clods, and planted her second vegetable garden, an exact replica of the first. We had to tiptoe around the ledge to get to our sylvan clubhouses. We also saw larger platters of despised bok choy, seared only until it released its juices, on the dinner table, along with thinly sliced flank steak and tomatoes, whose skins were wrinkled but whose flesh remained firm. This was a great departure. Green vegetables as prepared by my mother were leached rather than cooked; her "lightly sautéed" tomatoes stewed, even sauced, to a premature death.

Our front lawn was bordered by flower gardens, three separate and different ones: a straight line of red rosebushes; a circular plot of fragrant peonies and lilies of the valley; and a winding path of pink and lavender hyacinths, crimson tulips, sunny jonquils, and daffodils. Like our sandbox and ledge, this third and last garden would fall under Nai-nai's hoe. (Was nothing safe from it? Nothing sacrosanct?) Instead of red, yellow, pink, and purple blossoms each spring, the white and green oblong heads of bok choy and the round scarlet ones of tomatoes made their appearance every summer. In retaliation, my sisters and I went on a hunger strike against Nai-nai's ubiquitous bok choy. We ate as little as possible of the detested vegetable without attracting the attention of our parents, who would respond by filling our bowls with the stuff. And when we came home in the company of our non-Chinese friends (our

Chinese-American friends would have understood, and sympathized), we boycotted our front door and its embarrassing vegetable path for the back door.

Unfortunately, the path to the back door posed its own problems. On some days, my mother's umbrella clothesline was hung with drying laundry. On others, when Nai-nai got there first, it was strung with bok choy leaves in neat rows. Sometimes it supported cookie trays of chili peppers shriveling in the sun. The bok choy Nai-nai would pickle in Mason jars and add to stir-fried pork at dinnertime. The dried chilies she would use to enliven a number of dishes. The fresh ones she would mince, mash, and mix with garlic, salt, and spices (no oil), then bottle and squirrel away at the back of a kitchen cabinet to age until it became *la-jiao* — to be used very sparingly. Not because it was that hot, but because, even we had to admit, it was that good.

Nai-nai regularly engaged in another culinary pursuit that, if we were with non-Chinese friends, required our reconnoitering before we chose which route to take, front door or back. My father had bought her an expensive knife sharpener, but Nai-nai preferred honing her Chinese cleaver to a razor sharpness with a dribble of water, a steady supply of elbow grease, and the fine-grained flagstones at the edge of our back porch. A dull granite gray at the top of the blade, it turned progressively brighter and burnished in the middle until, at its cutting edge, it was the color of lightning, and possibly as trenchant. When its wooden handle split in two, my mother bought Nai-nai a new cleaver, which she relegated to the back of the knife drawer. There it lay, never to slice meat, dice vegetables, split firewood, gut and scale fish, crush garlic, flatten ginger slices, sharpen pencils, whittle new chopsticks, or otherwise fulfill its myriad purposes. Ever ingeniously waste not–want not, Nai-nai whittled part of a small branch from the front-yard sumac tree and stuck it onto the end of the cleaver. With the single-mindedness of an axe murderer, she then tested it by chopping a piece of pork butt until its consistency approximated a mash. She added minced dried Chinese black mushrooms, crisp water chestnuts, garlic, soy sauce, and spices, and steamed the large patty until it was bathed in its own juices, a sure signal that it was done. With a dish such as this, I could almost forgive her the humongous platter of bok choy that accompanied it.

It was a concession — the closest she ever came to compromise — for Nai-nai to accompany us to Chinatown to eat out. She didn't consider restaurant meals exactly wasteful, but dining out held less pleasure for her than eating in. (She did rise to the occasion, however, by wearing her royal blue jacquard silk cheongsam, apple-green jade earrings, and Shalimar perfume.) Nai-nai knew that her cooking was better, if less varied, and felt that the din of Chinatown eateries didn't allow proper digestion, much less full appreciation of the meal.

Chinatown nevertheless afforded her the opportunity to shop for necessities that she herself didn't raise in her three vegetable gardens. Like *guy-lan* (Chinese broccoli) and bamboo shoots. Like the hundred-pound sack of long-grain white rice that she stored in the shiny new garbage can she had my father buy specifically for that purpose. Like the meats that American markets didn't carry, such as *laap cheung* (pork sausage) and *char siu* (roast pork). For us, her grandchildren, she would always buy a tin of hard coconut candies, whose microscopically thin inner "paper" wrapper of glucose it delighted us to eat. And a box of licoricey preserved plums — sweet, salty, and sour all at once.

As for chickens, Nai-nai insisted on only freshly killed — an ultimatum which required a trip in the opposite direction, to Yonkers, where a Chinese émigré ran a chicken farm out of his large garage. One of us children would accompany my father and wade through the sea of clucking and pecking birds, a few of which would then be selected for the chopping block — thankfully out of sight and earshot — and ultimately for our dinner table. Not every chicken landed immediately in Nai-nai's wok, despite her obsession with freshness. One that didn't ended up pressed flat and dangling from the light fixture in the center of the back-porch ceiling. For over a year there it hung, season after season, in all sorts of weather, ostensibly to absorb the most salubrious northern breezes for best taste. We never did get to sample the results of Nai-nai's cured chicken, though we tasted more than once the bile that rose to our throats when we had to answer non-Chinese friends' queries as to what on earth was hanging from our porch ceiling instead of a light bulb.

One day my mother unhooked the sorry-looking bird and threw it out. She simply assumed that, after a year, Nai-nai had forgotten about it. Whether or not her assumption and deed were correct was never completely clarified.

That summer the pollen was especially prolific, which aggravated my mother's hay fever. On our next trip to Chinatown, Nai-nai entered a *yao-pu,* a Chinese medicinal herb shop, and bought a collection of roots, bark, seeds, and pods. At home she boiled them in water to concoct a "sure-fire" cure for hay fever which also caused the entire house to reek of a combination of curry, melting tar, and gunpowder. The result of Nai-nai's witch's brew was threefold: she was vindicated for the loss of her porch-cured chicken, my mother suffered a lot less from her sneezing fits, and all our nasal passages felt clean as a whistle, as if they'd been reamed.

Summer, a trial for my allergic mother, was a mixed blessing for us, all the more so now that Nai-nai had come to stay. ("Come to stay! Does that mean forever?") The season heralded the end of the school year and the commencement of a long vacation period. But it also meant mowing the lawns and cutting the English ivy and digging out the crabgrass and dandelions. It also marked the beginning of our visits to the dentist, not only for my sisters and me but for Nai-nai as well. Alone, it was a twenty-minute walk from our house to Dr. Savoy's office. When we accompanied Nai-nai, it was an unadulterated outing. On one such excursion, Nai-nai recognized *gow-gay* growing among the matted weeds and fallen horse chestnuts. *Gow-gay* is a cress-like, leafy green vegetable that grows in southern China and makes a fragrant soup. *Gow-gay*, Nai-nai discovered, also grew on Fieldston Road in the north Bronx.

From that moment on, Nai-nai's once immutable weekly schedule underwent a fundamental change. Sundays, she appeared before us wearing her version of a sunbonnet — a wool hat lined in flannel (she abhorred being cold) which she had sewn herself and that looked like a tea cozy — and carrying a large shopping bag. It was our duty to take turns accompanying her to the *gow-gay* patch beneath the horse chestnut trees that lined the road to Dr. Savoy's office. Nai-nai would forage like a squirrel until she had an adequate supply for a few evening meals, while whichever of her granddaughters who had been pressed into service waited across the street, pretending she wasn't hers.

When the *gow-gay* patch was picked bare, we thought we were home free. But no. Just as her gardening sights hadn't stopped with our sandbox, her gathering instincts strayed farther afield as well — to the grassy islands that divided Henry Hudson Parkway into north- and southbound lanes. How she divined that those oblong oases in the middle of a four-lane highway were fertile ground for her newfound soup greens is something I'll never know. I do remember, however, that when the coast was clear of cars, we scurried Nai-nai over to one of those tiny plots, where she would spend the next half hour or so — an eternity to us — placidly gathering her *gow-gay* while trucks rumbled and cars whizzed by us on both sides. Later, neither Nai-nai nor our parents added insult to injury by insisting that we eat the soup our expedition had made possible: *gow-gay,* chicken stock, and egg beaten to a froth. In fact, their contented silence while the three of them finished off the pot intimated better than words that they profited from our obstinate refusal.

Steamed Pork Patty with Water Chestnuts and Dried Chinese Mushrooms

1 pound pork butt, trimmed of excess fat and minced
    fine (or 1 pound lean ground pork, minced fine)
4 large dried Chinese mushrooms, soaked in boiling
    water for 10 minutes, stems discarded, caps
    minced
10 canned water chestnuts, minced
2 tablespoons dark soy sauce
2 tablespoons vegetable oil
1 tablespoon cornstarch
½ teaspoon sugar
1½ teaspoons salt
1 tablespoon fine julienne of peeled fresh gingerroot

In a bowl stir together the pork, mushrooms, water chestnuts, soy sauce, oil, cornstarch, sugar, and salt. Aerate the mixture by fluffing it with a fork.

Transfer mixture to a loaf pan or other baking pan that will fit in a steamer, being careful not to pack the mixture down. Sprinkle it with the gingerroot. Put the pan in a steamer set over boiling water. Steam the pork, covered, for 30 minutes.

Makes 4 servings.

2

FOOD SHAME AND SAND-WISHES

I was in seventh grade, no longer a child but not yet a teen, when Nai-nai came to live with us. Her arrival and my mother's abdication of the kitchen were evident in the lunches my sisters and I carried to school, which elicited curiosity and interest, some of it horrified. That is to say that, even though we tried to imitate our peers and sometimes had in our lunches the chemical additives we so admired in theirs, this follow-the-leaderism soon stopped. Instead of the Sno Balls and Twinkies from the local Shopwell or Grand Union, our desserts often came from faraway Chinatown. Some of these desserts were not sweet but savory, like dried beef, protected by thin paper packets that made exquisite rustling noises when you tore them open. Dried beef is no doubt an acquired taste, but one which I loved — enough to stand up to the put-down that "it looks like tree bark" by not only offering but daring the person who said so to try a bit. And with that, I would tear a strip from the thin, spicy beef square and extend it to the doubting Thomas or Theresa, who usually shook his head or turned up her nose — to my glee.

Not only was there that much more for me, I also managed to score a triumph of sorts, over my quietude, my shyness, my shame to be Chinese. "Tree bark" was the catalyst that made me overcompensate for my innate sensitivity, examples of which were legion and often resulted in tears: Strange children pulling at the corners of their eyes. Or singing "Ching chong Charlie sitting on a fence/ Couldn't make a dollar out of fifteen cents," which, the first time I heard the ditty, I failed to understand referred to me — a double degradation. Or, from one or two of my classmates, that my test scores, often the highest in class, "didn't count" since they weren't the result of diligent study, which they being American were constrained to do, but I being Chinese, "with a different brain," didn't have to do. "Tree bark" made me bold where my physical features and my mental makeup made me shrink. Dried beef gave me the courage to speak up, to challenge my intimidator. I became a veritable daredevil regarding the "weird" Chinese food I brought to school: "Want some? It's delicious. No?" The subtext was "How come I can eat it and you can't? Too bad. You're really missing out on something good." My lunch bag bravura bore another kind of fruit, one completely unexpected, with some of the boys in my class, those who still liked a one-of-the-guys, tomboyish streak in a girl but who a year later were smitten by the most feminine of my peers: Billy Berntsen waited for me at the shortcut to walk me the rest of the way home. Henry Sinkel asked me out to a dance at Neighborhood House. And that heartthrob James Burke smiled at me, twice. (To think that Nai-nai, via dried beef, was responsible for my newfound, short-lived popularity!)

Unlike dried beef, *guy-ying-gee* was much harder to feel confident about eating or offering, even on a dare. A double dare. *Guy-ying-gee* came in two forms: preserved purple plums which were wrinkled, moist, large, and sour with an undertaste of sweetness; and preserved purple plums which were smooth, dry, small, and salty with an undertaste of sourness. Respectively, they looked very much like a larger and a smaller animal's turds, wet and dry. In the case of *guy-ying-gee*, I enjoyed these preserved fruits in silence, as much silence and enjoyment as the outer rustley paper, then the inner crackly paper, and the rude but visually unimpaired verbal remarks of my classmates allowed. With weeks of practice, I was, when unemboldened to say something back, magnanimous enough to say nothing at all. I absolved them of their food fear, and I hoped to win them back — with mangoes, which in the fifties were hardly the popular fruit they are now. Nai-nai bought them in Chinatown — the big, oval, rosy, succulent mangoes grown in the Caribbean, not the small, lima bean–shaped, stringy mangoes shipped from Florida. Some days I opened my lunch bag to find a half of the fruit, cut longitudinally as close as possible to the tall, thin pit, scored in a grid, and turned inside out, each protuberant golden-orange cube just begging to be devoured.

"What's that?" Laurie, my best friend since fourth grade, asked, doubtful but nevertheless intrigued.

"Mango. It's a fruit. Don't worry. It's not Chinese. It's Caribbean. Have a bite." I lopped off a cube with the edge of a spoon and held it out to her. She bit the bait, held it in her mouth unchewed, then spat it out onto the waxed paper it was wrapped in. Her face was red; her expression horrible, a kind of seizure. Finally, she gasped: "Oh, it's awful. It tastes just like turpentine!"

I blinked at her and wondered if our friendship, after this near poisoning, would remain intact. I plucked a fresh cube from the peel with my teeth and bit into it. She was right: it did taste like turpentine. But she was also wrong: not just and only like turpentine. There was peach and pineapple, and the troika was delicious. Absolutely and even more delicious than before I knew the name of the mystery ingredient, which now I did, because of Laurie, who was still a bit gray, thanks to Nai-nai, the Lucrezia Borgia of the Li family.

Before Nai-nai came on the scene and started fiddling with our lunches, I was a hot-lunch girl, a cold-lunch wannabe, right from the moment I entered elementary school in the first grade. A great divide existed between hot lunchers and cold lunchers at St. Margaret's Parochial School. I remember it as clearly as if the line were drawn just yesterday.

It began the moment we first graders — essentially well behaved and lined up according to height and gender — arrived at the open doorway to the lunchroom. Once unified we were now divided: those who took hot lunches versus those who'd brought their cold lunches from home. I, who belonged, unhappily, to the former bunch, veered to the right; cold lunchers, to the left.

There were many reasons why I preferred to be a cold-lunch person. One was that sometimes my mother forgot, or I forget to tell her, that lunch money was due every Wednesday. This information was promulgated as law by Sister Anita, the principal. Though I brought twice the prescribed amount the following Wednesday, I suffered from guilt and shame at having committed an infraction, and I anticipated the omission's certain recurrence, which instilled fear, low-grade, latent, and persistent. My mother said I was sensitive. The Sisters of Charity who were my teachers said I was very quiet, shy, and timid.

Another reason was that my best friend at the time, Patty Cosby, was a cold luncher. Cold-lunch people sat on benches at tables on the opposite side of the room from hot-lunch people. This meant that I couldn't sit with Patty Cosby.

A cold-lunch person carried a sandwich, thermos of milk, apple, and cookies in a lunchbox, with Lassie, Roy Rogers, Hopalong Cassidy, Betty Boop, or some other much loved character on the lid. A hot luncher carried a tray with a small sweating carton of milk, half a white-bread sandwich (American cheese, peanut butter and raisins, peanut butter and grated carrots, plain margarine, or margarine with orange marmalade), a bowl of soup, and dessert, often canned stewed plums (either purple or greengage), cling peaches in syrup, or fruit cocktail in which the maraschino cherry was nowhere in evidence. The soups — when they weren't the obvious and commonplace cream of tomato, which I liked, served as it usually was with an American cheese half-sandwich, or lima bean, which I hated, no matter what it was served with — were a profound mystery to me, a challenge to identify in words (thus a spur to the verbal imagination, if not the gastronomic), and my best argument for bringing my lunch from home.

"Today, at lunch, they gave us alligator-skin soup."

My mother: "Oh, they did not!"

"It was thick and slimy and tough and had lots of ridges and it was greeny-black. It was alligator skin, all right."

My sister Marcy: "They never give us meat. In our soup or in our sandwich."

My father: "You just said they gave you alligator skin. That's meat."

In second grade, taught by Mrs. Rado, a non-nun, I was still a hot-lunch student, but Patty Cosby was no longer my best friend, having moved away. I got good marks, perfect scores on my tests, especially in catechism and spelling. I studied hard so that I'd know the answers. I didn't want to make a single mistake. Before tests, I developed butterflies in my stomach. I began pulling the belt to my school jumper tighter. I pulled it to the next to the last eyelet, then to the last. I even made a makeshift eyelet beyond the last one with my mother's scissors. My strange hourglass figure caught the eye of Sister Anita, who called me into her office and set my belt forward two notches so that I could breathe. Before and after school, I reset my belt the way I liked, an eyelet for an eyelet.

My third grade teacher was Sister Ellen, whose name didn't suit her. A man's name would have. Like Constantine. She was strict, severe, punitive. But it was fitting that Sister Ellen taught third grade. Third grade was serious, the first whiff of the steadily increasing sobriety and dread that was yet to come. There were more tests in third grade than in second, and they seemed to signify something more than whether or not you'd studied. The grades you received on these tests indicated whether you were smart or stupid. They were, in fact, the sole criterion on which you were judged intelligent or hopelessly incompetent. There seemed to be no way out of the latter, while it was very easy to be banished from the former: one false step and you were out, like the Garden of Eden.

Poor Kevin Cantwell belonged to the second category. As suggested by his name, he never did well, and he was punished mercilessly for it. Once, when he was unable to solve a homework problem in subtraction, Sister Ellen instructed him to take off his shoes and socks and count on his toes.

"Please, Sister Ellen," he whined, "please. I'll do my arithmetic homework from now on, I promise."

But the Sister of Charity was firm. Off came the shoes, exposing socks with holes in both toes. He whimpered abjectly, his multitudinous orange freckles dissolving in his pimiento-red face. Then the socks, revealing almost blue-white dirty feet and toenails thickly rimmed with grime. He blubbered unabashedly.

"Count," she ordered, having seconds before commanded him to place his unwashed feet on his desktop, for all to see. "No. Not to yourself. Out loud, so all of us can hear. And don't just point. Grasp each toe as you count it. Stop wiping at your eyes, Kevin. You'll lose count and then you'll have to start all over again."

Start all over again was what he did, several times — losing count while being publicly demeaned and debased was making him despair, and despair never gives you the right answer — before Sister Ellen permitted him to reshoe himself.

I studied hard for these tests, harder than I did in second grade, the fear factor having gone up a few notches.

I got good marks, sometimes even 100, though not as often as I did in first and second grades. Arithmetic was getting difficult, tricky. And then there was composition, which almost never merited a 100, though often a 98 if I'd written something with no mistakes in grammar, spelling, or punctuation. There were so many tests that my stomach was filling up with more and more butterflies. Ferocious ones. The injunction "Take every book and scrap of paper off your desks" bred new butterflies, as did the purple-inky smell of the mimeographed test Sister Ellen put on each of our desks. To keep them from fluttering — their wings were now razor-edged — I wrapped my legs around each other, like vines, like a vise, and hunched low over the mimeographed sheet, the test-taking smell of which was nauseating. Soon I was overcome by tears, to which I also bore the additional humiliation of being led weeping to the nurse's room by a fellow pupil, there to wait for my mother to pick me up and take me home. I hobbled to the nurse's office, doubled over, snuffling, my arms crossed over my brutalized stomach. I couldn't straighten up from the pain, which was exacerbated by the thought that I'd fail the test because I was too sick to take it. My mother came for me, an anxious look on her face, and drove me home. I was helped into my pajamas and into bed, fed clear consommé, unbuttered toast, and flat ginger ale. They took the edge off my shame, the threat of a goose egg as a test score, the razor-sharp butterfly wings.

These attacks of stomach cramps followed me to fourth grade — taught by jocular Sister Theodocia, who had wattles instead of cheeks — where they were less frequent, less painful, less debilitating. Then they stopped altogether. This rallying of my delicate digestive system may have been due to the fact that I no longer restrained my internal organs with the belt of my school uniform. Or that I'd simply outgrown a strong nervous reaction to the unpleasant but unavoidable scholastic task of test-taking. Or that I'd finally been granted cold-lunch status by my parents. No more remembering or forgetting lunch money on Wednesdays. No more anticipation of alligator-skin soup.

By fifth grade, taught by Miss Mulvaney, another non-nun, lunchboxes were considered babyish and, therefore, a social taboo. Lunch bags — waxy and sold as such, or plain brown paper bags that first held a small grocery item — were now the norm. Used brown paper bags had a certain cachet, but they couldn't be too thin, creased, or wrinkled; they had to be lunch-bag size; they couldn't have any grease spots, tears, or holes; and they could serve as a lunch bag only once. Hot-lunch money gave way to milk money, which I had no trouble remembering. Everything, in fact, was becoming more streamlined. Particularly by sixth grade, taught by Sister Philomena. Brown paper bags instead of clunky metal lunchboxes. Milk money instead of hot-lunch money. And, for some physically precocious girls, of which I was not one, carrying your books in your arms crossed in front of your breast buds instead of in a bulky leatherette or frankly plastic bookbag, as I did, down by your side.

Now that we were becoming young ladies (not altogether a term signifying increased maturity or status — the more severe teachers referred to a girl who committed an infraction or displeased them in some way as "young lady," said between gritted teeth, while they still referred to a laggard boy as "sonny," or "sonny boy," sometimes taking him by the knot of his navy blue tie and drawing him help-lessly close to their hot breath and burning face), we not only needed to act like young ladies but to look the part as well. That is, we had to wear hose. Not sheer nylon hose, but thick cotton lisle stockings — complete with clumsy seams which left a runnel up the back of our legs — the tops of which were held mid-thigh by that instrument of torture and misogyny, a garter belt. This demanding new level of apparel was inflicted year-round, no matter what the temperature, in June as in December.

Thus attired in calamine-colored lisle stockings over which we wore the requisite navy blue anklets and heavy oxford shoes, we young ladies of St. Margaret's Parochial School entered seventh grade, when boys began to figure strongly in our thoughts, when a single faux pas could make you a pariah forever, or at least close to a week. For my sisters and me, no matter what grade we were in, any faux pas we committed was doubled by one inherited and irrefutable fact: Nai-nai, who, among other unforgivable embarrassments she caused us, filled our lunch bags with "icky-looking tree bark," "disgusting animal turds," and turpentine-laced "poisonous" fruits. All of which we se-cretly loved (classmates' squeamishness be damned) and to which she added a fourth delicious offense. Wise woman. The best she saved for last.

Part of why it was best was that this last lunch-bag sur-prise provoked a more satisfying response from my cold-lunch mates than all the rest: a new variety of dried beef/tree bark, no longer packaged but homemade by Nai-nai. Flank steak was an inexpensive cut of beef of great versatility in Nai-nai's repertoire, combined as it was with tomatoes and black bean or *guy-lan* and oyster sauce, or served by itself after having soaked for a while in a bath of soy and spices. I didn't know what else conspired with the thin slices of meat to turn them into dried beef, but star anise probably played a part, and certainly soy sauce. The sun that beat down on the cookie trays of chili peppers and marinating meat was the alchemical agent that blended the different parts into a unified whole. That, and time.

When I emptied the contents of my lunch bag at school, instead of store-bought dried beef, there lay Nai-nai's version. And instead of strips of tree bark, my classmates insisted that I'd graduated to chunks of driftwood. I didn't counter the charge: the meat did not lie flat, as the pressed and packaged dried beef had. Nai-nai's was thicker, and in the natural drying process it had twisted and buckled and curlicued. But it was also far better than its pale substitute: thinly crackly on the outside, dense, moist, and chewy on the inside, and full of salty, spicy, licoricey flavor. This time, I didn't even offer the delicacy's detractors the compliment of the dare: "Want some?"

Beef and Tomatoes in Oyster Sauce

1 tablespoon cornstarch
1 tablespoon light soy sauce
1 tablespoon dry sherry
1 teaspoon granulated sugar

1 pound flank steak, cut across the grain into
     ⅛-inch-thick slices
3 tablespoons vegetable oil
1 onion, cut into 1-inch pieces
2 garlic cloves, crushed
1 teaspoon salt
2 tomatoes, cut into wedges
1 teaspoon brown sugar
2 tablespoons ketchup
2 tablespoons oyster sauce

In a bowl stir together the cornstarch, soy sauce, sherry, and granulated sugar. Add the steak. Toss the mixture well, and let the steak marinate for 20 minutes.

In a wok or heavy skillet heat 1 tablespoon of the oil over moderately high heat (hot but not smoking), and stir-fry the onion for 1 minute. Transfer the onion to a plate.

Add the remaining 2 tablespoons of oil to the wok, and heat it until hot but not smoking. Add the garlic. Stir-fry for 45 seconds, or until it is golden. Discard the garlic. Add the steak and the salt. Stir-fry the mixture for 1 minute.

Sprinkle the tomatoes with the brown sugar, and add them to the wok. Stir-fry the mixture until the tomatoes are just heated through. Add the ketchup. Bring the mixture to a boil. Add the onion and the oyster sauce. Stir-fry the mixture for 1 minute.

Makes 4 servings.

3

CHINESE NEW YEAR

Growing up in Riverdale and attending an elementary school where my sisters and I were the only Chinese made me ambivalent about celebrating Chinese (or Lunar) New Year, a holiday that our schoolmates, none of whose heritage matched our own, did not observe. Falling anywhere between January 21 and February 19, Spring Festival, as the period is better known in China, was a festive occasion that lit up the dreary winter months. My schoolmates had to wait until Easter for a similar reason to celebrate.

Chinese New Year included the best aspects of my favorite Western holidays. Like Easter, there was the requisite new set of clothes and a real parade, complete with a lion and a dragon dance. Like Christmas, we received gifts: for the children, *hong bao,* red envelopes containing "lucky money"; for the adults, the choicest fruits. Firecrackers went off with as big a bang as on the Fourth of July. Feasting on special foods with family members smacked of Thanksgiving. And like school vacations, the annual celebration varied in length from one day to two weeks, during which time celebrants paid their respects to ancestors and visited with relatives and friends.

As my family observed it, the Lunar New Year culminated in a sumptuous dinner party at Grampa's house. This impending family get-together always caused my sisters and me a measure of trepidation: Any visit to our grandfather's required good behavior. Chinese New Year demanded our best.

Best behavior, as we understood it, consisted of two tasks: wishing Grampa *"Gung hay fat choy,"* or "Happy and Prosperous New Year" in Cantonese (the full extent of our Chinese-language skills), and sitting in silence throughout the evening (Chinese children were meant to be seen and not heard, a rule enforced with far more rigor on us than on our more fortunate Western counterparts). The second task was harder.

Thankfully, Grampa, a brilliant military tactician for the Chinese Nationalists during the Sino-Japanese War, had devised a peaceable strategy to nip in the bud our youthful restlessness. No matter how garbled our *"Gung hay fat choy,"* he broke into a delighted smile, pinched our cheeks, and played finger games with us — rock-scissors-paper and find-the-index-finger — until he tired of them. Then he urged us toward the coffee table so that he and the other adults could retire to the winter garden to talk over many glasses of tea. The table was set with a blooming narcissus plant, which signifies good fortune and prosperity in the New Year, and an eight-sided "tray of togetherness." Forgetting all propriety, we raided the tray with abandon, gorging ourselves on candied kumquats, whose initial ideogram represents "gold" and therefore promises pros-

perity; coconut candy, which symbolizes family togetherness; and lotus seeds, whose homonym is "many children."
Totally ignorant of these semantic nuances, we thought we
were merely satisfying our penchant for sweets. Little did
we know we were also ingesting Chinese cultural concepts
and values. Eating our words, if you like.

Sated and sticky, we escaped the grown-ups' detection
and slipped up the stairs on tiptoe, headed for the adjoin-
ing bathroom of the master bedroom. We knew it was off-
limits, but that made our adventure all the more exciting.
There it was, on a table spread with all her beauty prepara-
tions — unguents, creams, lotions, potions — all of Chinese manufacture and so their labels indecipherable, all the
more mysterious. And treacherous, like her. We knew she
was treacherous and evil because our father didn't like her.

"How do you know that Daddy doesn't like Madam?"

My mother: "Precisely for that reason: he calls her 'Madam.'"

"What's wrong with that?"

*My mother: "She always wanted him to call her 'Mother.' And
that he would never do."*

*"If I didn't like somebody, I could think of a lot worse names
than 'Madam' to call them."*

Grampa and Nai-nai were physically separated about
a year after they were married. Grampa, who was on one or
another battlefield during the internecine regional wars
raging in China during the 1920s, met Dejie (Madam) and
took her as his second wife. She was beautiful, educated,
young (sixteen to his thirtysomething), and was a politi-
cally appropriate wife for the rising star that my grandfather was at that time. Except for one year in Canton,
Nai-nai never lived with Grampa again. Dejie was very

possessive of Grampa and did everything possible to usurp Nai-nai's place.

We spotted what we had come to see, the proof we ardently desired, and recoiled as if it were poison, before we drew near, since it was also irresistible. A small porcelain mortar and pestle. A glass of milky liquid, half empty. We examined the pestle closely for evidence.

"Don't touch it. You'll drop it, and it'll break," Marcy whispered. "Then won't we be in a fix!"

Sure enough, along the rim of the bowl was a trace of something finer than sand, coarser than talcum powder, and shimmeringly white. What we'd once overheard my mother say about Madam — that she was very vain, that she ate pearls to maintain her youthful complexion — was now verified, even if we hadn't found the raw proof, only the refined remnants.

"The Pearl-Eater," we tittered, both horrified and gleeful, listening with one ear cocked just in case she was on to us and was heading up the stairs at that very moment. "The Pearl-Eater!"

Usually it was my mother who found us, who knew what it was we were looking for and, by our Cheshire-cat smiles, that we had found it. We were then sent to the kitchen to "help" Aiying, Grampa's cook, and Regina, her English-speaking associate, prepare dinner. The two women had been forewarned of our arrival, along with Grampa's intentions for us, and were already at their battle stations, ready to work their wizardry while keeping us occupied. Standing in front of the wok, Regina guided us in dropping, one by one, hard pink and white disks the size of quarters into the hot, smoking oil, where they sizzled and sputtered and bubbled away. When she fished them out with a pair of long chopsticks and placed them on paper towels to cool and dry, the semi-translucent "food coins" had magically transformed into shrimp chips, feather-light pastel wafers that stuck to the tongue like Velcro and dissolved there like ice. As for Aiying, she manned the kitchen table groaning under hundreds of *jiaozi,* or dumplings.

Some she had already crimped shut, while the thin oval skins of others awaited our assistance, or interference, as the case turned out. The latter we sealed shut with egg yolk, then dropped into a pot of boiling water. Most of these *jiaozi* resurfaced shortly, in separate components — first a wad of soggy dough, then a mush of minced meat.

While Aiying disposed of the defective dumplings, Regina engaged us in a third kitchen game. This one employed another New Year specialty, one that augured long life, and required the winner of this contest to hold bean-thread noodles, or "silvery threads of longevity," in her chopsticks longer than the other contestants before inserting them into her mouth. The object of the game, as we played it, was simply to grasp the slippery strands between our chopsticks at all. Despite the potential for mischief, or at least distraction, that four children let loose in a kitchen were capable of unleashing, and despite the creative culinary entertainments they created for us to offset that possibility, Aiying and Regina managed to produce a full-scale Chinese banquet for a dozen or so people. Much of it had been prepared in advance, not because the two cooks knew that we would be invading their kitchen, but because the use of knives and cleavers is forbidden on Chinese New Year: no one wants to be accused of "cutting into" the family's luck by wielding a sharp instrument.

When everything was ready, the cry *"Chi fan!"* — "Dinner is served!" — went out, whereupon we all took our seats around the dining room table. We heaped oohs and aahs upon each dish that the beaming, if exhausted, cooks set before us. "Happiness to everyone" wasn't said but served in the form of shark's fin soup. Then came "Happy Spring Festival," also unspoken but more than implied in the shape of spring rolls. Next came a banquet favorite: a ruddy-brown lacquered Peking duck with the requisite pancakes, scallion brushes, and plum sauce. It preceded a concoction made with dried oysters, or *haosi* — a word that means "something good is bound to happen" — black mushrooms, bok choy, and *fat choy,* a black hairlike seaweed whose auspicious name not only signifies wealth but also provides half of the Chinese New Year greeting. Taken together, the ingredients comprise a dish appropriately called *gung hay fat choy.*

Midway through the meal came the pièce de résistance. Always it was a fish, or *yu,* homonym for "abundance," and always it was served whole, with head and tail attached, to assure a favorable start and finish. Usually it was a sea bass, steamed, scorched with piping-hot peanut oil, sprinkled liberally with slivers of fresh ginger and green onion strips, and bathed in soy sauce. The fish was followed by the bean-thread noodles — those that had not slipped through our chopsticks onto the floor or made it into our mouths — as elusive at the table as they had been in the kitchen and a clear indication that dinner was winding down. Nearly as slippery, and further proof that the meal's end was near, was the subsequent dish: *tangyuan*, a viscous, sweet soup whose glutinous rice-flour balls symbolize both the year's first full moon and family unity. By then we were full to bursting, but we always made room for the finale — long-life buns — sweetened steamed bread, tinted pink and shaped to resemble peaches, which connote longevity.

The food marathon of many dishes and (it seemed) as many hours was over. All that time, hardly a word was spoken. The grown-ups had been nearly as mute as we, reduced to an almost reverential silence that was broken only by an appreciative gustatory comment. We children regained the full use of our tongues and revived our scant knowledge of the Chinese language the moment we saw Grampa draw out of his sweater vest pocket four *hong bao*, one for each of us. *"Gung hay fat choy!"* we sang in chorus, as we ripped into the red envelopes. Silence, we discovered, had its compensation after all.

In 1965 Grampa returned to China at the invitation of Mao Zedong, but our Chinese New Year celebrations in New York did not end with his departure. Nai-nai took his place as keeper of the Spring Festival culinary flame. Keep it and fan it she did, in a way that was more elemental and less extravagant than when Grampa and his cooks had possession of it. The apparent simplicity of Nai-nai's life and of the meals she cooked was nevertheless deceptive. Such artful husbandry was highly labor-intensive. It was humbling to witness this tiny but determined woman who in her seventies and eighties rose with the sun to tend to her vegetables and retired from her gardens just before sunset. No doubt she took pride and satisfaction in diurnal rhythms. And justification: such bounty should require un-stinting effort. One reaped what one sowed.

The foundation of her vigilant simplicity was adapt-ability, no less at Spring Festival than at any other time of the year. Holiday delicacies, such as *fat choy* and shark's fin, were all well and good if you liked that sort of thing. But for this homespun woman who valued ingenuity over in-dulgence and economy over opulence, there was another way to welcome the New Year. Like Aiying and Regina, she would prepare a feast of dishes befitting the important oc-casion as generous in number as they were auspicious in name. Only she would use everyday ingredients, many of which she grew in her own gardens, plucked in the wild, or selected from Chinatown's most reputable shops.

As at Grampa's house, soup initiated the New Year meal. If it wasn't *gow-gay*, then it was wonton, or "swallow-ing a cloud," soup. This killed two birds with one stone, so to speak, since the wontons substituted very nicely for the customary *jiaozi*. Also similar to Grampa, Nai-nai served up a whole sea bass, head and tail intact. She did deviate, however, from Grampa's New Year feast — and official Chinese culinary canon — by offering boiled white rice, that common staple banished from Chinese banquet tables for being too ordinary. The simple reason for its inclusion, banal or no, at our banquet table is that we craved the great absorber, particularly to sop up the delectable juices in which her meat, poultry, and fish dishes floated. Another deviation from Grampa's method, we ate our New Year's dinner home-style, that is, all the dishes at the same time, rather than banquet-fashion, one dish after another. And instead of the usual whole chicken or duck for auspicious

30

beginnings and ends, Nai-nai's *see yao gai* chicken wings invited us to "soar one thousand miles." Closer to earth, Nai-nai also slow-simmered pig's knuckles, whose homonym means "treading the azure clouds of good fortune." Perhaps Nai-nai made this unusual porcine choice for Spring Festival in deference to my mother, who not only loved eating feet — chicken, duck, pig — but who as a professional tap dancer in her youth had trod the more solid floorboards of the stage. As for dessert, gone were the long-life buns, replaced by a better bet for longevity than the sugar-flour-food-coloring confection: golden-hued fruits au naturel. "Prevents colds," Nai-nai declared. "Better for the teeth."

Though the dishes placed before us at Nai-nai's table differed in both style and content from Grampa's, the atmosphere of pleasure, bounty, and accord prevailed at both, as well as an almost unbroken silence. I didn't then, but now I understand this camaraderie without conversation, this communion without comment: At a Chinese table, it's the unspoken words that count. The meal is the message.

Grampa's and Nai-nai's Chinese New Year banquets are a thing of the past. Today I celebrate the holiday in Chinese restaurants with family and friends, or with a few simple Chinese dishes that I cook at home. Still, despite the many years since I sat down to *chi fan* with them, the message of my grandparents' meals remains audible, and all the louder for Nai-nai's and Grampa's absence: May you enjoy good fortune and prosperity say the New Year fruits and seeds and flowers. Happiness for all declares the shark's fin. Abundance intones the sea bass. Family unity says the slippery-ball soup. Long life murmurs the peach. To say more would be superfluous.

Whole Steamed Sea Bass

15 slices fresh ginger
2-pound sea bass, cleaned and scaled, with head and
    tail
5 spring onions or scallions
¼ cup peanut oil
⅓ cup chicken stock (See Note.)
¼ cup light soy sauce
¼ teaspoon ground black pepper
a few sprigs of cilantro

Peel ginger and cut into slices the thickness of a quarter. Put 5 slices inside the fish cavity. Finely shred the rest. Place two of the spring onions on a large plate. Lay the fish on top of them. Shred the remainder of the spring onions.

Set the plate on the steamer rack of a wok full of rapidly boiling water. Steam for 18–20 minutes. Remove plate from wok. Garnish fish with shredded spring onion and shredded ginger.

Heat the peanut oil to sizzling and pour over fish. Mix chicken stock, light soy sauce, and black pepper in a bowl. Heat in wok, then pour over fish. Garnish with cilantro. Serve immediately.

Makes 4–6 servings.

Note: To make basic chicken stock, put 1 chicken, 3 stalks green onion or scallion, 1 tablespoon salt, and 2–3 quarts water into a pot so that the water just covers the chicken. Bring all ingredients to a boil. Turn down heat and simmer 2 hours, skimming off fat and scum. Remove chicken. Adjust seasonings to taste.

Pig's Feet with Ginger and Sweet Rice Vinegar

3 pounds pig's feet (pork knuckles)
2 pounds fresh ginger

Seasoning:

6 cups sweet rice vinegar
2 cups Chinese brown vinegar (or 1½ cups white
    vinegar)
¼ cup sugar
3 cubes chicken bouillon

Drop pig's feet into pot of boiling water for 2 minutes. Remove and scrape off any remaining hair. Cut into 2-inch pieces. Place in empty pot, cover with cold water, and bring to boil. Simmer for 35 minutes. Drain and rinse with cold water.

Peel ginger and cut into 2-inch pieces. Pour vinegars into pot and bring to boil. Add sugar and chicken bouillon. Mix well. Add ginger and simmer 25 minutes. Add pig's feet. Bring back to boil. Reduce heat and simmer until pig's feet are completely tender. Remove from heat. Let stand 3 hours before reheating to serve.

Makes 6 servings.

4

Three Short Fish Tales
(and One Shrimp Cocktale)

*F*ish, whether freshwater or salt-, occupies an exalted place at the banquet table and the uppermost reaches of China's protein pantheon. Perhaps that's because that quintessential Chinese icon, the dragon, is covered in fish scales. Or because the spoken word for fish, *yu*, is the homonym (same sound, different ideogram) for "good fortune." Surely because its flesh, whether sweet or briny, is succulent and delicate, a unique gastronomic experience.

Fish tales, on the other hand, occupy the dunce's corner in Li family lore. Our pelagic stories fly in the face of what is probably the most famous Chinese fish folktale — not surprisingly, a study in Chinese filial piety.

Once upon a time, there lived a widow and her little son. The widow loved her son very much and gave him the best ears of corn to eat and the softest grains of polished rice. And the son in turn loved his mother very much, as good sons will. One year, a plague of locusts stretched across the land, eating everything in sight: every kernel of corn, every grain of rice. Famine bent people's heads in unrelieved sorrow, and many of them went hungry. To make matters even worse, it was a particularly cold and cruel winter that year, and the widow lay wrapped in her blanket on her bed of straw, for she was very sick from lack of food. Her son knew that no food was to be had anywhere, for the locusts had eaten the fields and the paddies clean, and the land lay under a thick layer of snow.

"If I might just have one fish to eat, I know I would get well," the woman told him. She was so weak she couldn't lift her head from her pillow. But when he went to the river to cast his net, his heart sank: the river was frozen solid. He was near despair when an idea came to him. He walked to the middle of the river and lay down, vowing to lie there until the heat of his body melted the thick ice. He lay there all winter long, then through the first days of spring. He felt neither cold nor hunger, so great was his resolve, so deep was his love for his mother.

Then one day, he felt the current flowing beneath him. He plunged his arm into the water. When he raised it, he held a great squirming fish. He ran home with his catch and cooked it for his mother, whose strength returned as quickly as she ate it. And so it was that the filial son saved the life of his starving mother.

My mother has her own fish, or rather shrimp, story to tell, which in its own way proves her to be as dutiful as the aforementioned Chinese son. Her father-in-law, a candidate for the vice presidency at the time, arranged a banquet in honor of his daughter-in-law, who had just arrived in China and whom he was meeting for the first time. The banquet would be a formal affair, with many guests and a strong potential for mishap, particularly since it was not a secret that my grandfather had opposed the marriage, my mother being neither Chinese in culture nor (completely) Han by blood. Worse, she had made her living on the stage. She had been an entertainer, a *le hu*. The dinner party, her first public appearance in Chinese society, where first impressions also tend to be the last, had two goals: to welcome my mother to, and to test her suitability for, her new home.

The banquet was opulent and lengthy. One course followed another in almost interminable succession. One of the dishes served was salt-and-pepper shrimp, still in their shells, for succulence and best taste. Chopsticks poised, my mother watched as the other dinner guests suavely placed whole shrimp in their mouths and, with a minimum of maxillary activity and solely with their teeth, removed transparent exoskeletons, spanking clean and miraculously whole, which they daintily spat out onto small plates, there specifically for that purpose. Since she was new to China, a novice to the difficult language as well as to the dexterous feat of shelling shrimp with her teeth, she ate, as discreetly as she could, all the shrimp she was plied with, shells and all.

If my mother's "shrimp cocktale" demonstrated her adherence to local propriety, her conscientious yielding to foreign ways, it was her "fish diplomacy" at the same event that won my grandfather over in the end, and through a brilliant stratagem my mother had unwittingly employed. To welcome her daughter-in-law to her new home, Nai-nai had given my mother a heavy chain — *sautoir*-length — of Chinese gold, so soft it was malleable, a quality upon which this fish tale hangs. Attached to the chain at regular intervals were short lengths of finer links at whose ends dangled different Chinese coins, also of 23-carat gold. To set off the necklace, my mother had had a dress made, a silk *chipao* in a subdued color. On the day of the dinner party, she tried on both dress and parure in front of the mirror only to realize that they were suitable for an evening out but not quite grand enough for a banquet at which she was the guest of honor. What to do?

Dejie, my grandfather's second wife, had also given my mother a welcoming present, and on that very day: a goldfish — bulbous-eyed and luxuriantly finned — carved from copper-colored jadeite and big as a child's fist. With a few bends and twists of a few links in the chain, my mother attached the jadeite fish to the gold *sautoir*.

When my mother appeared at the banquet wearing the combined gifts from both his wives, my grandfather beamed with undisguised pride, pleasure, and, possibly, relief. Any reservations he might have had regarding my American mother's ability to grasp the subtleties of Chinese manners and mores were dispelled by this eloquent tribute she unknowingly gave to both women and, by association, to the man who had married them. What might have been a recipe for domestic disaster (Dejie's vindictiveness was legendary when she felt slighted) turned out to be a diplomatic coup. Seated between my mother and his second wife (my grandmother was not present due to Dejie's maneuvering), my grandfather took his daughter-in-law's hand and patted it paternally. *"Hen piaoliang. Hen congming."* "How beautiful you are. And how intelligent." From then on, he never questioned my mother's Chinese-ness nor her appropriateness as a daughter-in-law. And all because, on the night of a big dinner party, my mother's aesthetic sense told her to hang a jade fish on a gold chain.

Unlike my mother, I did not acquit myself so graciously in my own fish test, though there were certain similarities. My gastronomic gaffe also occurred at a banquet, one not in my honor nor in Shanghai, but for a Czech painter and his pianist wife in Paris. I blame this example of food shame on my personal social ineptitude and agoraphobia, though to be fair, having been raised in an insular Chinese household, I was ill-prepared for dining out in the Western world.

Mealtimes at our house meant eating. Speaking was almost always out of turn, both before food went into one's mouth and after one had swallowed it. Silence was broken now and then by my father and Nai-nai, who spoke in Chinese, a language unintelligible to the rest of us. Silence for us children at mealtimes was therefore not only the cultural norm, it was reinforced by our linguistic ignorance. What a rude awakening it was then when, invited to a grammar school friend's house for dinner for the first time, I discovered that I was expected not only to say something but to engage in a lengthy conversation. More like the Spanish Inquisition! My friend's parents must have thought I barely spoke English or, worse, pitied me for being slow.

And the surprise, the disorientation, the terror I felt when, as a high school student, I was called upon to pass bowls or platters of food around the dinner table of a classmate — a bit like buckets in a fire brigade, only in this case it was to put out the fires of hunger in our stomachs. Which could only smolder, given the inefficiency of such a method. Compare it to reaching out with one's chopsticks and plucking the desired, pre-cut portion from the various dishes set in the middle of the dining table, accessible to everyone. Oh, the interminable waiting demanded of you while your neighbor spooned onto his plate the desired portion from the heavy, slippery bowl you held for him, since there was no place on the table to set it down, given the profusion of cutlery, china, and glassware. With the disconcerting array of bowls to pass around, and the varying time each person took to transfer his portion from bowl to plate, there was always a bottleneck or two somewhere along this human food chain. This meant cramps in one's arms from holding aloft tottering platters while the viands they bore turned a shade paler or congealed before one's very eyes. After these pre-consumption prerequisites called proper table manners were dispensed with, you would think it was finally time to eat what had taken so long to find its way onto your plate. Surprise: that slab of roast beef you had swung off the meat platter required cutting before it could enter your mouth. This feat required not only dexterity of both hands, but the frequent shuffling of knife and fork back and forth between them. If right-handed, you cut your meat with that hand while, with your left, you plunged the tines of your fork into it to hold the chunk of meat steady. Once you had a bite-sized piece on the end of your fork, you then had to transfer that implement into your right hand, which raised the morsel to your mouth, which then removed, chewed, and swallowed it. Caveat: before you could switch your fork from your left to your right hand, you first had to set down the knife already in your right hand, laterally, on the right edge of your plate.

For another forkful of meat, or any food that needed dismembering, you then transferred the fork from your right hand to your left, picked up the knife lying on the edge of your plate with your right hand, and repeated the sequence of events described above. After a few such repetitions, your veal cutlet, lamb shank, or chicken breast was stone cold. And if it wasn't, it would soon be, for inevitably one of the invited guests would pipe up, sweetly, "Excuse me, but would you mind passing the butter?" Or the salt. Or the dish of mashed parsnips. Multiply this request for extra condiments or second helpings by the number of guests seated around the table, and you will have some idea of how I experienced my first American dinner party.

I attended my first French banquet soon after I graduated from college and went to live in Paris. Here I appreciated the Continental version of knife and forkery (no shuffling of cutlery between hands — a definite step up in eating efficiency) and took pride in using it in all my usual cheap eateries: the various self-services in my *quartier,* the more garrulous bistros, the cafés redolent of Gauloise and Gitane smoke. Mine was the life of a student at the Alliance Française sou-ing and centime-ing it. Eating out was a relative extravagance. Dining al fresco with a *copain* on a banquette near the Seine with an oblique view of Notre Dame was more in line with my finances and, often, my preferences. Dinner ingredients, fresh and inexpensive, came prêt à manger from the market stalls — street theater, in disguise — that flanked rue Mouffetard, rue de Seine, or Place Maubert-Mutualité: a slice of *terrine du canard* or *pâté du porc,* a wedge of Brie or Gruyère, a *baguette pas trop cuite,* a handful of grapes, a half bottle of a serviceable red

Bordeaux, and thou, O *Ville Lumière*. What could be better?

That last sentence was not a rhetorical question. It required an answer, which happened to be, in my book at least: a French banquet that pulled out all the stops. A French banquet held in a *grand hôtel particulier* in the sixteenth arrondissement where all the French women are terribly *soignée* and wear cocktail dresses, understated diamonds and pearls, and their hair in upswept chignons; where all the Gallic husbands are smartly but soberly attired to set off their wives, where both sexes dispense scintillating anecdotes as well as cultivated conversation. This was in great contrast to me, a Chinese-American version of Claudine à l'Ecole who spoke French like a *vache espagnol*. But I was too naive and too enchanted by my fellow guests, the iced champagne, the gilded foyer, the elaborate crystal chandelier, the baroque silver nameplates, and the single perfect red rose on my plate — and on the plate of every other woman present — to notice. I felt like a child let loose in a toy shop. Indeed, in locating my place at table — there were more than twenty of them — I likened the search to the children's game of musical chairs. Once seated, I looked for my escort at table, peering around what seemed to be a small topiary garden, complete with Hellenic statuary. When I peeked, he did too. *Chouette!* In addition to musical chairs, blindman's bluff.

The French, as everyone knows, take eating very seriously. As seriously as do the Chinese, but without manifesting their gusto. "In so many traits the Chinese resemble the French," the English writer Osbert Sitwell noted. "They are original, self-indulgent, fond of food and good things and gossip, kindly and deeply attached to their families, interested in the arts and commerce." He continues: "The Chinese are witty, in their lives, the things they make, if not in conversation; which [like the French] resembles a game of cards. I pull out this card, a philosophical tag, and you pull out the opposite one."

At this French banquet, I wondered if there were aspects of the Chinese variety, where the meal is the message, where talk is superfluous, indeed impolite, unless it touched upon the meal itself. Faced with the regiment of platters and plates before me, the battalion of glasses and goblets, the armaments of knife, fork, and spoon, I had my answer: not very likely. As if to underscore the fact, the first course was a soup — *crème de champignons* — ladled from a porcelain tureen by a young man in livery. The tureen was set on a rolling cart pushed by another and identically dressed young man.

Soup at a traditional Chinese banquet, unlike at Li family dinner parties, is served at the tail end; it is set in the middle of the table; and if it is melon-ball soup, which it often was in my family, it comes in its own tureen. I knew I shouldn't be doing this — comparing and contrasting the French and the Chinese — but I couldn't help myself. It seemed the farther from my heritage I journeyed, the stronger its influence on me. It was perhaps for the same reason that artist, writer, and solitary traveler Gontran de Poncins settled in Cholon, a riverbank community of Chinese outside Saigon, to study and record the lives of his expatriate subjects: he suspected that the ancient customs of a national culture are best preserved and endure longer in diaspora rather than in the motherland.

A cheese soufflé and its accoutrements came and went,

entering and exiting in the white-gloved hands of the same two young men. Around the table there was polite talk in measured tones — not the American effulgent discourse that conceals a complete background check that haunted my adolescence. Much of the talk concerned food, as consumed at this meal. Silence reigned at comfortable intervals, in moderate amounts. No heavy bowls or platters to pass or hold for one's neighbor. No requests for second helpings. My wineglasses and water goblet were refreshed before they were half empty by unobtrusive hands.

The next time the door opened, it was to emit a young *serveuse,* in ruffled organdy cap and matching starched apron, bearing before her an immense domed silver platter. This was a deviation from established procedure. Her burden would have been more appropriately borne by the two young men. Here was my first clue that something if it was not yet amiss would be soon. My adrenaline level rose; my eyelids lowered. I prayed. The maid removed the silver dome, like a prestidigitator in a magic show, to the oohs and ahhs of the guests and the satisfied grin of our host. *"Turbot à la meunière,"* she announced, then began to circumambulate the table. This was like theater. No. It was theater: the fish was getting a round of applause. We were clapping. We were actually clapping. The women with their perfect maquillage, the men with their urbane repartee. I clapped too, hoping all the while that so secular a display of appreciation in no way weakened the efficacy of my fervent prayer: Please let her stop at someone else's chair. Please let her pass me by.

She stopped to the right of my chair. I was still looking down at my lap. She tilted the platter at an angle that, without being insistent, was a clear invitation to me to view its contents. I turned my head and looked. Despite my adrenaline level, which urged me to flee, I maintained enough presence of mind to remain in my chair, there to discern that what she was presenting to me was a whole fish, which if this were a Chinese banquet would have made its appearance toward the end of the meal. But this, I reminded myself, was not a Chinese banquet, where the fish would have had eyes, white and jellied from poaching. This fish's eyes had been removed, which, to my adrenaline-addled brain, was one step closer to the Chinese tradition of leaving them in, but was three steps further from the American practice of removing not only the eyes but also the head, tail, and spine. I tried to take succor in this, but couldn't. I was too aware that the young woman holding that heavy silver platter of whole but eyeless fish was waiting for me to do . . . what? Take the tray from her and set it in the middle of the banquet table for each of us to serve ourselves, the Chinese way? Take the platter from her and pass it around, American-style? Or take it from her so she could serve me, friendly American-style?

I looked from the sightless fish into the maid's seeing eyes, hoping for kindness, a sign, a clue. That she dropped the platter.

"C'est joli," I said, softly. I steeled myself and waited for the walls to come tumbling down.

"Mademoiselle ne voudrait pas partager?" She looked down and nodded, just perceptibly, toward the platter, toward the serving fork and spoon. She looked into my eyes and smiled graciously. *"C'est très bon, je vous assure."*

I smiled back, in gratitude. I picked up the fork and

spoon, extracted a small portion of the delicate flesh, set it on my plate — though not as deftly as she had maneuvered me out of my predicament — and returned the utensils back onto the platter, which she must have felt was lighter by more than just the ounce or two of fish I'd removed. At least, so it seemed to me by the ease with which she carried it to the next, and knowing, guest.

Chinese culture is rife with pithy maxims, sound bites with significance, the most memorable of which were not uttered, stereotypically, by Confucius or any of the other lofty sages but sprang from the lips of the common man. It is these earthy folk sayings, not the pearls of Eastern philosophical wisdom, that formed my earliest consciousness, that infiltrated the very marrow of my bones.

Aphorisms like "first the flower, then the fruit," proffered to console the parents of a newborn baby girl (the flower), to diminish the disappointment that it wasn't a boy (the fruit), and to encourage them to try again. Which was to say that the birth of a baby girl was tantamount to a failure, and a grave one at that.

When Nai-nai was born at the end of the nineteenth century, a fourth and unwanted daughter of a poor peasant family, her mother, who knew she must either drown or smother the infant, was wily enough to devise a way to keep her. When my mother gave birth in the middle of the twentieth century, she felt compelled to apologize to my father four times, once for each daughter. Compensating for being only half Chinese, she believed that "four candles do not take the place of one lamp." The culture of her Cantonese father had infiltrated her bones, too. His Polish wife, who nonetheless knew something about Chinese patriarchy, was another story. My Slavic grandmother bore five daughters, leavened by a single son, the penultimate child. Each time she gave birth — at home with a midwife in attendance, in Minneapolis — she summoned her husband to her side, unwrapped the swaddling clothes upon the newest squalling family addition, and announced in a defiant tone, "See? A girl." (Or "Another girl.") She then dismissed my grandfather with an imperious, "You may go now." Even in confinement, Nana was secretly formulating a master plan for her girls, one she felt she would encounter little ardor for and therefore little interference from a husband constitutionally interested in lamps.

I was the one who came closest. Second in line, thus first to fulfill the Chinese horticultural adage, the flower's exegesis. The one requiring my mother's most heartfelt apology for having held out my father's greatest hope, only to snatch it away. For my dereliction of duty, I was tacitly given certain privileges, and I silently assumed certain burdens that my sisters didn't share. Not that they wanted those medals of honor that came with being a tomboy: the calluses on my hands big as walnuts; the scabs and bruises that healed only to make room for larger, uglier ones; the smug knowledge and titillating and incautious use of swear words, curses, and dirty jokes. The acceptance of these privileges was not without its equal share of punishments. Reciprocity, after all. With a semi-blind eye, my father allowed me to ice-skate on Indian Pond after school, before I did my homework, before it got dark. But he grilled me mercilessly after I completed each homework assignment. He permitted me, encouraged me, to grow into the tomboy I became. But I had better not come home crying if I was bested by or hurt in a fight with a boy or in a contest of kinetic skill or a match of wits. When he caught me filching one or two cigarettes from his packs of Kents so I could smoke them in the woods with the boy who lived next door, my father shut me in the master bathroom with a full pack of cigarettes and told me I could come out only when I had smoked them all. (I was let out after two cigarettes and the promise never to smoke again.) He also invited me to accompany him in Katrinka, the old Buick, to pick up my mother at the subway station at the end of her workday, so that he could teach me how to drive. At eleven years of age, it was my calloused hands on Katrinka's steering wheel, my father's foot on the gas pedal. My life has probably always been that way: my father providing the impetus; I directing its course.

I read somewhere that there are fathers who cherish their children and those who educate their children; that each type loves them in his own way, thinks it the better one. My father belonged to the second category, to offset what he believed to be the deleterious effects of the soft love, the leniency, the latitude my mother gave us. He feared that we would grow up to be weak — powder puffs unable to withstand life's hard knocks, rude disappointments, crushing rejections. To harden us, to prepare us, he saw to it that we received them from him rather than from a complete stranger. My father was nothing if not cautious. "It's better to be safe than sorry. It's better not to take any chances. If it's not perfect (our test scores, our school grades), it's not good enough." From those maxims, I extrapolated: Not good enough is close to failure. Close to failure is worse than death.

An eleven-year-old child thinks this way. The eleven-year-old child I was didn't know that my father's near-military sense of discipline was both an awkward way of loving us and a symptom of his unremitting preoccupation with the obligations he bore as the single head of two households — his own and his aging father's — whose ranks swelled or shrank according to which second cousin or third nephew was fleeing China for the United States, required introductions, English lessons, a place to stay, a job, a college education. My father, as eldest son and head of the Li clan, was honor-bound by filial piety to provide these services to extended family members, those interconnected strands in a wide and sticky web of distant relatives whose requests were summarily honored before his obligations to his own nuclear family were even considered.

"What can I do?" my father would say when my mother protested yet another refugee to feed and house and send to college before any of her own daughters had the chance — and might not, if this free flow of finite funds continued. What will people say if I don't do what they ask? is what he meant, and my mother knew it. Everyone back home will talk. They'll speak against me. They'll say that Yau Luen is a miser. They'll say that I'm not fulfilling my filial obligations. With privilege comes obligation, and I have the privilege of being Li Zongren's son. Not only would I lose face, my father would lose face. All of us would. What can I do?

This last was a rhetorical question. My father's mind was made up and my mother could do nothing to change it, for it concerned the most intransigent icon and underpinning of Chinese culture — face: its maintenance, its gain, its loss. My mother understood: these distant relatives, these people he didn't even know, mattered more to him than his own family because of what they would say. What we, his immediate family, said or thought didn't matter, precisely because we were immediate family. And we were American. Therefore what we said or thought didn't count, wouldn't reach the ears of people in China, the "they" of what-will-they-say whom he barely knew. They, not we, had the power to diminish or increase his face and thus control his fate. Our fate. We meant more to him, but they mattered more to him.

This realization coincided with the growing importance my mother gave to her position as a clothing buyer at Saks Fifth Avenue and the personal satisfaction and financial remuneration she received from it. It was also at a time when production at the factory my father owned in Hong Kong was slack and profits were down: the electric condensers that he manufactured were becoming obsolete; computer chips were on the rise.

It was my mother who made dinner when she came home from work, which was later than my father, who did the shopping. But one night a week when her store remained open until nine o'clock and she worked until closing, my father assumed both tasks. Only during inventory, when my mother worked every night way past nine, arriving home after ten or eleven o'clock, did my father cook dinner for us daily. They were meals which, had we been able to decipher the acrid and bitter emotions that seasoned them, might have softened our hearts toward him.

"Where did you go to college, Daddy?"

"University of Chicago. And Beloit College."

"What did you study?"

"Political science."

"Will I go to college, too?"

"Of course. If you're smart enough."

"At college, what did you do for fun?"

"I would go to the apartment of one of my Chinese friends. Everyone would be there. All our Chinese friends. There were few Chinese restaurants, and no decent ones. American food! (A sour face.) We couldn't eat it. So we would cook a real Chinese meal together."

"That doesn't sound like fun. That sounds like work."

A wag of his head. "What do you know?"

That my father couldn't eat American food. At least not until he married my mother and she made her version of it for him. But on her late nights at work, American food was what he made for the five of us. We all ate it, like a penance, in silent suffering. One such meal stood out in particular, served on Fridays, but capable of insinuating itself into another evening of the week: frozen fish sticks, baked; egg noodles with melted butter; and frozen string beans boiled within an inch of their life, wilted and gray with fatigue. I hated those Friday dinners and, despite my best intentions, despite the knowledge that my father was watching, silent and disapproving, I picked sullenly at my food. I would manage to get a forkful of the dubious fish and greasy bread crumbs or some limp, sodden noodles into my mouth. I tried not to chew but simply swallowed, or tried to. Instead I gagged. Out came the fish stick, nearly intact, back onto my plate. When I looked up, my father's eyes were bulging in their sockets, his nostrils were flared, his breathing had stopped. This indication of his anger was all the more frightening because it was so quickly suppressed, gone almost as soon as it had appeared. No verbal tirade. No physical violence or the threat of it. Just his usual cold self-control and the withering request that I excuse myself from the table.

One night during inventory week when my mother phoned my father to pick her up at the station as was customary, he didn't lift the receiver off the cradle but let the phone ring, which woke us up. Eventually the ringing stopped, but soon it started up again. My father forbade any of us to answer it and instructed us to go back to bed. We were wide awake when some time later my mother, who must have taken a taxi, rang the doorbell. Like the phone, the doorbell continued to ring. We crept downstairs to the kitchen where my father, seated at the kitchen table, pretended to read the paper.

"Mom's buzzing the doorbell. Why don't you let her in?"

My father frowned and shook his head. When we moved toward the door, he forbade us to open it and commanded us to move away. By this time my mother was pounding on the door, crying and pleading with my father to let her in. We started to cry, too.

"Please, Daddy, please let Mom into the house." His mouth was set and, by his bulging eyes, his flared nostrils, I could see that he was holding his breath, holding back his anger.

Dinner that evening had consisted of the detested trio — fish sticks, buttered noodles, and string beans. Detested but consumed. Now out it came, not just a mouthful, but the full meal. Not nearly intact, but mostly digested.

No one noticed, much. Not with everything else going on and everyone coming apart, except for my father. Or, in retrospect, especially my father. Covertly but inexorably, as time would tell.

My father let my mother cry and pound on the door until he felt she had learned the lesson he wanted to teach her, that is, long enough to feel that he was in the driver's seat. Then he nodded at us, affirming yet dismissive. We rushed to the door, unlocked it, and let my mother in. We gathered around her, sobbing and hugging her, and my mother wept and hugged us back. My father stood a few feet away, expressionless, wordless, alone.

Sautéed Prawns in Their Shells

1 pound prawns, with shells
2 stalks green onion or scallion
2 tablespoons fresh gingerroot, slivered
1 teaspoon salt
1½ teaspoons light soy sauce
2 tablespoons rice wine or sherry
3 tablespoons peanut oil

Remove legs from prawns but leave intact shell and tail. Shred green onions (or scallions) lengthwise and cut into 1-inch pieces. Mix light soy sauce and rice wine (or sherry) together.

Heat wok. Add oil and heat until very hot. Add salt

and garlic and cook 1 minute until the garlic is golden but not brown. Discard garlic. Add prawns, green onions, and ginger. Sauté prawns on both sides till pink. Quickly add soy sauce mixture. Stir-fry for 30 seconds to blend all the flavors. Serve immediately.

Makes 4 servings.

Note: Cooking prawns this way traps the flavor of the sauce inside the shell while protecting the flesh from direct contact with the wok. This makes the prawns juicier and tastier. The proper way to eat the prawns is to place one in your mouth and remove the shell solely with your teeth while you are sucking (noisily — it's the polite thing to do) the sauce trapped inside. Gastronomic, no-hands multitasking.

5

AGAINST THE GRAIN

The status of noodles in Chinese cuisine is a complicated affair. Noodles exist in a culinary limbo. On the one hand, they are dismissed as snack food, not a real meal. On the other, they are banquet fare, the feast's grand finale. Noodles in their long form are de rigueur at birthday celebrations and anniversaries, since their length connotes long life, which along with health and wealth is the appropriate triad of wishes for such occasions. No dim sum brunch is complete without their short form — silver pin noodles, made from wheat gluten and tapioca flour and rolled under a knowing palm to no longer than a bean sprout. While they always end a banquet, noodles can also begin a day, as Nainai chose on occasion. Her breakfast noodles, or *gee ma wot mein* in Cantonese — which my sisters turned into a juvenile joke, "Gee, Ma! What? Mein again for breakfast?!" — were cut from wonton wrappers into half-inch strips, boiled in water, bathed in oyster, soy, and chili sauces, laced with sesame oil, and flecked with toasted sesame seeds. Besides a day, noodles can also begin a life. The *sub gum* variety — egg noodles in chicken or pork stock — is traditionally served to guests at a baby's one-month "coming out" party.

But noodles as the foundation of a "proper" meal? Never! That Buddhist maxim — "there is no chance; there is only law" — could well have been applied to Nai-nai's kitchen. As incontrovertible as a law of physics, rice ruled at dinnertime. That other starch was banished from the table or, at most, to the bottom of the soup tureen.

Why this preference for rice, this bias against wheat, at a Chinese table? Primogeniture, for one. Rice was cultivated in southern China as early as 5000 B.C., whereas wheat was grown in northern China only by the end of the second millennium B.C. A second reason is that the techniques for making wheat-based *ping fu,* or noodle food, such as the large-scale grinding of wheat into flour and the art of baking bread, wasn't indigenous to China but borrowed from lands on its western frontier, possibly Persia. A third reason is the snob factor. As late as the Tang dynasty (A.D. 618–907), wheat and millet were China's primary staple grains, and rice was a luxury item available only to the upper classes. But when the Sung dynasty (A.D. 960–1279) fled its northern court at Kaifeng and established its new capital at Hangzhou, a southern city in the country's rice-growing belt, *Oryza sativa* became the preeminent grain for the first time in Chinese history. The noodle was now both commonplace and secondary.

Naturally, there arose from Nai-nai's "rice law" — rice for meals; noodles for snacks — the desire to break it. This I did time and again, with impunity, when I lived in Italy, where the culinary tables of my upbringing were turned. My favorite snack-on-the-run when I lived in

Rome and in Acireale on Sicily's eastern shore consisted of rice — *arancine,* those savory balls of boiled rice with a hefty center of meat, cheese, and peas dipped in batter and bread crumbs, then fried to a golden turn. As for dinners, I often ate as my entire dinner a wheat-based pasta or, occasionally, baked polenta, made of cornmeal. But rice for dinner? Even risotto? Never.

Little did I know then that my personal argument concerning pasta had a historical precedent: who invented noodles, the Italians or the Chinese? The most commonly told, believed, and erroneous, story is that Marco Polo introduced pasta to Italy after his long sojourn at Kublai Khan's court during the Yuan dynasty (A.D. 1271–1368). Historical evidence decrees otherwise.

Varieties of *ping fu* already existed throughout Asia: Russian *pelemeni,* Jewish kreplachs, and Tibetan *mo-mo* are just some of the examples. Proof positive remains elusive, but opinions about the origin of noodles abound, with the top contender for that honor being, in addition to China, Etruscan Italy, which, if the scant evidence proves true, would predate the Chinese claim by five hundred years.

What is noteworthy about China and Italy, the two countries most contentious about the matter, is that, ironically, both countries share the same low regard for pasta. The *insalata* of Italian and Latin spoken in certain quarters of sixteenth-century Italy was termed macaronic Latin because, like Venetian macaroni, it was coarse, rustic, and rough. Adolescent aristocrats dispatched to Italy to absorb classical art and high culture were disparagingly called "macaroni" — Eurotrash seicento-style — by many of their countrymen. Similarly, in China, noodles and their cousins wontons, dumplings, and steamed or fried bread were considered poor man's fare — fast food sold by street vendors from open-air stalls or ambulatory snack carts.

Another irony is that, in China, the secondary position of wheat and the lowly status of noodles worked in their favor, and in the same dynasty which had demoted them, the Sung. Employing the cosmological principle of yin and yang, scholar-gourmets created a culinary concept of balanced opposites — a synthesis of rustic simplicity and gastronomic extravagance. How to reconcile these two opposing tendencies? Cooks would offer, for example, a simple dish of wheat noodles in soup at the same meal where they served that esoteric delicacy, swallow's nest. This paradoxical paradigm of the earthy paired with the ethereal, the healthy with the hedonistic, has remained a guiding principle of Chinese culinary philosophy to this day.

Actually, the commonplace noodle found its way into imperial haute cuisine even before the Sung dynasty officially sanctioned its consumption with the equation: frugality + refinement = elegant simplicity. The Han dynasty (202 B.C.–A.D. 220) emperor Wang Meng ate the slippery strands, and his imprimatur helped noodle sales zoom off the charts and provided a precedent for future pasta-loving Sons of Heaven. The Qing (A.D. 1644–1912) emperor Kuang-hsu liked a light *ping* breakfast of milk, rice porridge, and flat wheat cakes. And a typical repast consumed by his successor Ch'ien-lung included steamed dumplings stuffed with bamboo shoots and pickled Chinese cabbage. Tired of the usual feasts produced in their kitchens, imperial majesties were not above sending a runner out of the Forbidden City and into the local night market to buy a bowl of Old Man Wang's Spicy Beef Noodles or Pock-Marked Mama's Bean Curd, culinary icons of savory simplicity that no imperial chef deigned to reproduce.

China's last emperor, Pu Yi, possessed the most austere palate of all. He never touched the sumptuous dishes brought to him by a procession of eunuchs bearing silver platters set on porcelain trays. Reporting back to the emperor's chefs after one such occasion, his eunuchs delivered this withering report: "The Lord of Ten Thousand Years consumed one bowl of old rice viands, one steamed bread roll, and a bowl of *congee*. He consumed it with relish."

Nai-nai would have approved. She too favored the pristine over the pretentious, the economical over the excessive. My grandmother had grown up in Guilin, Guangxi province, one of the few regions denied its own cuisine, unlike Canton, Sichuan, and Beijing. But Guilin, Guangxi province, is close enough to Canton, Guangdong province, that adoption of that most refined of Chinese cuisines, Cantonese — requiring only the freshest ingredients and unburdened of elaborate techniques or the aggressive use of condiments — seemed more like a birthright. After all, the two provinces combined constituted the single area known in ancient times as Lingnan. Historically and geographically, Lingnan was China's rice bowl, so perhaps it was also out of a sense of regional pride that Nai-nai preferred rice and pooh-poohed noodles. But there was at least one occasion when Nai-nai's incontrovertible law — the proper consumption of noodle food as a snack — was if not broken then at least modified by her son, who served it as the foundation of a memorable midnight supper.

It happened one summer, on a torrid Friday night. I

sat up in bed. I was hot and, having picked at that evening's fish-stick dinner and been sent upstairs, hungry. To solace myself whenever sleep evaded me, no matter what the cause or season, I climbed the walls. Literally. The pebbly walls of the second-floor corridor had just the right width and traction, and with my sweaty hands and feet I scaled them like a gecko. I climbed to ceiling level and there I stayed and sniffed. Someone was cooking. I tiptoed downstairs — the light from the kitchen drew my creeping silhouette on the wall as I descended — and peered through the doorway. My father was standing at the gas range, his back to me, in his undershirt, shorts, and flip-flops. He didn't look like the man who ruined our summers by insisting we swim the width of Tibbetts pool without once treading water, or who taught us how to ride a bicycle, the one English ladies' version he'd bought for the four of us to share and fight over. This was the same man who wore a suit and tie to work five days a week and walked briefcase in hand to the subway at 242nd Street to spend eight hours in his cramped Broad Street office at the tip of Manhattan, after which he made the same long subway trip back to the top of the Bronx to walk the mile or so home, this time uphill all the way. Who would then turn around an hour or two later to drive Katrinka down the hill to the same subway station to pick up my mother and drive her back home, at which time we had to clear the dining room table for dinner. During that hour or so between the two trips, this was the man, before whom I stood rigid as a martinet, who would then quiz me on my catechism lessons and the spelling of the score of words I needed to know for class the next day, who was quick to let me know when I'd made a mistake and silent when I hadn't made one. But he was also the man who would sometimes ask me or one of my sisters if we wanted to accompany him down to the subway station to pick up our mother. None of us relished receiving, let alone dutifully accepting, the invitation and often employed the one acceptable excuse — homework — to refuse; not, that is, until he sweetened it with the prospect of letting us steer. For a while, the bribe worked, but after a few weeks, only with me. I loved sitting beside my father on the front seat in command of Katrinka — instead of standing in front of him being grilled — his foot depressing and releasing the pedal coordinated with my hands on the steering wheel as I turned it left and right. I did one thing; he did another toward the same end; we were a team. On evenings when I steered particularly well, he might say so. Or there might be only the most subtle of smiles, or not even that, just a relaxed expression on his usually closed, tight face. On evenings when I steered badly, he might even assure me that I hadn't, or that it was all right, I'd do better next time. When the next times came, the relationship between my parents having grown worse with each one, I steered erratically. I dreaded accompanying my father to the subway station at all — the tension when my mother entered the car sucked all the air out of Katrinka and made it hard for me to breathe. Yet I couldn't bear not to, not because it was my obligation to accede to my father's request but because I understood that the invitation, automatic by now, in fact a blunt command, issued from a well of loneliness so deep that it precluded even the thought of my refusing.

Something on the stove was crackling and sputtering;

on another burner something else sent up plumes of steam. When my father turned around, he didn't seem surprised to see me.

"I couldn't sleep," I stammered. "It's too hot upstairs."

I walked over to the kitchen table, pulled out a chair and sat down. In front of me were two plates, both of leftovers: sautéed pork with Chinese string beans, as bumpy as the walls I'd just climbed; and *laap cheung,* savory Chinese sausage mottled with tasty, translucent globules of fat.

"What are you making?"

"Chinese food," he said.

"It smells good."

"If you're eating with me, get me another egg from the refrigerator."

I did as I was told and got the egg, which he cracked on the side of the skillet where another egg already sizzled, its white creamily opaque, its bright yellow yolk glassy as a jewel. The pot of boiling water writhed with billowing strings of noodles.

"Get me another bowl."

He divided the boiled noodles into the two bowls, scraped half of the leftovers into each bowl, and placed the fully fried egg on top of one of them, which he handed to me. He did all this with a practiced efficiency, an automatic sense of ritual.

"Start, before it gets cold."

I broke the yolk with my chopsticks and let the viscous liquid seep into my noodles, along with the drippings from the pork and string beans. My father watched over the egg cooking in the pan. When it was done, he jiggled it into his bowl, sat opposite me, and lanced the yolk. Then he plucked a cube of fermented bean curd, *dow see,* from an open jar on the table. The cube — its consistency that of the thick white paste I used for art projects at school, the kind that came in a squat round jar with a brush attached to the lid — was the color of a mole, and I could smell it from where I was sitting: musty, pungent, overripe, decayed. He placed the cube on the rim of his bowl, pried away a dab of it, and swirled it into his food.

"May I try some?"

"It's very salty. You won't like it."

"Just a tiny bit."

My father extracted a dot of *dow see* from his cube and placed it on the rim of my bowl. I poked at the taupe smear glued to my bowl with the tips of my chopsticks, then stroked them against a thin slice of *laap cheung.* Not as bad as I thought it would taste. I bowed my head and began to eat in earnest, as my father did. Our silence was broken only by the ambient noise of our vigorous mastication, the refrigerator's steady hum, the rasping of crickets outside the open kitchen windows, the whir of the small rotating fan. The food in my bowl was originally destined for my father's, and I knew that I was depriving him of half his Chinese midnight supper. But my sense of shame was not so great that I ever considered relinquishing the half in my bowl which properly belonged in his. After all, as creator and enforcer of the punitive fish-stick-and-buttered-noodles dinner, he was responsible for my present hunger — it was fitting that he should satiate it. I also didn't want him to have to eat alone, not when my parents' marriage was dissolving, like the pierced egg yolk seeping and disappearing into his noodles. And so I ate with him, almost in

tandem, my lips to the lip of my bowl, my clicking chopsticks, like his, shoveling into my avaricious mouth the Chinese leftovers, the freshly boiled noodles, the bits of crisp
and runny egg. And as I ate, I watched my father eat with
undisguised relish, his single-minded pleasure increasing
my own. That he had reprimanded me only hours before
for turning up my nose at a tasteless American supper only
to invite me to consume a delicious Chinese one in his
company surely had something to do with it. But even if a
sense of vindication had not been an ingredient, still this
midnight repast would have been satisfying, less in what it
consisted of than what it meant. Without words I was apologizing for my inability to swallow his Friday fish-stick dinners. Without words he was forgiving me my rejection of
those fish sticks with which he punished us and poisoned
himself, each bite a door slammed against us, locking us
out, so that he might hide unseen and unknown behind it.
This late-night supper was the first time, and the last, that I
would share a meal with my father, just he and I alone, in a
silence arising from and infused with, if not communion
exactly, then a rare and precious accord.

Gee Ma Wot Mein (Breakfast Noodles)

¼ pound wonton skins (20–24 skins)
1½ teaspoons oyster sauce
1½ teaspoons light soy sauce
2 teaspoons sesame oil
¼ teaspoon Guilin *la-jiao* (hot chili sauce)
1 teaspoon toasted sesame seeds

Cut wonton skins into ½-inch-wide strips.
Bring small pot of water to boil. Drop wonton skins into water. Boil 1 minute. Rinse quickly with hot water. Drain. Transfer to bowl and add all other ingredients. Mix well.
Makes 1 serving.

Old Man Wang's Spicy Beef Noodles

12 ounces flank steak
peanut oil (enough for stir-frying noodles)
1 ounce bean-thread noodles
¼ teaspoon salt
2 teaspoons cornstarch
⅓ one egg white

1 teaspoon rice wine or dry sherry
1½ teaspoons fresh ginger, finely minced
1 teaspoon garlic, minced
2 scallions, cut in 1½-inch strips
1½ cups bamboo shoots, cut into matchsticks
½ red or green bell pepper, cut in ¼-inch-wide strips
2 dried chili peppers, torn into small pieces (keep
    seeds)

Sauce:

½ teaspoon cayenne pepper
½ teaspoon sugar
2 teaspoons rice wine or dry sherry
1 tablespoon cider vinegar
1 tablespoon black soy sauce
1½ teaspoons sesame oil

Slice flank steak against the grain into paper-thin slices. (To slice flank steak thinly, freeze the meat and slice it when it is partially thawed.) Cut the slices into matchstick-size pieces. Set aside.

Heat peanut oil in wok till sizzling. The oil is hot enough when a piece of bean-thread noodle dropped into the wok pops to the surface and turns white. Pull the rest of the bean threads apart and deep-fry in batches, about 10 seconds on each side. Drain on paper towels, then place on a serving platter.

Mix together beef, salt, cornstarch, ⅓ egg white, and 1 teaspoon of sherry in a bowl. Set aside.

Reheat oil in wok till sizzling. Add beef mixture, stirring to separate the slices. Cook briefly, only until beef is no longer red. Remove with slotted spoon to bowl.

Remove all but 2 tablespoons of oil from wok. Reheat oil, then add the ginger, garlic, scallions, bamboo shoots, bell pepper, and chili peppers. Stir-fry 15 seconds. Add sauce mixture, except for the sesame oil. Cook, stirring, several seconds. Add beef to wok. Mix thoroughly. Add sesame oil. Spoon all ingredients in wok over the fried bean threads. Serve hot.

Makes 4–5 servings.

Pock-Marked Mama's Bean Curd

1 rounded tablespoon fermented black beans, rinsed
    in warm water and mashed
2 teaspoons oyster sauce
2 teaspoons garlic, minced
2 teaspoons ginger, finely minced
1 teaspoon hot chili sauce
¼ cup vegetable oil
½ pound ground round
1 leek, white and light green parts only, chopped
    medium-fine
1 pound firm bean curd, cut into ½-inch cubes

several sprigs cilantro, finely chopped

Seasoning:

1½ tablespoons soy sauce
1 tablespoon rice wine or dry sherry
½ teaspoon salt
1½ teaspoons granulated sugar
1 cup chicken stock or water
1 tablespoon cornstarch

Combine seasoning ingredients in a bowl and set aside. Combine black beans, oyster sauce, garlic, ginger, and hot chili sauce in another bowl and set aside.

Heat the oil in a wok or large frying pan. Stir-fry the beef till slightly brown, but still pink. Add the leeks and stir-fry another 30 seconds. Add the black bean, oyster sauce, garlic, ginger, and hot chili sauce mixture. Stir-fry another 30 seconds.

Add the seasoning mixture and bring to a boil. Simmer for 1 minute. Add the bean curd and reduce heat. Simmer till the sauce is thick and its flavor permeates the bean curd. Sprinkle the cilantro on top. Serve with rice or noodles.

Makes 4 servings.

6

THE SOUND OF ONE STONE FALLING

*F*or most of my life, my father and I inhabited two different continents over which we had constructed, each from our opposite shores, a stone bridge, unstable and unfinished. I wanted, I expected, my father to, Superman-like, leap over the gulf that separated us, that yawned between his raw end of the bridge and mine. If he were a good father, he would make that leap of faith, of love. No doubt, he expected the same of me, were I a dutiful daughter. But the most we were capable of was to stand, each on our most recently constructed patch of bridge, beckoning to each other, shouting entreaties that were half-heard in the wind's whistle and the ocean's roar so that in the end we returned, masking our disappointment with bravura or indifference, to our separate shores.

With each retreat, in our frustration we'd kick at a freshly laid stone which, lacking the mortar of communication and comprehension, of compassion, dropped off the bridge with a defeated plop. With time, the bridge grew shorter, as did our tempers; the gulf, wider; and the remaining stones looser, like our tongues. I say tongues in a figurative sense. More often than not we employed nonverbal communication: a gesture, a glare, a slouch. We utilized moods: irritable, sullen, repressed rage. We used, to great effect, utter and unbroken silence, that vacuum impervious to sound, that infinite void.

Which was the critical stone that, once jettisoned, destroyed the arch which supported the bridge and brought it tumbling down?

The one among many. Was it an early one, setting the stage for those to follow, which could only form a crumbling foundation?

My sister Marcy and I were invited to a party given by our next-door neighbor and my classmate at St. Margaret's, George Sansone. My father insisted that we dress "appropriately" — i.e., a skirt, with a crinoline underneath — and that we take a large box of chocolates, wrapped in gold paper and tied with a bow. Marcy and I were not only the only two girls wearing puffy skirts, while all the other girls were wearing slim pedal pushers, we were also the only guests to have come bearing a gift, ostentatious at that. It was bad enough to be wearing the wrong clothes, but the extravagance of the box of chocolates demanded that Mr. Sansone, George's father, march us right back next door to our house to explain to my father, Chinese immigrant that he still was after several years in the United States, that the occasion was just a little get-together, not a party per se, an informal occasion where, lovely thought though it was, any gift was unnecessary, actually, out of place. I could feel the box of chocolates I gripped in my hand melting in the heat of my shame to have a grown man, an American man, tell my father, a grown man, a Chinese man, what to do and what not to do, what was proper and what was not, patronizing words which sounded like ridicule to my ears and which my father accepted not only in submissive silence but grating gratitude as well.

Or was the crucial stone the time when Wendye, Gerrie, and I had gathered on Old Baldy above our back hill and Gerrie lost her balance, toppled into the blackberry bushes below, and began to bawl at the top of her lungs? We heard my father shout at us. He stood at the back door holding one of the bows from our bow-and-rubber-tipped-arrow play sets. He commanded us to come into the house, "right now." Whimpering, Gerrie passed through the door first, then Wendye, who for all her silent submissiveness still received a lash across her legs with the bow, as did I — two lashes, since I was last in line and the oldest, and he could rear back in his anger and let loose a second time. What stung worse than the force of those blows were his words — "That will teach you to push your little sister off the rocks" — words I was forbidden as dutiful daughter of a Chinese father to question, contradict, or correct. His mere accusation was tantamount to, and unimpeachable proof of, my guilt. My ensuing silence was the only acceptable response, and I smarted at the injustice.

Or was it a later stone? The one when the World's Fair had come to New York and Marcy and I, looking for summer jobs in the hope of avoiding the agony of a second stint at my father's boring, sweltering office on Broad Street, had seen an ad in the paper: the American pavilion was looking for "Oriental" high school girls to man the Hawaiian information booth and concessions stands. We'd received my father's halfhearted permission to fill out the application. But when we breezed through the personal interviews and landed our first real jobs, he forbade us to accept them. No daughters of his were going to cheapen themselves by ca-vorting in public wearing leis and a sarong. (When we at-tended the World's Fair and visited the United States pavilion, the "Hawaiian" girls were clad in muumuus.)

Or was the sundering stone the one not long after that, when I was a freshman in college and Wendye a junior in high school? "Discovered" in Saks Fifth Avenue by a fash-ion photographer, we were invited to model the season's look in the *Mademoiselle* magazine fall fashion show. With my mother running interference for us and with her assur-ances that fashion models and prostitutes were not synony-mous, my father grudgingly gave his consent. At the end of the *défilé*, all the beautiful professional models left the glamorous hotel by the side entrance, there to be met rap-turously by their handsome husbands or breathtaking boyfriends, or otherwise to saunter insouciantly into the autumn night in chosen, enviable, Garboesque solitude. Not my sister and me. The evening's euphoria vanished in a single humiliating moment when we saw, waiting in Ka-trinka to drive us home, our glowering father — lest we turn into streetwalkers on the subway between midtown Manhattan and the north Bronx — whose eyes suggested just such an ignominious end for us if he hadn't come to prevent it.

No. No to all of the above, though they were surely stepping-stones to the single critical stone which I now re-call with unwonted clarity, perhaps because it possesses a déjà vu quality. It is also a stone I do not share with my sisters, at least one of whom helped me bear up under the stones I've just recounted. This stone I bore alone: the collective "we" of my sisters and me became the solitary "I" of myself. (It is interesting to note that in traditional Chinese thought no "I" exists unless there is an "other" to validate the fact, the Eastern equivalent of the Western conundrum: if no one heard the sound of a tree falling, did it fall?)

The stone that took the entire bridge down tumbled off just a few months after the *Mademoiselle* fashion show fiasco. I was a freshman in college, and it was the last day of the year, December 31. I had been invited to a New Year's Eve party given by the parents of Laurie and Diane Roizin, sororal twins and my closest friends of long standing. I'd known them through grammar school, which we attended together, and high school, where we separated — they to a Catholic academy, I to Bronx High School of Science. Despite different high schools, we hung out together after school when light homework permitted and on weekends.

I had no problem wresting permission from my father to go to the party. He gave it without a second thought. After all, he knew the Roizins, their house was less than a block away, and our exurban neighborhood was unquestionably, boringly safe. But permission came with two conditions: because it was a New Year's Eve party and because I'd be coming home after — "right after" he insisted, and I promised — the glittering ball descended in Times Square, I was to take the key to let myself back into the house on the more than fair chance that my noncelebratory parents and sisters would be sound asleep. And "No champagne. A sip at most."

The party was fabulous. Laurie and Diane's aunts and uncles and cousins were incredibly interesting, particularly because they showed interest in me. And why not? I was a college girl. I was knowledgeable and sophisticated, or at least I was on my way there. They used big words I loved hearing and that I'd only read in books. They held important jobs I couldn't imagine holding myself. But most of all, they talked. They talked a lot. They talked to me, and they waited, with bated breath surely, for my pearls of wisdom, my bons mots. Why shouldn't they? What I said was important. What I said was fascinating. I could see it in their eyes, beneath the thickening glaze. Silence was unacceptable. Silence was impolite.

Right before midnight we all gathered around the television set and counted down the seconds to the New Year in loud, champagne-ready voices. When the hour struck, we drank the bubbly, linked arms, and do-si-doed. We tooted toy horns and donned ridiculous hats that we strapped under our chins. We laughed. We sang "Auld Lang Syne."

When I remembered to consult a clock, it was past one in the first morning of the New Year. When I checked the pocket of my coat, no house key. I had forgotten it at home, on the sideboard in the kitchen where I'd put it so that I would remember to take it on my way out the back door.

The long three-quarters of a block to my house, I hoped and prayed that someone would be up to let me in when I knocked quietly on the back door. Preferably one of my sisters. Perhaps I wouldn't even have to ring the bell and alert the whole house to the fact that I'd forgotten my key and, worse, that I was returning more than an hour after I promised I would. Perhaps my mother was waiting up for me, even though I was a college freshman and beyond such protective behavior. Perhaps my father was, suspicious of my unself-protective own. How dare they? How dare they treat me like the child I no longer was? Why couldn't they behave the way Laurie and Diane's family behaved in my presence? With interest, appreciation, even admiration. Perhaps a trace of reverence, possibly awe. What was one hour's tardiness on New Year's Eve anyway? Didn't they know that the fun only started after midnight? I should be angry with them — not my parents with me — for imposing impossible, outlandish, infantile conditions on my one night out. Didn't they trust me?! As for the key, I shouldn't be expected to think of everything, not when one year was ending and another was beginning, and on such a festive note as my first New Year's Eve party, unescorted and alone, without my parents and sisters to dampen my spirits, to remind me of who I was. That's what I would say when I knocked on the door and my mother or father opened it. If my sisters did, I'd say nothing at all. I'd just breeze by them like the cat that swallowed the canary, with champagne as a chaser.

When I arrived home, the house was completely dark. I walked to the back door (the night light above it was also extinguished) and knocked, quietly. Nothing happened. Half a minute later, I knocked again, a little more forcefully. Again, nothing happened. I took off my glove and rapped on the door with bare knuckles, with the same results. This half-measure wasn't working. They were all

asleep. I would have to ring the doorbell and wake someone up, someone who would come down the stairs and let
me in, hopefully someone not my father.

I rang the doorbell, its sound shrill and aggravating. It
wasn't a melodic, bell-chiming doorbell, but a buzzer that
could wake the whole block if the windows were open,
which thankfully they were not. Though I winced to hear
it through the thick wooden door, the jarring vibrations
didn't manage to wake a single member of my family. I
buzzed again, longer. I waited. No light went on. No sound
of slippered feet padded across the kitchen linoleum to
open the back door. It was cold. I hadn't noticed the cold
before, but I was feeling it now. I put my glove back on. I
turned up my collar. I wished I'd worn a hat. I fought with
myself about whether or not to buzz a third and longer
time. I felt sheepish to have forgotten the key. I was angry
at my parents, who were sound asleep, or pretended to be
to teach me not to come home late ever again; and I was
afraid that they were truly sound asleep and that I'd have
to spend the night outside, perhaps to freeze to death. Anxious, I gave in and buzzed again, keeping my finger on the
button for at least a minute while I stamped my feet, ostensibly to warm my benumbed toes, but more out of help-
lessness and frustration. I thought of shouting up to my
parents' bedroom window. But what if the Sansones heard
me caterwauling? I was just about to walk to the front door
and try that doorbell when my parents' bedroom window
swung open. My heart, and my breath, stopped. In relief.
In fear.

"Who's there?"

It was my father's voice. As if he didn't know. My

throat contracted to the diameter of a drinking straw. It refused to answer. It balked to be so humiliated. But I wanted to come inside. I wanted to be safe and warm.

"It's me," I rasped in a high-pitched voice, one that, insult to injury, cracked.

"Who?"

My cold face burned in humiliation. I'd return to Laurie and Diane's house. They'd still be up. They'd let me in. They'd welcome me. That's exactly what I'd do. I didn't move. Not a single cowardly muscle.

"Me. Leslie," I said in a feeble, wavering voice.

I heard the window slam shut. I waited — between self-loathing, fear of my father, and relief, knowing I would be safe once more — for my father to come down the stairs and let me in. And I waited. And as I waited, realizing that this prolonged ostracism out in the cold was but partial punishment for my dereliction, my self-loathing for my weakness and my dependency on my father, my fear of his wrath, and my anticipation of the warmth and the safety that were his to bestow were all transforming into hatred for him. What had contracted my throat to the narrowness of a straw was strangling my heart to the same bitter size, dislodging and extruding from it a deeply buried memory: Though I was locked out, I witnessed myself on the other side of the door, inside the house. The person outside wasn't me but my mother. My mother, whom my father wouldn't let in. My mother, who was crying, begging to be let in after a long day's work, to which my father was no longer privy, of which he was envious. He was punishing her for her work, in which she took pride and pleasure, as he was punishing me for my play, my ability to take pleasure in the preferred society of my friends instead of the forced familiarity of his Chinese relatives and business associates. My friends, who were Americans.

Outside the back door, when I saw the vestibule light go on, I had steeled myself for the encounter with my father. The time he had let me wait in the cold and dark had not been punitive but fruitful. Those long, humiliating minutes had closed my heart to him completely. If at one point I had been near tears to recall those of my mother and those that I'd shed in response, that moment of weakness and vulnerability had passed without a trace. My eyes were dry; my heart was ash. I ignored the cold. The numbness in my feet and fingers had spread to the rest of my body, infiltrating my feelings but one: I despised my father. This knowledge warmed me, as did its corollary: my refusal to be my mother.

I heard the slide and the tinkle of the chain being drawn back and released, the turn and click of the lock being sprung. The door opened. My father, in his robe and slippers, stood before me. He waited several seconds: for me to speak, to explain about forgetting my keys, to apologize for coming home late and waking him up.

"You're late," he said, finally. "Do you know what time it is?"

I continued to look at him, expressionless, indifferent, giving nothing away.

"No." It was the first time I remember lying to my father. Later, to soften the blow, to cover up my cowardice, I told myself it had been a half-lie and so a half-truth: yes, I knew it was later than I promised, but, no, I didn't know the exact time.

"It's after one o'clock," he said. "Where's your key?"

"I forgot it, on the sideboard."

I clamped my mouth shut. My upper and lower teeth clicked together like castanets and ground upon each other. I'd come close to apologizing — a reflex action, a learned response — but I'd caught myself just in time. I was learning. I'd get better at this. He would not humiliate me like he humiliated my mother.

"You woke me up. Did you know that?"

I bit my lower lip. I was sure I'd woken up my mother too, but he would have forbidden her to open the door for me. Just as he'd forbidden my sisters and me to open the door for her. I bit the inside of my cheek. My jaws ached. But I would not say I was sorry. If I even thought the words, I would begin to cry, on both counts: I would be me, timid and obedient, and I would be my mother, meek and submissive. I would not be my mother, to beg and plead, to be humiliated in front of her tormentor, in front of her children.

My father waited in the doorway, unmoving, expectant. I thought: He'll close the door on me if I don't give in. He'll lock me out of the house if I don't apologize. I feared he would, he wielded such power as patriarch. I hated him, my dependency on him. My hatred must have been greater than my fear. He must have known this, even if I didn't. He must have felt it, because he stepped back from the door as though the force of my hatred had pushed him away to allow me to enter. For a split second, I hesitated, disbelieving. I'd won. I had triumphed over my father. As I crossed the threshold and walked into the house that first morning of the New Year, I felt that I had breached a second boundary, one invisible but more substantial, a barrier that, once broken, forbade me to return to the other side of my father's fatal concession and my empty victory.

When I got into bed, after my father had mounted the stairs and returned to his, I began to cry silently into my pillow, so I wouldn't wake Marcy, who was asleep in the dormer of our bedroom. Why was I crying? I should have been happy. I should have felt jubilant.

Tears falling. If no one else sees them, do the tears exist?

7

BITTER RICE, SWEET RICE

When I was in China, I learned to end a meal with pure rice, quite plain, and to taste every grain. It is one of the most beautiful tastes in the world, freshly-boiled rice. I don't know if it would be if it was all you had every day, if you were starving. It would be differently delicious, differently haunting, don't you think? You can't describe this taste.

—from "The Chinese Lobster" by A. S. Byatt

*I*n 1984 I was a single mother working at a public affairs company in New York as a research associate, churning out synopses of current events in the countries we represented — the Sudan, Venezuela, Costa Rica. Before then I worked at a variety of clerical or secretarial jobs, so I could give my son the attention and energy that such jobs didn't deplete. When he was old and independent enough and began attending a private school, I was able to give him greater latitude and take for myself a more responsible and demanding job, one that would both pay his tuition and engage my understimulated faculties. It was at this time that a magazine called *Rice,* geared for Asian-Americans, hit the newsstands.

"*Rice!*" Sharon, one of my coworkers, snorted. "What kind of name is that for a general-interest magazine! Here. Take a look."

I leafed through the first edition. *Rice* was indeed a general-interest magazine, like the old *Look* or *Saturday Evening Post.* Sharon, who watched me, arms folded across her chest, was Irish-American. Would she have been so scornful if the magazine were dubbed *Potatoes?* Or how about *All-American Meat and Potatoes?*

"Actually, I think the name is well chosen," I said. "Rice is common fare among Asian-Americans — perhaps the one across-the-board common denominator that we of Asian extraction share. Other than rice, what do we have in common? Certainly not religion. We're either Hindu, Muslim, Buddhist, or Christian by conversion. Physical features? A Chinese-American will hardly be mistaken for an Indian-American, or a Filipino-American for a Japanese-American. And our secular customs and political systems differentiate us further still. But we all eat, much and often, rice."

I was shaking and red in the face. I could feel the radiant heat that had risen there. This seething anger made manifest shamed and embarrassed me. Normally, I spoke little on the job. Platitudes. Pleasantries. I didn't want to be the nail that was hammered down, a person who stood out. Now I'd gone and done it. Shown that I had emotions, strong ones.

"Well, you don't have to get defensive about it," Sharon said, smiling, like the Cheshire cat who'd caught the mouse, the timid mouse who'd shown she had sharp teeth after all. She cast *Rice* a deprecating glance. "Keep it," she said before she sashayed down the hall.

Research was what I was paid to do at my company. Well, research was what I'd do, this time for my own purposes. I bought the book *Food in China: A Cultural and Historical Inquiry.* I meant to validate, if only in my mind, the appropriateness of *Rice* as the name of a general-interest magazine geared for Asian-Americans, with the assistance of a bit of rice cultural anthropology. My anger served as the wind in my sails, the fire in my belly. What I was angry about was not so much Sharon's dismissive remark about *Rice,* which, in my eyes, was dismissive of the billions of people who eat it — Asians certainly, and mostly — as the fact that I knew more about the culture and history of the Sudan, Venezuela, and Costa Rica than I did about China. I'd never felt this way before: I wanted to know about China and my Chinese heritage, something that had been foisted upon me, something I'd either taken for granted or forgotten because I was "assimilated," because I was brought up short by a subliminally snide or openly racist remark.

According to *Food in China,* there are two species of cultivated rice: *Oryza sativa,* which was domesticated on mainland Asia between northern India and southern China; and *Oryza glaberrima,* grown first in West Africa and apparently independent of its Asian cousin. While *Oryza sativa* has long been cultivated in South, East, and Southeast Asia, the following images are universal, and to me intensely personal and symbolically Chinese: a lone man behind a wooden plow, strapped to a water buffalo, turning over the soil of flooded paddies; rows of bent women up to their knees and elbows in muddy water, planting the rice seedlings every several inches, in relentless rows; bamboo-hatted laborers harvesting the mature plants, then threshing the kernels from the stalk, and finally winnowing the chaff from the grain.

"I'm full. May I be excused ... to finish my homework?"

My father, peering over into my bowl: "Finish your rice."

"But I'm not hungry anymore."

"Leave the meat and vegetables, then. But finish your rice."

When my father was a boy, my grandfather wanted him to see how the Chinese agrarian majority lived. Particularly, he wanted his son to witness the cultivation of rice, which the Chinese had grown and consumed at least as early as 5000 B.C. During vacations, my father would leave the private Presbyterian boarding school he attended in Canton and return to the family home in rural Langtou-cun, outside of Guilin. There, he saw in the paddies all around him the backbreaking stoop work that the cultivation of rice required and the daunting ratio of effort to reward. There, he needed to be admonished only once by Dashao, Nai-nai's cook at the time, to eat all his rice, if nothing else, "because every grain of rice in your bowl is a drop of sweat from a poor peasant's brow." Though he had to remind us more than once to eat the remaining grains of rice in our bowls, my father omitted to tell my sisters and me the why and wherefore which that particular injunction from his youth would have clarified. He also spared us yet a second admonition (if he ever knew it himself), which I found in the pages of *Food in China*: "If you don't eat every grain of rice in your bowl, your future spouse will have a pock-marked face."

Why this near-sanctity of rice? I read on and discovered that until the Yuan and the Ming dynasties, rice ranked first in status among the six grains, above wheat, barley, two kinds of millet, soybeans, and red lentils. Because it was labor-intensive and difficult to grow, and then only in southern China, it was expensive and consumed almost exclusively by the nobility. Highly nutritious, especially in its brown, unmilled form, it was easily digested. Subtle in flavor, it was an "absorber," a bland medium which took on, emphasized, or unified the flavors of other foods with which it was prepared. In other words, rice was a nutritional tabula rasa offering unlimited possibilities for culinary creativity, a blank slate ready to receive the artistic strokes of whichever dishes accompanied it. Thus did rice become the foundation of the *fan-tsai* principle, a Chinese gastronomic concept that decrees that any meal be divided into two unequal parts: *fan*, which literally means "cooked rice," but which is in fact any grain food in any form; and *tsai*, which originally meant vegetables but now includes meat and fish as well. *Fan* is fundamental and therefore the meal's more abundant component; *tsai* is supplemental, a flavor enhancer, a gourmet grace note. Without *fan*, one doesn't feel full; without *tsai*, the meal lacks taste. Only at Chinese banquets are the proportions reversed, and not till the end of the meal does a speck of *fan* appear — too ordinary to be prominent but too basic to be ignored — a hedge by the host against the possibility that a guest might walk away from the table without both consummated taste buds and a sated stomach.

Which brings up another kind of nourishment provided by a shared meal: communication, albeit nonverbal communication of the Chinese variety. Often has an Occidental come away from a meal offered by a Chinese host starved for talk more meaningful than pleasantries and platitudes, not understanding that the meal itself — the quality and the quantity of the food, the number of guests invited, the degree of formality, the importance of the occasion — was the message. Food eaten in the company of others is much more than the mere satiation of one's hunger; it is the great social facilitator. A shared meal can (1) initiate or maintain interpersonal relationships; (2) express the host's status, whether economic (how much can the host afford?), social (how much does he owe his guests?), or cultural (is she patrician or plebian in her gastronomic pleasures?); or (3) reward, punish, or in some way influence the behavior of the invited guests.

I remember my father telling me about an incident where Nai-nai was able to employ all three of these non-subsistence food factors — to her advantage and her rival's dismay — involving that simple staple, rice. The incident occurred not long after Nai-nai, who was my grandfather's primary wife, learned that he had taken a secondary one, Dejie. At that time Nai-nai was living as a dutiful daughter-in-law in the house of her in-laws, while Delin, her husband, was away on a military campaign. Even though polygamy was a common practice, my grandmother was devastated by the news and helpless to change it. All the power rested with her husband, simply because he was a man. If she pouted or made a scene, he had ample grounds to divorce her. Then where would she be? Better to accept life as it was than yearn for the impossible. And so, urged by her mother-in-law, Nai-nai left the tiny village of Langtoucun for the much larger town of Kweiping, where Delin, now a brigadier general, was posted and living with Dejie. His house was large, befitting his rank, and could easily accommodate the two weary travelers who presented themselves on his doorstep: his primary wife, my grandmother, and their young son, my father, Yau Luen. It was understood that all three adults would fulfill the duties and responsibilities demanded by their particular station and status in life and reap the rewards and privileges inherent therein. My grandfather's position was that of patriarch, with all the honor, respect, and obedience that word implied. My grandmother's was mistress of the house, the smooth running of which included the hiring of servants, cooks, and a nursemaid for Yau Luen — tasks which she, daughter of poor peasants, had never had the occasion to perform. As for Dejie, her principal duty as secondary wife was to be of service to the first. She accompanied Nai-nai on her social rounds, helped her receive visiting family members and honored guests, and ran errands for her. At first. But Dejie preferred shopping sprees, mahjong parties, and soirées at the theater or the opera. She also preferred the company of her peers, the citified concubines of Delin's officers, many of whom resented their inferior marital status, who put the bee in her bonnet: "Why do you attend the same functions as your husband's first wife? There they treat her like a queen, and you like a lady-in-waiting. Is that the position you wish to hold? Have you no face? Refuse to accompany her. What could you possibly have in common with a farm woman like that?"

Their barbed stinger struck, stung, and stuck. Dejie stopped accompanying Nai-nai anywhere. She neglected all her responsibilities to my grandmother, which Nai-nai chose to overlook, realizing that Dejie's recently acquired independent turn of mind would not long go unnoticed by Delin, or unremarked upon.

"When do I have time to fulfill my obligations to her?" Dejie replied when confronted by her husband. "My service to you takes up all the hours of the day and night. I accompany you to all your functions. I give speeches in your name. I dedicate schools and hospitals on your behalf. I receive and entertain important visitors when you're away. Do you begrudge me the little time I spend with my friends? To befriend the wives of your fellow officers is to foster good relations between you and their husbands. As for your first wife, I sincerely doubt she wants my company. She prefers women like herself — simple folk from the country."

My grandfather, who had been seated, came to his feet. "You will show more respect for my wife. I, too, am 'simple folk from the country.'"

Nice of him to stick up for Nai-nai but, true paterfamilias that he was, for the wrong reasons. Of course it didn't end there. Family dramas rarely do. The unresolved issue hovered in the wings of my grandfather's household, forgotten but not gone, only to reemerge center stage some time later in a different form — that of food, rice specifically — the depiction of which requires a slight digression. As mentioned previously, part of Nai-nai's duties at this time was to employ and oversee the household help. Because of his position and status, my grandfather encouraged her to employ a large contingent of servants. Dejie readily embraced having people attend to her every need.

She had already hired, for her exclusive use, two maids, a secretary, two cooks — one for Chinese and one for Western food — and two tutors, one to teach her the English language and the other the King James Bible. Since my grandmother's position was superior to Dejie's, she was naturally expected to have the larger household staff, yet Nai-nai insisted on employing a staff of one. But such a one! Dashao. A woman who wore numerous hats, and always at the appropriate time and the proper angle, including that of good cook.

"You must taste Dashao's cooking," my grandmother told Delin one evening after he was feeling the effects of a particularly heavy meal that Dejie's Western chef had prepared. "It's common knowledge that men make the best cooks, but Dashao is an exception to the rule."

Delin understood the remark to be the thinly veiled invitation it was and presented himself at Nai-nai's table the following evening. For his delectation, Dashao had prepared a feast: diced chicken and cashew nuts, minced pork and bok choy with mushrooms, served in a bean curd jacket; deep-fried fish with five-spiced salt; watercress soup; boiled rice; and for dessert, sweet walnuts. Thereafter, at my grandmother's direct request, Delin and Dejie dined once at week at Nai-nai's table, where there was a fundamental change in the menu.

"Ah, brown rice," Delin sighed the first evening the ménage à trois dined together. "I'd almost forgotten how good it tastes."

"Do you really like it?" asked Nai-nai, who was taking great pleasure in watching Dejie poke dejectedly at the contents of her bowl. "Unpolished rice is grown by simple country folk. They don't eat it, however. Oh, no. They sell it at market so that city folk can have their fill. If simple farm women didn't grow rice of this kind, city folk would never know how good it tastes."

"Don't I know it," Delin replied. "Don't forget, I was a farmer once myself. And I remain a farmer at heart. If it weren't for China's growing pains that have pulled me out of the rice fields and onto the battlefield, what would keep me from retiring from military life and returning to the rice paddies?"

A rhetorical question which forced an infuriated Dejie to set down her ivory chopsticks for fear her fellow diners would see them trembling in her hands or hear them clatter in bitter defeat against her porcelain bowl, and which permitted Nai-nai to digest her gratifying triumph even before she finished her meal. Nai-nai had wooed and won, with rice. And why not? Would Silvana Mangano have been as voluptuous and alluring in the film *Bitter Rice* had she been plucking potatoes from sandy soil instead of ankle-deep in a toe-sucking, flooded rice paddy? Then again, food has often served as a metaphor for sex — or sometimes sex's twin sibling in that whither goes one, the other is never far behind — and never anywhere longer, or more closely, than in the Middle Kingdom.

During the Shang dynasty (1523–1027 B.C.), the ruling house indulged in orgies so extreme that gluttony, drunkenness, and debauchery are cited as principal reasons for the dynasty's downfall. The depraved Shang was followed by the virtuous and longest-lasting Chou dynasty (1027–256 B.C.), who were the first to apply Chinese philosophical and cosmological concepts to food — the harmonizing principles of yin and yang and the balancing aspects of the five elements: fire, air, water, earth, and metal. Like its predecessor, the Chou dynasty didn't divorce human sexuality from the sensual appreciation of food. The fifth-century philosopher Kao-tze explained the inclusion of sex with (and often while) eating in simple mathematical terms: "Food plus sex (without excess of either component) equals nature." The Shang concupiscent glutton had become the Chou sexually moderate gourmet.

By the Tang dynasty (A.D. 618–907), food was more than just good-tasting; it could be good for you. Physicians and pharmacologists rather than cooks and gourmets became the prime authorities on correct eating practices, which now served the causes of physical health as well as hedonistic pleasure. Still, the new food-as-medicine theory did nothing to change Kao-tze's food-and-sex equation. Even Tang aphrodisiacs had surefire medicinal properties, such as crab apples soaked in honey and cinnabar served promptly after dinner. In fact, a criminal headed to the execution ground was given a string of crab apples for his last meal, so that he might feel elevated and cheerful during his last journey on earth.

Scholar-gourmets and professional cooks replaced medicine men as keepers of the gastronomic flame in the subsequent Sung dynasty (A.D. 960–1279), China's Golden Age. The sophisticated Sung were responsible for the conscientious development of regional styles of Chinese cuisine, as well as a principal paradox in Chinese food philosophy: complex culinary extravaganzas of common ingredients artfully prepared.

An invasion of the Mongol hordes ushered in the

brief, barbaric interlude of the Yuan dynasty (A.D. 1271–1368), where dining habits included eating hacked carcasses of lamb barehanded (with a little bit of help from the handy pocket dagger). The ultraconservative Ming dynasty (A.D. 1368–1644) followed, reviving the traditional Confucian culture of their Chinese forebears, including the ceremonial uses of food offerings to the spirits of the dead and the further refinement of dishes destined for the palates of the living.

By the time my grandmother was born at the end of the Qing dynasty (A.D. 1644–1912), the culinary principles and techniques espoused and adopted over five millennia had transformed the Middle Kingdom into a country of gourmets, no matter if one were rich or poor. In fact, it was the peasantry who through sheer necessity, ingenuity, and improvisation invented innumerable delicious dishes composed of simple, inexpensive ingredients for which Chinese cuisine is renowned today; and *chao*, or stir-frying, a method of quick cooking which is not only fuel-efficient but also blends the various flavors of the principal ingredients without sacrificing their texture. In other words, the kind of dishes Nai-nai herself made in both China and New York, and which she had Dashao prepare, whether she ate alone or had guests to dinner. In either case, both women agreed with Qing philosopher Yuan Mei's basic tenet: "A good cook cannot without the utmost application produce more than four successful dishes in one day.... It's no use to give him a lot of assistants; each of them will have his own ideas, and there will be no proper discipline. The more help he gets, the worse the results will be."

My grandmother's sweet victory with brown rice the first evening she invited Delin and Dejie to dine with her not only satisfied all three nonsubsistence food factors — improvement of her relationship with her husband, increased social standing for herself, and deserved comeuppance of Dejie — it also had far-reaching effects. It was unthinkable for Dejie not to reciprocate and return the invitation. But which cook to employ? Her Western cook, whose meals Delin found heavy? Or her Chinese cook, who served boiled white rice? If Dejie ordered him to make brown rice, which she now knew Delin preferred, that would be tantamount to admitting a second defeat to my grandmother. And if he cooked white rice, Dejie would be deprived of the lusty accolades which Delin had heaped upon Nai-nai. Nothing less than all-important face was at stake, and the prospect of attaining it seemed to be receding. The fact that she employed two cooks to Nai-nai's one, formerly a matter of prestige, was now a cause for shame: my grandmother's abstemiousness had proven superior to Dejie's extravagance. Or if not quite shame, then at the very least a diminution of her status — an indication of her epicurean ignorance or arrogance, or both. Which just goes to show what a long, long way a little rice can go.

"Leslie." It was the president of the company who had spoken my name, who came into my tiny office and sat in the chair opposite my desk, rolling his unlit cigar between his right thumb and forefinger.

I slammed *Food in China* closed on (too late to sweep it off) my desk and got back to work snipping out articles from the *New York Times, International Herald Tribune, Wall*

Street Journal, Washington Post, Economist, and other publications that had to do with our clients, of which China was not one.

"Whatcha reading there?"

"It's a book on China," I said in a slightly husky voice. "Chinese cultural anthropology."

Which at least sounded more serious than if I'd said Chinese food. If I was about to be fired for neglecting to do work for which I was being paid, it might as well be for something serious. My boss never came into my cubbyhole of an office. He sent for me to come to his suite. With the shoe on the other foot, it could mean only one thing: he'd come to boot me out of my job, now that he'd found a good reason.

"China, huh. That's an interesting coincidence. How'd you like to write a briefing paper on China?"

So that's how you were fired from this company. Pierced and bleeding and carried out the door at the end of a barbed sarcasm.

"The president of the Sudan is going to China in three weeks. He needs a crash course in Chinese history, economy, and politics so he can sound knowledgeable when he meets with Deng. But he also needs to know something about Chinese customs so he doesn't make an ass of himself at state dinners and the like. You're Chinese. I'm sure that you know a lot about these things."

He paused, twirling his cigar.

"Of course," I said.

"And what you don't know you can find out through research, which is what we're paying you for. Not that you'll do the research. Someone else in the company will do it for you. You'll be too busy organizing it, editing it, writing it up in a briefing paper that Nimeiri can read on the plane. After all, you're the expert."

"Of course."

"So you'll do it. You'll take it on. It'll mean a lot of work. How much, I don't know. This is the first time we're doing something like this. It could mean longer hours at the office. Maybe a weekend. You'll be exempt from your present duties, of course. This briefing paper is primary. Crucial. And we're in a time crunch. We need the paper in two weeks, and we haven't even started on the research, which will probably take a couple of days. Think you can handle it?"

"Of course."

"Good," he said and sprang out of the chair. "So who do you want to do the research, all the research, and nothing but the research? They'll have to get on it right away."

"Well," I said, drawing out the word, as though I was thinking of possibilities, "it should be someone who's already interested in China."

"Got someone in mind?"

I held up the copy of *Rice*. I told him who'd brought it to my attention just a few days prior.

"Sharon it is," he said.

There was a happy and unexpected ending to this story. The result of Sharon's research and my writing wasn't a briefing paper but a briefing book weighing in at some 140 pages. It took eight long days but no weekends to complete, and I finished the project well within the time allotted. The paper contained not only the original four chapters on Chinese history, economy, politics, and customs but also chapters on geography, foreign relations, government, ethnic minorities, and culture, which was the longest. My boss was elated with the finished product, which became a prototype for two more such books I would compile: on Venezuela and Costa Rica. For my labors, I received a generous bonus and a new title: director of communications and publications. But the source of my greatest satisfaction lay in neither one. I had, during those eight days of nonstop immersion in all things Chinese, become obsessed with learning all I could about the land of my forebears — so much so that I wanted to write another kind of book. Now that I had 140 pages of preliminary background research, I wanted to write a biography of Li Zongren, my grandfather, the first popularly elected vice president of China. His military autobiography already existed. I wanted to make his extraordinary life available to a readership wider than West Point cadets and veterans of foreign wars. What had once been inconceivable had become, in eight days, a distinct possibility.

And to think: it had started with a grain of rice.

Cantonese Fried Rice

4 tablespoons peanut oil
1 beaten egg
½ cup onion, diced
½ cup celery, diced
½ cup roast pork (*char siu*) or ham, diced
½ cup cooked shrimp (not canned), diced
3 cups cold cooked rice
1 teaspoon salt
½ cup peas, fresh or frozen
3 stalks green onion or scallion, diced
2 tablespoons dark soy sauce
1 tablespoon light soy sauce

All solid ingredients should be diced to pea-size.

Heat wok. Add 1 teaspoon peanut oil till sizzling. Stir-fry beaten egg 20 seconds. Set aside. Add 1 teaspoon oil, heat until sizzling, and stir-fry onions and celery 1 minute. Set aside. Add 1 teaspoon oil, heat till sizzling, and stir-fry roast pork and shrimp for 2 minutes. Set aside.

Add 2 tablespoons oil to wok, heat until sizzling, and stir-fry rice, breaking up the clumps. Season with salt, stir till heated throughout.

Add all other ingredients. Season with light and dark soy sauces. Mix thoroughly.

Makes 4–6 servings.

Seven-Treasure Rice

3 dried Chinese mushrooms, soaked in hot water for 2
    hours
4 strips bacon
1 packet chicken giblets (liver, heart, and gizzard)
¾ cup long-grain white rice, washed and rinsed
¾ cup glutinous rice, washed and rinsed
2¼ cups water
½ cup celery, diced
½ cup onion, diced
3 stalks green onion or scallion
½ teaspoon salt
2 tablespoons light soy sauce
1 teaspoon sesame oil

Remove stems from mushrooms and finely dice caps. Slice bacon into thin strips. Dice liver, heart, and gizzard.

Cook rice in 2¼ cups water. While rice cooks, heat wok. Stir-fry bacon strips with giblets till done, about 3 minutes. Set aside. Using what remains of the bacon fat (if there are no remains, add 1 tablespoon peanut oil), stir-fry celery, onions, and mushrooms 2 minutes. Add giblets and bacon.

Add cooked rice when done and still hot to ingredients in wok. Add salt, soy sauce, and sesame oil. Mix well.

Makes 4–5 servings.

8

In the Forest of Osmanthus Trees

Under blue mountains we wound our way,
My boat and I, along green water;

—Wang Wan, Tang dynasty poet

Y ou must go when the osmanthus trees are in bloom,"
my father told me when I said I wanted to visit Nai-nai,
who, after fifteen years in the United States, had returned
to her natal town of Guilin.

But that was only half the story. The other half was
that for the past few months I secretly had been writing
what I hoped would be a joint biography of both my grandparents. Originally it had started out as a biography of my
grandfather, but the more I tried to keep Nai-nai out of it,
the more she intruded. Besides, she was alive and Grampa
was not, and what questions I had I could ask her myself in
my spotty Mandarin or employ Daddy as my intermediary.
He was proud that I'd finally taken an interest in my
Chinese heritage, though he wouldn't say so. And I was

certainly not ready to tell him the reason for my interest. He'd only pull a long face and make that scornful "toc" sound deep in his throat. There was a third reason why Nai-nai couldn't be left out of the biography: she was left out of most of Grampa's life. Here was a way to reunite them. To know Nai-nai, both for myself and for the book I was writing — a book which was, in part, an apologia for not having known her, not having wanted to know her all the years she lived with us — I had to set her in the proper context: on home ground. For that, I had to go to Guilin.

I arrived in Nai-nai's terra cognita in the autumn of 1986. Thirteen years had passed since she left our home in Riverdale to take up residence in the house she had had built as a wedding present for my mother and father. That house, which my parents never occupied due to the Sino-Japanese War, was my home for a full month.

"Tell us about where you lived, Daddy, when you were a little boy. Tell us what your home was like, in China."

"When I was little, I lived in Guilin. I didn't like taking a bath. I would run outside behind our house and hide in one of the big earthenware jars, bigger than me, one that wasn't full of rice. One day I ran away from my amah and jumped inside one of those big grain jars. But she had filled the jar halfway with warm water, so I got my bath anyway.

"When I was little, I saw a tiger behind our house. When the tiger saw me, it started to chase me. I ran as fast as I could and jumped inside an empty grain jar to hide. I could hear the tiger growling and sniffing, but I was safe inside the jar. When the tiger went away, I climbed out."

"That's not true, Daddy. There aren't any tigers in China. Only in Africa."

"You're telling a story."
"You're making it up."
"We don't believe you."
"What do you know? You're not even Chinese. All of you are juk sing.*"*
"Mommy, what's juk sing?*"*
Silence. Then a shrug of her shoulders that says, I don't know. Or, I won't tell.

I followed my father's advice: I timed my visit to coincide with the flowering of the osmanthus trees. That's what Guilin means. *Gui* = osmanthus. *Lin* = forest. So when I stepped out of the plane on that moonless October night, my first sensation was olfactory. I smelled the city of my forebears before I saw it. Orange blossoms but subtler, more nuanced. I walked down the rollaway staircase onto the spottily lit tarmac toward the airport arrival and departure building. I knew they were there. Not Jiaqiu and Tanmin, Nai-nai's nephew and his wife, sent to collect me, but the hundreds of limestone karst formations thrust up from their seabed some 300 million years ago and weathered and eroded into their present-day configurations. They would assure me of what the pervasive, sweet orange fragrance strongly suggested: that I was indeed, at last, in the Forest of Osmanthus Trees.

Already I knew some of their names, some of their shapes, some of their legends. Old Man Hill, who sat facing the sea awaiting the return of his unfilial son for so long that he'd turned to stone. Piercing Rock, whose gaping hole was the result of a general's arrow shot in a contest of strength that reestablished the allegiance of a rebellious tribe to the emperor. Elephant Trunk Hill, the kindly pachyderm that deserted the emperor's ranks to help Guilinese farmers plow their paddies during a famine, only to become petrified when a vengeful general thrust a sword into the back of its neck — the hilt of that sword the Buddhist reliquary tower that stands there today. Taken all together, those limestone cliffs that invisibly but palpably surrounded me were once stones carried from the country's vast interior by conscripted laborers to throw into the South China Sea. The laborers got only as far as Guilin, and the stones have remained here ever since.

Guilin's importance as a commercial and cultural center began in 214 B.C., when the first Qin emperor built the nearby Lin Canal to connect the Yangtze and the Pearl rivers, thereby establishing a north-south trade route for military transport and trade. From the Ming dynasty (A.D. 1368–1644) to the 1950s, Guilin served as the capital of Guangxi province, which, located in southwestern China, was far from Beijing's administrative authority and cultural influence. The headquarters of an American air force unit in World War II, Guilin was described by author-historian Theodore White, then a foreign correspondent, as "the most lovable and abandoned city in the Orient. For intellectual Americans there was always good conversation; for Americans of a more earthy sort there were women." And for a group of Chinese liberals who took advantage of Guangxi's reputation as a prickly thorn in authority's side, Guilin was a safe haven from which to irritate Chiang Kai-shek's central government.

For most of its history, Guangxi has been known for four things: the aforementioned aversion to authority, its extreme poverty, the quality of its fighting men, and as a way station for opium shipments passing from India to Guangxi's neighbor to the east, Guangdong province. Given Guangxi's rebellious nature, it's not surprising that the Taiping Rebellion, which hastened the downfall of the decadent Qing dynasty (A.D. 1644–1912), began here. Nor that the Northern Expedition, the purpose of which was to unify China and rid the country of its fractious warlords, had its starting point in the then provincial capital of Guilin. Despite the Northern Expedition's success, Guangxi, dissatisfied with the policies of Chiang's Guomindang government, threatened more than once to secede. Even today the independent-minded, multiethnic province, many of whose citizens belong to the Zhuang ethnic minority, is officially known as the Guangxi-Zhuang Autonomous Region.

All this I knew because I'd read it in scores of books, in hundreds of magazine and newspaper articles, in miles of microfilm — the background I needed to write the briefing book for the president of the Sudan's visit to China. I had done my homework. But standing on the stone terrace outside my room, fresh from my mosquito-netted bed, I saw that my homework had been the Zen-proverbial "finger pointing at the moon." What I'd read about, what I had seen reproduced dozens of times in photographs and in paintings, was now reality, and right before my eyes. The "moon" itself. The improbable, impetuous limestone towers for which Guilin is famous.

I looked at them as one should look at a vertical Chinese landscape scroll: from top to bottom, from far to near. In the distance, to the west, was Folded Brocade Mountain — layer upon layer of soft greens, grays, and violets, like so many quilts folded neatly, one piled atop the other. To the east, on the riverbank, the straight, proud shaft of Wave Restraining Hill was more than adequate to contain the Li River, which, due to the dry season, was almost at a standstill. Nai-nai had her house built close to and equidistant from the two peaks for both aesthetic and practical purposes: both contain caves that were natural air-raid shelters when the Japanese bombed Guilin during the Sino-Japanese War.

I gazed below me, to the middle ground. Folded Brocade Street, broad and winding, was already a cacophony of bleating truck horns and trilling bicycle bells, already a swollen current of drivers, cyclists, and basket-bearing or child-carrying pedestrians. I took in the foreground, the high, thick, whitewashed wall that surrounded Nai-nai's half-timbered, two-story, brick-and-stucco house. Chinese Tudor, I thought, and déjà vu. The resemblance to my childhood home in Riverdale was uncanny, though that house lacked this one's thick outer wall, onto which was built a row of small rooms that traditionally had no place in a Chinese house: a storage room for coal, a privy, a washroom with a new shower, a kitchen, and a larder. Inside the house proper were a full bathroom and a half bath with Western-style toilets, a distinction Nai-nai's house was the first in Guilin to possess.

I performed my morning ablutions in the upstairs half bath, dressed, and descended the curving staircase. Tan-min was waiting for me in the dining room with my breakfast: a bowl of *mi-fen* — rice noodles — in consommé with roast pork and bok choy. When I took a bite of bok choy, it tasted better than I remembered. It was, in fact, delicious.

"A Guilinese specialty," Tanmin said about the savory dish. Guilin dialect was thankfully closer to Mandarin than to hard-voweled Cantonese, with its impossible seven tones instead of Mandarin's mere four. She and Jiaqiu had eaten breakfast earlier, she told me. As had Lizi, their son, and his wife, Nannan, and their son, Liqi. Except for Tanmin, the adults were all at work; the sole child, at school. It struck me that I was living just one generation shy of what the traditional Chinese family once considered ideal: five generations under the same roof. And that I hadn't yet seen Nai-nai, having arrived too late the night before, when she was already asleep.

Tanmin slipped into Nai-nai's room, which was toward the back of the house, while I ate my *mi-fen* at the dining room table. I heard her voice, raised several decibels, as she prepared Nai-nai, who was clearly hard of hearing and lying in bed, for my visit.

"Sit up," I heard, followed by the creak of springs. "That's better. Let me help you put your sweater on. Lay-zuh-lee is here to see you. Lay-zuh-lee. You remember Lay-zuh-lee. Your granddaughter. Mah-cee, Lay-zuh-lee, When-dee, Jeh-lee," Tanmin chanted (approximating Marcy, Leslie, Wendye, Gerrie), plying Nai-nai with mnemonic clues.

I heard some rustling noises, after which Tanmin scurried into the dining room, smiling encouragingly, to lead me into Nai-nai's room. The shades were drawn; the room was in semi-darkness. It smelled strongly of Tiger Balm, weakly of urine and subtropical mustiness. Gradually, my eyes adjusted to the change in light. Nai-nai was sitting in the wheelchair that Marcy and I had bought for her in

Hong Kong and had shipped to Guilin. The chair looked too big for her, though it was the smallest model we could find, collapsible, tidy. Despite the heat, Nai-nai was wearing her tea cozy hat and a gray wool cardigan over her flannel nightgown. She was smaller and thinner than I remembered. She was, I told myself, ninety-six years old, after all. I knew she didn't recognize me, despite Tanmin's encouraging and loud repetitions of "Lay-zuh-lee. You remember Lay-zuh-lee." I, too, had changed, after all, but I knew that wasn't the reason. I bent down and kissed her on the cheek, breathed in the scent of Tiger Balm, my cheek brushing slightly against the tea cozy's black velvet. Now that I had the Chinese words, I wanted to say, but I did not say: Did Daddy really take baths in a rice storage jar when he was little? Were there really tigers in Guilin then? And did a tiger really chase Daddy when he was little? What was Daddy like, when he was a boy? Was he smart? Was he so smart that he didn't have to study that hard and could spend a lot of time playing tennis? He said he studied all the time at college, but the one college photo I have of him, he's on a tennis court wearing white flannels and swinging a racket. That he studied all the time, was that a made-up story? Was the tiger?

Tanmin accompanied me to, but did not climb, solitary Single Beauty Peak, whose summit towers above the campus of Guangxi Teachers College, which was once the palace grounds of a fourteenth-century prince, nephew to the emperor. I was winded when I finally reached the top, but the view was more than worth the flight of 306 high-riser stone steps. Single Beauty was Guilin's sheerest climb, highest peak, and, because there was no other promontory nearby to obstruct the view, best vantage point from which to see for miles and miles. From here, and in the blue-gold haze of late morning, I saw that the Chinese word for "landscape," *shan-shui* — literally "mountains and water" — was, likewise, to be taken literally. Rimming the horizon, hundreds of jagged, denuded crags or rounded, plant-lush peaks soared straight up without warning from the verdant plain. The sluggish Li River, stippled with rickety houseboats and fishing boats made from lengths of bamboo lashed together, wended its jade-green way among them. Closer by were Fir Lake and Banyan Lake, both embroidered with walkways, flowerbeds, and pergolas. No wonder Guilin had for centuries been the destination of Chinese painter-poets in quest of immortality, the kind achieved by setting down on silk, paper, or stone the "fragment of eternity" to be found there. A Chinese art historian once told me that four elements were necessary to a Chinese garden: rocks (or mountains), water, plants (trees, particularly), and buildings. Viewed from above, Guilin was one grand garden, on a grand scale.

As I descended Single Beauty Peak, the Edenic qualities of the city as seen from above transformed to the Brueghelesque the closer I came to ground level. Never had I seen, not even in small-town Sicily, my address for half a year, life lived so openly, so completely in the public eye as in Guilin. Private life extruded from the doorways, spilling out onto the streets. Everywhere I saw Guilinese cooking and eating their midday meal, washing their dishes as well as their clothes, hanging the latter on ropes strung between trees to dry. Tanmin and I turned down another larger, more commercial street, where seamstresses hunched over treadle sewing machines making or repairing clothing, and cobblers affixed shoe soles and heels. Bed quilts were dragged out of a house for a thorough wash and rinse. Even the storefronts had no fronts: al fresco barber shops, restaurants, pharmacies — testament to China's infatuation with free enterprise and Deng Xiaoping's responsibility system.

Once we crossed the threshold of Nai-nai's compound the frantic activity and sensory overload ceased. The dining room table was set with six bowls and sets of chopsticks. On a side table was a tureen of bitter-melon soup. At the center of the dining table, platters of pork sautéed with more bitter melon, *see yao gai* chicken, *guy-lan* in oyster sauce, and a big pot of boiled white rice. I thought of Jean Cocteau's *Beauty and the Beast,* where the banquets appeared as if by magic. Who had prepared this collation, and, by the steam rising from the various dishes, right on cue? Jiaqiu came down the stairs. Lizi, Nannan, and their son, Liqi, entered, nodded, smiled, then settled into their chairs. Tanmin insisted I do the same.

"And Nai-nai?" I said.

"She's already eaten," Tanmin replied, and ladled some soup into my bowl. *"Chi fan."*

"Chi fan," the others repeated.

We bowed our heads over our bowls. In the avid silence of eating, I heard, just barely, someone humming and shuffling about in the outdoor kitchen, or larder. The ghostly prestidigitator who had prepared this very real meal.

I sat on the front porch after my postprandial nap, a daily household custom. The others were still sleeping.

Nai-nai, who slept for much of the day and night and of whom I'd seen the least in actuality — brief morning greetings such as we exchanged the first day of my visit — I saw symbolically, all around me. I was struck by how much her house in Guilin resembled my childhood home in suburban New York City. Like the rose garden in the front yard, its dense, heady fragrance intermingling with the lighter perfume of the osmanthus tree nearby. Like the vegetable garden — rows of tomato, bok choy, bitter melon, and Chinese string bean plants — dominating the backyard, where I spied a chicken coop, an improvement in self-sufficiency over our New York residence. I took in these relics or remnants of the tiny but obstreperous woman who once controlled, if not our lives, at least our mealtimes — occasions at which she no longer presided, and surely no longer prepared, though the dishes I'd been served at every meal since my arrival assured me she was present in every bite. The bok choy, of which I gladly took second helpings, the succulent spareribs, with black beans and soy sauce, that literally slid off the bone, even the *la-jiao* tasted of Nai-nai's cooking.

By the Tang dynasty (A.D. 618–907), cooking in southern China — unlike in the north, where the superior position of men granted them a monopoly on all the arts — was a specifically female endeavor. If a northern woman was admired for her golden lotuses, her tiny broken and bound feet, a southern woman was honored for her skill in the kitchen. Small wonder that Nai-nai, when she lived with us in New York, was happiest boiling, steaming, roasting, pot-stewing, stir-frying, deep-frying, salting, pickling, or drying food in her kitchen, and planting, weeding, hoeing, and watering in her vegetable gardens! If she was unimpressed by the specialties offered in Chinatown's restaurants, she pored over the selection of produce offered in its shops. And why not? During the Qing dynasty (A.D. 1644–1912) the scholar Yuan Mei declared that the credit for any fine meal must be divided two ways: sixty percent to the cook and forty percent to the person doing the marketing. Nai-nai, then, could rightfully claim one hundred percent of every meal she made; in addition to food preparer and purveyor, she was food producer as well.

I peeled myself from the wicker chair and walked behind Nai-nai's house, where someone in a loose shirt and baggy pants was bent over a tomato plant in the vegetable garden.

"Chi le fan le ma?" she asked, when she saw me. She was tiny, though not as tiny as Nai-nai. Her face was crosshatched with many fine wrinkles, though her hair, bluntcut to her chin and held away from her high-boned cheeks by long hairpins, was jet black. Her age was difficult to guess. I was mistaken. She was not bent over a tomato plant but hunchbacked, with one shoulder blade that looked like it had buckled and been thrust up and away from her spine, which was askew.

"Chi le," I assured her. *"Ni ne?"*

This bit of civility serving as an introduction between two people may be translated, literally, as: "Have you eaten yet?" "Yes, I have. And you?" Figuratively, what we had exchanged was: "How are you?" "Fine. And you?"

I asked her her *mingzi,* her given name. Jiunyang, she said, and explained that she was a distant relative of my grandmother. She was also, clearly, the invisible chef, Nai-nai's caretaker, vegetable gardener, and, by the limp fowl at her feet, its neck broken, chicken-coop tender.

"You are Lay-zuh-lee," she told me. "Are your baths hot enough?" In addition, she was also responsible for the pails and kettles of boiling water (only cold water ran out of the faucets in Nai-nai's house) that I found in the downstairs bathroom next to the tub, its surface moss-green from an omnipresent mold that elbow grease might have effaced but that Guilin's raging humidity would only replace in a matter of hours. This was the same mold that coated the leather soles of my shoes which, once scraped off with walking, reappeared the following morning. My cotton clothes, washed the night before, never dried completely, not even days afterwards, but at least they didn't grow short green fur.

"Yes, thank you," I said. "Very hot." "*Shi, xie-xie. Hen re.*"

I told her that nevertheless I would prefer to bathe outdoors instead, in the al fresco shower stall. I told her that my father took his baths outside as a boy, in a big earthenware rice jar half full of water.

"Tell me when you want to take your shower, and I'll supply buckets of hot water so you can soap yourself with it, then rinse with the cool water from the shower. You can usually find me in the outdoor kitchen, or around the vegetable garden or chicken coop, when I'm not taking care of your grandmother."

I told Jiunyang that her garden looked just like the one Nai-nai used to grow behind our house in New York, that at one time there were nine people living at our house and that, astonishingly, she'd fed us all from less than an acre of land.

"It's your grandmother who taught me how to cook . . . that is, cook the dishes she liked, the way she liked them," Jiunyang said. "At first, after she returned to Guilin, she did most of the cooking. I helped her. She also planted this garden. I helped her here, too. Then, bit by bit, she handed over both jobs to me. Before I came here from the countryside, I didn't live in a place like this." She encompassed Nai-nai's compound with a sweep both of her arm and her gaze. "Not many people do, you know. When your grandmother came home, there were five families living in this house, and it was very run-down. But your grandmother is a venerable personage. The wife of Li Zongren. The families moved out. The house was repaired. Her nephew, Jiaqiu, and his family were sent for, to take care of her. I came later."

I'd passed Jiunyang's bedroom, hidden among the storage rooms on the third floor. It was unlike the other family members' rooms, unlike my room. It was tiny, without windows or a terrace. In it was a rudimentary bed with a penitentially thin mattress. Piled at its foot were all of Jiunyang's possessions: a few sticks of rickety, rustic furniture, a few wooden boxes and cardboard cartons, a threadbare quilt rolled up and tied with twine. A room befitting a distant relative, a poor relation.

"But why 'astonishingly'?" Jiunyang asked me, rather astonished herself. She picked up the wrung chicken at her feet. "I feed the seven of us with half a *mou* (one-sixth of an acre). It's not the amount of land you own. It's the amount of work you put into it."

She sniffed in satisfaction, then walked off, toward the outdoor kitchen: there was dinner to prepare, a portion of which drooped pathetically from her hand. Her remark corroborated what I'd read: not only does the southern Chinese diet support the highest population density on the least land but southern Chinese crops have the most nutritional value for the least land. So it seemed only fair that so much bounty on so little acreage should require such intensive labor. Little wonder that in New York Nai-nai rose with the sun to tend to her vegetables and retired from her labors only when it had started to set.

I heard water running in the outdoor kitchen. Jiunyang had turned on the tap above the bath-size stone basin. At ninety-six, Nai-nai was no longer a fixture in the kitchen — hers in Guilin or ours in New York. Nor did she putter about in the vegetable garden. Or forage along the roadside for *gow-gay*. She had, however, passed on her recipes to Jiunyang: beef and tomato with oyster sauce, pork and bok choy, which Jiunyang sometimes bastardized by substituting bitter melon. Nai-nai had even divulged to her successor the secret of her excellent *la-jiao*, which warmed the palate without searing the tongue, whose subtle but spicy heat was without the burn of store-bought chili sauce. In fact, I could tell no difference between Jiunyang's meals in Guilin and Nai-nai's in New York. There was a disparity, though, one that had nothing to do with taste. It was this: Jiunyang's cooking under Nai-nai's tutelage, besides whetting my appetite, evoked memories which otherwise would have remained dormant. By anointing my tongue with familiarity, she awakened my mind to recall.

Stir-Fried Pork with Bitter Melon

1 pound bitter melon
6 cups water
½ teaspoon baking soda
3 tablespoons peanut oil
2½ teaspoons garlic, minced
2 scallions, minced
8 ounces lean pork, thinly sliced (about 1 cup)
1 tablespoon cornstarch
2 teaspoons black soy sauce
½ teaspoon sugar

Sauce:

½ teaspoon granulated sugar
4 tablespoons water
1¼ tablespoons black soy sauce
2 tablespoons rice wine or sherry
1 teaspoon cornstarch

Cut bitter melon lengthwise. Scoop out soft center and seeds, and cut melon crosswise into thin slices. Bring water to boil. Add bitter melon and baking soda. Reduce heat to medium-low and simmer 3–4 minutes to reduce the bitterness of the melon. Remove bitter melon from pot, rinse briefly under cold water to stop cooking. Drain.

Heat wok over medium-high heat. Add oil. When sizzling, add garlic and scallions. Stir-fry until garlic is golden but not brown. Add pork, cornstarch, black soy sauce, and sugar. Cook, stirring, until pork loses its pink color. Remove with slotted spoon, pressing so oil drips back into wok. Set pork mixture aside.

Mix sauce ingredients together. Turn heat up to high. Add sauce mixture. Cook, stirring over medium-high heat until sauce thickens and bubbles. Add bitter melon, then add pork mixture. Stir-fry about 30 seconds. Serve hot.

Makes 6 servings.

Spareribs with Black Beans

1 pound spareribs, cut into 1-inch pieces
2 tablespoons salted black beans
2 cloves garlic, finely minced
1 tablespoon fresh ginger, minced
1 teaspoon dark soy sauce
1 tablespoon cornstarch
1 tablespoon rice wine or dry sherry

Trim fat from spareribs. Place spareribs in heat-proof dish.

Wash and rinse black beans 2–3 times. Mash together with garlic, ginger, soy sauce, cornstarch, and rice wine. Add to spareribs and mix thoroughly.

Place heat-proof dish with all ingredients on steaming rack. Add water to wok, cover, and steam for 30 minutes. Serve hot.

Makes 4 servings.

9

Dashao

*A*lready my brief but vital encounters with Jiunyang were bearing fruit on the tree of my joint biography-in-progress (the "joint" of which is a bit misleading: Nai-nai remained leading lady, but Grampa was falling from equal prominence and becoming a supporting player). Hybrid fruit. I was melding her with Second Cook — the wife of Nai-nai's First Cook when my grandmother lived in Hong Kong in 1949–50 — and together the two women were beginning to serve as the model for Dashao, Nai-nai's cook and confidante for a quarter of a century and a character as essential to my book as she was important in Nai-nai's life. Jiunyang I saw every day over that month. I needed to "see" Second Cook, whom I knew in Hong Kong but didn't remember, in order to bring Dashao, whom I'd never met, to literary life.

What I did remember of Second Cook was her likeness in a few photos taken during the years when my grandmother lived in the penthouse of a sleek art deco building on Link Road. Her apartment overlooked Happy

Valley racetrack, where on high-betting days we could hear the lusty roars from the stadium. Not that we ever went — Nai-nai, my older sister Marcy, and I — though we did pass it on our walks to and from a public park which I remembered, not for its proximity to the race course but for the life-sized stone animals that appeared, sometimes malicious, sometimes benign, along the graveled walks. I recalled two stone deer in particular, one standing, the other's forelegs bent gracefully under her proud breast. Marcy, being older and taller, got to sit on the standing deer. I never understood the rationale in that, since I, being lighter and smaller, was the logical choice for Nai-nai to lift up and set on the higher animal's back. This injustice, this loss of physical and psychological stature, caused me to pout and whine, to sometimes burst into tears as I straddled the prone deer, stamping my feet miserably and solidly on the ground instead of having them dangling along the other deer's flanks, in midair.

My pulling a long face often shortened Nai-nai's by a broad grin. Otherwise she imitated me. Mimicking my foul mood didn't stretch her face any between forehead and chin, while it added inches to mine. (I would one day dislocate my jaw in this way.) When I cried, my mouth wide open, my father would laugh, similar to Nai-nai, and call me Joe E. Brown after the rubber-faced comedian, which of course only made me cry all the harder. After she'd had her fun with me, Nai-nai relented and lifted me onto the back of the standing deer, which my sister had vacated with her help and which now only had to bound away to make me eternally happy.

Recalling this interlude in my childhood reminded me

of the photographs taken of Nai-nai's servants. There they were, in black and white. Sho-lan, grinning, hair-plaited, *siming*-jacketed, no more than fourteen or fifteen, held Wendye in her arms. Sho-lan, who was blamed for having spoiled my sister by picking her up whenever she cried or threatened to, which happened so often that the two of them appeared as one — a set of asymmetrical, unchronological Siamese twins. Sho-lan, our amah whom Wendye monopolized, upon whom we later conferred the unkind but apt sobriquet Pie-face. Her broad face was a single plane decorated, as a child would draw on a sheet of paper, with eyes, eyebrows, nubbin of a nose, mouth — features that lay flush with that shadowless surface. Next to Sho-lan and towering above her, First Cook (his name having escaped my mother's memory), as scrawny and tall as Sho-lan was round and squat, his gaze good-natured and sheepish, his protruding Adam's apple pendulous beneath the slanting shelf of his receding chin. It was First Cook who, alerted by my mother's scream that something was amiss, had come running from the kitchen armed with a broom. My mother had peeked in on me in the nursery and found a giant spider the span of a hand on the wall above my crib. It was swat, and swat again. No more spider. Unfortunately, First Cook was not on hand the night I was bitten by a similarly outsized mosquito. I scratched and scratched until it bled — not a good thing in steamy, subtropical, summertime Shanghai.

My mother: "It was wartime (between the Nationalist troops and the Communist revolutionaries) and penicillin was in very short supply, and very expensive. Only a few hospitals had it, and then for the war-wounded. Or you obtained it on the black market at an even more outrageous price. Your infection was spreading rapidly. And you wouldn't stop scratching. You were delirious. You had a raging fever. We had to tie your hands to the bars of your crib. We could actually see the infection spreading, moving up your leg. If we didn't get penicillin — thank heavens for Grampa — before it reached your heart . . . well, thank heavens for Grampa."

And rounding out the portrait, there was Second Cook, First Cook's wife, almost as tall and bony as her husband. A long head, a square, almost lug jaw, large, intelligent, skeptical eyes practically challenging the camera, wide, firm mouth shut tightly in discretion or suspicion, possibly disdain. A handsome woman. In the photo of Second Cook, I saw Dashao in words. She "dictated" them to me, this lanky stand-in for Dashao, whose photo didn't accompany Nai-nai when she came to the United States nine years after the success of the Communist Revolution. By then, maid and mistress had been separated by an ocean and a quarter of a century — the same number of years Dashao had spent in faithful service to my grandmother.

Unlike with Jiunyang, it wasn't through shared if diluted bloodlines that Dashao entered my grandmother's service as a maidservant and left it as a friend and confidante. China made widows out of women who were once wives, women displaced if not from actual home and hearth then certainly from a decent position in a rigidly patriarchal society where a husband was required for status, authority, inclusion, and where the lack of one was a stigma, a literal shame, and a sufficient cause for ostracism. Dashao was one such woman when she arrived at Nai-nai's door.

Strangely enough, both Nai-nai and Dashao had much

in common. Like Baba, Nai-nai's father-in-law, Dashao's father had also been a teacher who had failed the imperial examination at the end of the Qing dynasty (A.D. 1644–1912). He was also enlightened enough, as was Baba, to want his daughter to be literate and was literate enough himself to teach his daughter to read and write. Like Nai-nai, Dashao learned sewing and needlework from her mother, became a skilled seamstress, and supplemented her family's income with her handiwork. She, too, married an officer in the Nationalist Army, but her husband was killed in the provincial wars, leaving her a widow at twenty with two infant sons, both of whom died not long thereafter, one in a bombing raid, the other from smallpox.

Dashao bade me take up my pen and resuscitate her back into being. She had me describe her plight to my grandmother, who is interviewing her for the position of maidservant: "When I was a child and living in the house of my parents, I witnessed the wedding procession of a well-born maiden to a dead man. They had been betrothed since infancy, but soon after their engagement, he died of tuberculosis. I was touched by the pomp and dignity of the ceremony, and I vowed that if my husband-to-be died before I did, I would be an honorable widow and never again marry. Little did I know that my husband would be taken from me so soon after our wedding. And when he was, I wished I had been so lucky as to marry a groom who was deceased, for then I wouldn't have had to be lonely without him. I wouldn't have had to grieve on three separate occasions within five years: first, when I left my family to be wed; second, when I learned of the death of my husband; and third, when I buried my two sons."

Nai-nai conducted the interview thoughtfully and thoroughly. Not only was she looking for indications of the candidate's qualifications but also, equally if not more important, clues to her character. She had already formed a good first impression of Dashao, who had arrived with a letter of recommendation and the greeting, "My humble respects to the august mistress of the house." She also exhibited propriety and the bearing of someone superior to the position she was seeking, as if she were at home in luxury, familiar with wealth. When Nai-nai asked Dashao how she was able to support her two sons after the death of her husband, the prospective servant replied, thus explaining the reason for her ease: "Madam, I worked in this very house. General Lu Jung-ting was warlord of the whole province at the time, and I found employment as one of the many maidservants in his enormous household. I received no pay — just two meals a day and a roof over my head and the heads of my two children. When I heard that the wife of the man who had defeated General Lu was now living in his house and looking for a maidservant, I came straightaway."

And straightaway was how my grandmother hired her, with commensurate fiduciary compensation in addition to room and board, as her personal servant, her son's nursemaid, and, when she discovered what turned out to be Dashao's trump card, their cook as well. That position had figured strongly in the "rice wars" that raged between Nai-nai and Dejie for the gustatory affections of my grandfather, and it initiated a strong alliance between mistress and maid against my grandfather's second wife, to whom Dashao had taken an immediate aversion.

Dashao had me take up my pen again and write down

the following: Just one week after the first "rice war," Dashao entered Nai-nai's room and announced, "Guo Yi Tai-tai (Dejie) stopped me in the hall the other day. It was in the corner of the hallway at a time of day when no one passes. She asked me to work for her so that General Li could eat my good food every day."

"And what did you reply?" my grandmother inquired.

"I told her that I was already employed, that I worked for you and my young master, and that I was very happy with my job."

"And did she accept your answer?"

"She asked me how I would have responded if General Li had put the same question to me. I told her if General Li wanted to eat my food, then he should be the one to tell me so."

The era of the New Life Movement — a socioreligious movement that combined aspects of Christianity and Confucianism — was in full swing at the time. It included the improvement of personal conduct and the cultivation of virtues such as courtesy, service, honor, and honesty for the betterment of oneself and society. It was a movement that Dejie, who was in thrall to Chiang Mei-ling, Chiang Kai-shek's Christian wife, was quick to support.

"Except a man be born again," Dejie quoted to Dashao, whom she had decided was in particular need of salvation, especially since the servant's snub, "he cannot see New Life." Dressed modestly in a long-sleeved cheongsam despite the hot, humid summer's day, and with a King James Bible in the crook of her arm, she had stopped Dashao in the hallway. "I saw you watching that gaudy funeral in town yesterday when you should have been running errands for

your mistress. Don't you know that such expensive celebrations are wasteful and superstitious?"

Dashao shrugged her shoulders. "I like lighting joss
sticks and firecrackers and burning spirit money. Now that
I work for a wealthy family, there are lots of things it would
be improper for me to do but, thank the gods" — a heresy
which made Dejie clench her jaw — "enjoying funerals
isn't one of them. At the temple fairs and outdoor theatri-
cals, I'm forced to sit in a special section reserved for the
well-to-do and their servants, far from the stage and the
excitement. I must be on my best behavior not to shame my
mistress or make her lose face because of me. Sometimes I
think I would rather trade places with the beggar women.
They have a front-row seat, practically right up onstage.
They have no face to save, and so they can have a grand
time, laughing, chattering away, slapping their knees, without fearing what others will think of them. Even if I'm having a good time, it wouldn't do for me to show it."

That was hardly the end of their mutual antagonism.
When Dashao shuffled, Dejie told her to pick up her feet.
If her bun was less than a tight and perfect knot, she told
her to fix her hair. If Dashao cooked more than four dishes
and a soup for Nai-nai and her son Yau Luen, Dejie accused her of being frivolous and wasteful. When Dejie
came upon Dashao scrubbing her face and hands, drying
them, then repeating the procedure two more times, the
servant greeted yet another admonition this way: "Didn't
you tell me that I must bathe once a week, wash and boil
my vegetables before eating them, and wash my hands and
face three times a day? I thought I'd get the last rule over
and done with all at once so I would have time to do my

chores." When Dejie came upon Dashao scolding the serving boy for being slow or lazy, Dejie chided, "If you were Christian, you would be more charitable in your dealings with others. If you become a Christian, you'll grow a good heart, save your soul, and go to heaven."

To which Dashao replied, "I've seen Chinese who are Christian and Chinese who are not. The good actions of one are no better than the good actions of the other. And the same holds true for the bad actions: they are no worse. As for heaven, what do any of us know about what awaits us after death? Who's to say that your Christian heaven is any better than our Chinese spirit world?"

On another occasion, Dashao was sitting in the courtyard mending a pair of Nai-nai's cloth shoes. She was holding the needle very close to her eyes so she could thread it when Dejie, under the nearby willow tree, raised her eyes from her Bible and, seeing Dashao's effortful squint, remarked, "In the Christian religion, in order to enter the kingdom of heaven, the rich of this earth will have to pass through the eye of a needle, but the poor of this world will wear a gold crown set with as many precious stones as the number of people they've converted to Christianity. Those with the most gems in their crowns will sit closest to God the Father."

Dashao dropped her hands into her lap and burst out laughing. "No wonder you're so anxious to convert people! All I know is what is here and now. And what I see is the rich of the world passing through thresholds whose doors are held wide open for them, while we poor must slip round to the back entrance and pound with all our might for someone to open up."

"There are rich who believe, and there are poor who believe," Dejie countered, undeterred.

Dashao wet the end of the thread with her tongue. "The rich think it's fashionable to dress in Western clothes and eat Western food. Why wouldn't they think it fashionable to believe in Western religion as well? As for the poor who believe, their faith is seasonal. When the harvest is bad and there's little rice to be had, they believe, and the Christian missionaries give them rice. When the harvest is good and their bellies are full, they revert to burning incense in front of the ancestral tablets."

Dejie threw down the hefty King James in sheer frustration. "You should be ashamed of yourself — sewing in the courtyard for all to see when today is the Sabbath, the day of rest. If you must sew for your mistress, can't you at least sew in the privacy of your own room?"

Dashao pulled the thread through the needle's eye and knotted the two ends together. "What difference does it make if I sew here in the courtyard or alone in my room, since your God sees everywhere?"

"It's better that you're not a Christian," Dejie said, picking up her Bible with an angry swipe and rising to go inside. "You'd make a very bad one."

"Now there we are in complete agreement," Dashao said, slapping her thighs in confirmation. "For one, I cannot tell my hands to be still on the Sabbath any more than I can any other day when there's work to be done. They simply wouldn't listen. For another, Christians, so you tell me, always tell the truth. When I go to market, how could I tell a merchant who wants fifty cash for an article that I have only forty cash, when that is not true? My mistress Li Tai-tai entrusts me with the family budget. What kind of manager would I be if I paid all that the merchant asked?"

How Dashao felt about Dejie's New Life Movement was also how she felt about Western food, especially after Da Mama — my paternal great-grandmother — developed a fondness for French cuisine, a taste she had acquired from the days she lived in Shanghai. Now she had brought it with her to Hong Kong, where her family had moved so that my father could receive a good education, a Western one at that.

"Eating in a Western restaurant is much more hygienic than eating in a Chinese one," Da Mama explained, hoping to whet her family's appetite for a new gastronomic experience. "A waiter serves each person at table his own portion on his plate. The diner's eating utensils touch only his own food."

In fact, Da Mama so enjoyed eating at French restaurants that she devised a game — a game within a game — to induce her family to take her on these gastronomic "foreign expeditions." The game she taught to her youngest son, Solin, his English wife, Emma, her youngest daughter, Yifu, and her daughter-in-law, my grandmother, was mahjong, but with this rule: quarreling or losing one's temper was strictly forbidden. The penalty: the violator of this regulation must treat all the other players to a meal at a French restaurant. Most of Da Mama's mahjong parties were peaceful affairs, but occasionally one of the players, feeling a craving for coq au vin perhaps, or *moules marinières,* might contest a certain move or speak out of turn. Then all of them, my father included, would hop into the roadster and head down Mead Mountain to one of Hong Kong's

French restaurants at the invitation of the penalized party.

The first time, Nai-nai, her coevals, and my father sat down to a French meal, they discovered that not only was the cuisine entirely different from Chinese food but that the two styles of eating varied widely as well. Bread was served instead of rice. Meat, whether white or red, appeared at table not in bite-sized morsels but in a crude slab, which had to be cut into pieces with metal instruments before one could eat it. A dish, called a course, wasn't accompanied by others, family-style, but was sequential, banquet-style, served only after the preceding one had been consumed and cleared away. And the clattering abundance of porcelain! Plates of different sizes for bread, soup, appetizer, and dessert; platters for meat and fish. The near-blinding array of lead crystal and blown glass: tumblers for iced drinks and water, goblets for aperitifs, wines, digestifs. The armaments of silver plate and silverware: the huge domed tray for the roasted carnivore or herbivore; different knives to butter one's bread, to slice one's meat or fish; different spoons for sipping soup, plunging into pudding, or stirring sugar into one's coffee or tea; different forks for hors d'oeuvre, entrée, first course, second course, and dessert. To make matters even worse, each piece of the seeming arsenal of silverware had to be set at a specific location around one's place setting. Compared to the Chinese single porcelain bowl and single pair of ivory chopsticks, eating Western-style was complicated and inefficient to an extreme. It was not without a certain theatrical charm, my grandmother admitted when her first Western meal came to an end, the finale a crystal bowl of warm water in which a single slice of lemon floated, and she sighed as much in emotional relief as in physical satisfaction. Here was the cue for Dashao to help me advance what was quickly becoming Nai-nai's biography.

"An adequate meal," Nai-nai informed Dashao when they arrived home, "but nothing compared to your Chinese home cooking."

"I knew that," Dashao replied, displaying her gold-rimmed, overlapping teeth in a smile. "Did you think I doubted it? My concern wasn't which cuisine is better — Chinese or French — but the state of your stomachs and your bowels following your 'foreign expedition.'"

The Li foreign expeditions to Hong Kong's Western restaurants, once occasional, became frequent when Emma became a member of the family. Chopsticks proved too unwieldy. She replaced them with knife and fork, then suggested the replacement of Chinese food altogether. She wanted to eat strictly Continental fare, which meant dining out. Which meant that Solin was forced to ask Da Mama for an increase in his allowance. Her home cooking summarily rejected, Dashao retaliated by informing her young master: "Our household budget doesn't include so many meals at expensive restaurants."

"But Emma can't eat Chinese food," Solin replied, addressing his remarks to Da Mama. "It doesn't agree with her."

"How does she know?" Dashao quipped. "She has yet to get a chopstickful into her mouth."

Emma did not last very long as Solin's wife, or in China for that matter, but returned in fairly short order to England to enjoy the bangers and mash and the fish and chips she was used to. Dashao was not sorry to see her go.

Nor, eventually, was Solin, who remarried not too long afterwards, this time a woman who was content to eat home-cooked Chinese food with chopsticks.

But there was another *guailou*, or foreign devil, looming on the Western horizon of Dashao's Eastern world. Or so Dashao dictated. A woman whom my father met while attending university in the United States, married, and brought back with him to China along with their starter family — my older sister Marcy and me. Having waged and won the culinary war against Emma, Dashao was well prepared to meet and make mincemeat — in the kitchen if she had to — of her mistress's new daughter-in-law. My mother, however, was nothing like Emma. For one, she was half Chinese on her father's side. For another, Nai-nai took to my mother as early as their first encounter, which occurred in Shanghai. For this all-important meeting my mother wore an elegant cheongsam with a repeating pattern of the Buddhist eternal knot woven into the silk jacquard fabric. Circling her neck was a double strand of pearls. She had stayed back, waiting for her husband to introduce her. At his beckoning, she approached her mother-in-law, not rushing forward aggressively as so many Westerners tend to, but not hanging back timidly either, as so many Chinese were wont to when meeting someone for the first time. Truly, this Eurasian daughter-in-law of mine is half Eastern and half Western, my grandmother thought. And I don't have to be a physiognomist to know that she is blessed with good fortune. Nai-nai took my mother's hands in hers and, with Yau Luen translating, welcomed her into the family and to China, hoping she would be happy in both. By the expression in the young woman's eyes, Nai-nai knew that my mother understood, if not her words, then certainly her sentiments. My mother thanked her in very simple Mandarin and called her *"Muqin."* Mother. All the way home in the chauffeured limousine which my grandfather had hired for his enlarged family, Nai-nai held and patted my mother's hand and tried to make simple conversation with her. To everything her daughter-in-law said, Nai-nai leaned over to my father and remarked, "She speaks Chinese very well, doesn't she? And to think — she's only just arrived!"

Though my mother won Nai-nai over easily, Dashao was not so ready to succumb to the half-*guailou*'s charms. No doubt she was as impressed as she was skeptical when thundering trucks arrived in front of the house on Haight Road and discharged huge crates and boxes, two of which contained a refrigerator and a stove. Another crate housed an American automobile, a purchase which Nai-nai attributed to my mother's exemplary foresight and thorough preparation. "But did she think that our country didn't have cars?" she asked her son, out of earshot from his wife.

Other aspects of Western living as revealed by my mother's standards of housekeeping were also perplexing. Americans, it seemed, were very particular about their bathrooms. For them, bedrooms could be rudimentary, but well-appointed and immaculate bathrooms, with flush toilets and hot and cold running water, were de rigueur. And if the bathroom was important, the kitchen was crucial. "Hygiene is essential to food preparation," my mother explained to Nai-nai, with Dashao right by her shoulder hanging on every word. "One's health depends on it. A proper kitchen must have good circulation, lots of sunlight, and spotless utensils."

In fact, one of my mother's first tasks as second mistress of the house was to teach Dashao how to wash dishes the Western way — in very hot water to which was added dish detergent, a substance Dashao had never used before, then how to dry them, with a clean dish towel used specifically for that purpose, another first. During these strange initiations, Dashao performed her duties without question or fail, thanks to my mother, who, though inexperienced in much of the culture and customs of her newly adopted country, was a paragon of tact, diplomacy, and intuition. Yet surprisingly it was she, not Dashao, who threw down the kitchen mitt and declared the "chicken wars."

Though it was customary for my family to eat the meals Dashao prepared, one day my mother, who loves Chinese food but who was also homesick for simple, straightforward meat and potatoes, decided to whip up a Western-style dinner. Dashao's duties were thus reduced to after-dinner cleanup: she was not to prepare a thing. Her long, lanky arms folded across her chest, she followed my mother with eagle eyes as her usurper traversed the kitchen many times: from refrigerator to stove to toaster to electric oven to cake mixer to ice-cream machine. The menu her young mistress had planned was hors d'oeuvres on toast points, leg of lamb, julienned vegetables, roast potatoes, chocolate layer cake, and vanilla ice cream.

"It's surprising to me how many machines, big and small, foreigners need to cook a good meal," Dashao said, finally, "while we Chinese need only a wok and a cleaver."

"For example?" my mother asked, basting the leg of lamb.

"For example, mistress, that great big refrigerator. I can see the purpose it serves if the weather is hot all year long, but in Shanghai winters are very cold. Yet foreigners, I hear, rely on their refrigerator year-round."

"It's true. An American family would be lost without a refrigerator. We don't shop as you do — once, even twice a day. We don't have the time, so we shop for most of our food once or twice a week."

"Foreigners say that a refrigerator keeps food as fresh as just-picked or just-killed. But I don't believe it," Dashao continued. "Can you honestly tell me that a box that's cold inside is the same thing as a plot of earth enriched with a nice thick layer of night soil? Or that a chicken that lies in the electric winter of an icebox will be as tender as one that's still warm, whose neck has just been wrung? I don't mean to criticize, mistress, but despite all your fancy machines and exotic ingredients, the dishes you can make are proportionately few."

"That sounds like a challenge, Dashao," my mother said, smiling. "Remember, although I'm American, my given name, Genevieve, is French, and French cuisine is among the best in the world."

"As is Chinese cuisine," Dashao was quick to reply.

"And justifiably so. Perhaps we should put your theory to the test — a contest. There's no question that you are a better cook than I," my mother conceded. "However, national cuisine is the question here, not personal cooking skills. You say that, with all the ingredients and all the machines I have at my disposal, I am able to cook only a limited number of dishes. Let me cook them, then. You, as the better cook, may make as many vegetable dishes as you wish to prepare, but as for meat, you are restricted to chicken, and chicken only."

"Not just any chickens," Dashao qualified, not to be denied her say in the formulation of the rules of the game. "Only fresh-killed, unrefrigerated chickens."

"Of course. The contest will last ten days. We'll each cook dinner for five alternating days. Agreed?" My mother held out her hand.

"Agreed!" Dashao boomed, grasping it in hers and pumping away.

When Yau Luen and Nai-nai learned of the gastronomic contest that my mother and Dashao had devised, the latter attributed it to her daughter-in-law's Chinese sense of protocol. "To defuse potential rivalry, she employed a form of rivalry — a challenge — the result of which will be that Dashao will become her loyal servant and unwavering ally, just like she became mine."

Yau Luen disagreed. "More likely it's her Polish charm and her American rigor. A blend of Western spiritedness and seriousness."

"Whatever the reason," Nai-nai replied, "we will never eat more thoughtfully prepared meals than those concocted in this house over the next ten days."

Or more anticipated ones. The electricity generated wasn't just in my mother's American-bought range or mixer, it was palpable in the air in the Li kitchen. My mother created her Western-style meals — a variety of meat, fish, and poultry, exotic (for China) fruits and vegetables, and a vast array of condiments and confectionery — with the aid of her many culinary appliances and gadgets. Dashao, on the other hand, remained well within the limits my mother had set: chicken, common Chinese vegetables, such as bok choy, *guy-lan,* and celery cabbage; the usual condiments of soy sauce, black bean, chili paste, oyster sauce, garlic, ginger, and five-spice powder; and her wok and cleaver. But such wizardry she worked with her few implements and ingredients! Cold shredded chicken, chicken with cashews, *see yao gai* chicken, steamed chicken with mushrooms and lily buds, drunken chicken, chicken medallions with snow peas. At the end of the ten-day trial, my mother graciously conceded that Dashao was not only the far better cook but also that Chinese food was the better cuisine. The winner of the cooking contest, however, would not be outdone in international relations and replied, "I may be a somewhat better cook than my young mistress, but I also understand that she is an excellent dancer."

Given this unexpected compliment and cue, my mother changed into her tap shoes and set a big band tune on the Victrola; Dashao and my father rolled up the dining room rug; and my mother set to work a second time, beating out a rhythm on the parquet floor with her rapid feet to which Nai-nai kept time by slapping her hands on her bouncing knees. When the recording and the lively performance came to an end, who should be applauding loudest and longest but the winner of the chicken wars.

It was wars of a very different sort — the Chinese Revolution of 1945–49 and the Cold War that succeeded it and continued to be waged until 1971 — that separated Nai-nai and Dashao in the end. Shortly before the Chinese Communists took power in 1949, my entire family sought refuge in Hong Kong. We had moved steadily southward — from Beijing to Shanghai to Hong Kong — as the Red Army rolled through the country from north to south and east to west. Leaving Dashao behind while she made ready to travel to Hong Kong was for Nai-nai almost as wrenching as the many times she had said her temporary farewells to her immediate family, with whom she was almost certain she would be reunited. But leaving Dashao in Shanghai offered little promise that the two women would ever see each other again.

I sensed Dashao's presence, felt her tap me on the shoulder. I rolled over in bed, opened my eyes, switched on the lamp. She placed the pen on the night table between my fingers, opened my notebook, dictated the final chapter to her story: "You've been more than a trusted servant," Nai-nai told the weeping woman. "You've been more than a family member. You've been a wonderful friend to me, and I will miss you very much."

"Li Tai-tai," Dashao said, pressing her palms together and bowing repeatedly, "return to China when we have won it back. Send for me, and I will come. I will wait till I hear from you. And I will serve you for the rest of my days."

See Yao Gai (Soy Sauce Chicken)

3-pound chicken, washed and patted dry
1 cup dark soy sauce
1 cup light soy sauce
1 cup water
¼ cup plus 3 tablespoons firmly packed brown sugar
1 whole star anise
3 tablespoons dry sherry
2 cloves garlic, crushed
2 slices of peeled fresh gingerroot about the size of a
    quarter
sesame oil for brushing the chicken
1 scallion, shredded lengthwise and cut crosswise into
    1-inch pieces

Hang the chicken from the neck on a hook over a bowl for 20 minutes to tenderize it. In a heavy saucepan or kettle just large enough to hold the chicken stir together the soy sauces, water, brown sugar, anise, sherry, garlic, and gingerroot. Bring the mixture to a boil. Add the chicken. Simmer, covered, for 15 minutes. Turn it over and simmer, covered, for another 15 minutes.

Transfer the chicken to a colander and let drain. Cut the chicken through the bone into 2-inch pieces. Brush the skin with sesame oil. Sprinkle with scallions. Serve the chicken on a platter with the soy sauce mixture on the side.

Makes 4 servings.

Drunken Chicken

2 whole chicken breasts, with skin and bones
½ teaspoon sugar
1 cup *shaoshing* (or white) wine
2½ teaspoons salt
sprigs of cilantro

Rinse chicken breasts and pat dry. Cut breasts in half through the bone. Rub salt evenly into the breasts. Refrigerate overnight.

Place chicken breasts on rack in wok filled with water. Cover and steam for 15 minutes. Transfer breasts to a bowl.

Mix sugar and wine. Pour over chicken to soak and cover for one, preferably two, days, turning the breasts several times to soak evenly.

Drain chicken breasts and chop crosswise into ½-inch pieces. Garnish with sprigs of cilantro and arrange on a serving platter. Serve cold or at room temperature.

Makes 4–6 servings.

10

MOON CAKES, JADE RABBITS, AND ELIXIRS OF IMMORTALITY

From a pot of wine among the flowers
I drank alone. There was no one with me —
Till, raising my cup, I asked the bright moon
To bring me my shadow and make us three.

—from "Drinking Alone with the Moon"
by Li Po (A.D. 701–762)

*W*hen the osmanthus trees are in bloom — "the best time of year to visit Guilin," according to my father — is also when the Moon Festival is celebrated. With autumn comprising the seventh, eighth, and ninth months of the lunar calendar, the Moon Festival falls precisely in the middle of the season — on the fifteenth day of the eighth month. This is the day of the year when the moon is full, or "completely round," as the Chinese would say. The celestial orb is also at its greatest distance from the earth and at its lowest angle to the horizon, making it appear bigger and brighter than at any other time of year. And I was in Guilin to see and to celebrate it "the Chinese way," as my father would say, to differentiate the real from the fake, the wheat from the chaff, Eastern values from Western ones.

Of course, we observed the Mid-Autumn Festival, as it is less poetically called, in New York when Nai-nai came to live with us. That is, we bought *yuebing*, or moon cakes, from a Chinatown bakery and ate them at home washed down with glasses of chrysanthemum tea. I wasn't terribly fond of moon cakes — round pastries stuffed with various fillings: orange peel, red-bean paste, date paste, egg yolk, coconut, lotus seed paste — until I stopped eating them like cookies and began nibbling at them like cake — fruit-cake, Chinese-style, which is the Western dessert they most resemble. Cut in very thin slices, moon cakes become the satisfying and substantial delicacy they are, whereas con-sumed in generous bites, they're capable of gluing one's jaws shut and, once swallowed, sit heavily in the stomach like a stone.

If my family's observation of the Moon Festival on Fieldston Road in New York City was prosaic, celebrating it at Nai-nai's house on Die Cai Lu in Guilin was as poetic as the names of her street address and her natal city trans-lated into English: Folded Brocade Road in the Forest of Osmanthus Trees. As twilight fell, Tanmin, Nannan, and Jiunyang hung red-and-gold paper lanterns from the eaves of the terrace, then dragged the dining room table and sev-eral chairs out of the house and into the front yard, careful to place them near but not under the blooming osmanthus tree — the better to view the moon. On the table they set five platters — one each of apples, mandarin oranges, pomegranates, grapes, and melons.

"It's strange that there are no pears," I remarked, to call attention to the irony of the profusion of people bearing our surname (the ideogram for *li* signifies "pear") and the absence of the actual fruit. In fact, I was wearing the heirloom bracelet my mother had given me years after she and my father separated. He had given it to her soon after they were wed. Cast in Chinese silver, the richly fruited and intertwined boughs of a pear tree encircled my wrist.

"No pears. Never pears," Tanmin replied, taking me literally. "Only round fruits, like the round moon. Round shapes symbolize family unity and harmony. Besides, the *li* that means 'pear' sounds just like the *li* that means 'separation.'"

My parents had been separated for nearly two decades, but when I first arrived in Guilin, Tanmin greeted me by saying, "I met your mother when she accompanied your father last fall. You look just like her." I hid my confusion and displeasure as best I could behind a protracted smile and deflected the charge by switching to another subject as soon as it was polite for me to do so. It was not my mother who had traveled to China with my father but the woman he had been living with for the past several years. Not only had my father concealed the fact that his marriage had disintegrated, he had produced an ersatz "wife" as proof that it was intact.

Several teacups and dessert plates, two pots brimming with hot tea, a tray bearing a dozen or so moon cakes completed the table setting, the centerpiece of which was a

141

porcelain rabbit. When I asked Tanmin about the figurine (the alluded-to change of subject) she smiled, delighted to withhold the answer while divulging a secret: "One of our invited guests lived in London and teaches English at Guangxi Teachers College. She's also an amateur ethnologist. She will be the best one to tell you."

"Ah, the Jade Rabbit," the lover of myths said when we were introduced.

She and the other invited guests — all women, and bearers of more moon cakes — had taken their places at the table and were admiring the luminous orb in the indigo sky while they nibbled at the cakes and fruits and sipped their tea.

"In your country, you see a man in the moon. In China, we see a rabbit. Perhaps that's because in America, you see one side of the silvery satellite, while we in China, half the world away, see the other, where a short-tailed rabbit pounds the elixir of immortality with a mortar and pestle under the branches of an osmanthus tree" — she looked over her shoulder — "much like this one."

"I prefer the Chinese vision," I admitted. "It's more imaginative. How did the rabbit get to the moon?"

"Through a story, of course. In this case, an old Buddhist tale. Would you like to hear it?"

I settled back in my chair, indicating yes. She leaned forward in hers, ready to begin.

"One day, the Buddha, who had assumed the form of a bodhisattva, appeared in a forest glade, where he made a fire to warm himself. He asked the animals living there if they might give him some food and drink, for he was hungry and thirsty. The otter brought him seven fishes. The jackal shared part of his kill. When it was the rabbit's turn, the timid creature deeply regretted that he could give only herbs and grasses, the simple food he ate. Noticing the fire, the rabbit realized that there was something more that he could offer and, with that thought, he jumped into the flames. For this selfless act, the Buddha announced that henceforth the image of the rabbit would forever emblazon the surface of the moon as a shining example of modesty, compassion, and self-sacrifice."

After a sip of tea, the woman continued. "The Taoists went the Buddhists one better. Their rabbit received a second life, which is why they say he lives on the moon. He also was given the recipe for immortality — an elixir he pounds into a pill, a jade pill, under the shade of an osmanthus tree. Tell me now, when you look at the moon, what do you see? Look carefully before you answer."

I looked up, then at the masterful storyteller. She held out a philosophical tag, like a card in a game of cards, and I took it up.

"That's difficult to say. What I saw there when I looked a few minutes ago has changed into something else." *Luna è mobile.*

"Ah!" She clapped her hands together with pleasure. Evidently, I had plucked the right card. "A different image. A different image requires a different story, doesn't it? One that's just as memorable. Could it be a woman that you see? If she's beautiful and wearing flowing white robes, then she's the Moon Lady, the goddess Chang E."

I nodded, indicating that this was so. Whether or not it

was, I was eager to hear Chang E's story. The amateur ethnologist settled back in her chair, nibbled at her moon cake, and continued.

"She wasn't always a goddess, you know, and she didn't always live on the moon. How she came to be there is quite the opposite of the Jade Rabbit's story. Chang E used to live on earth, with her husband, Hou Yi. With his magic bow and quiver of arrows, he was the archer nonpareil of the Imperial Guard. One day, ten suns appeared in the sky. Ten! Our poor planet Earth! Drought withered the crops. Lakes and seas dried up. Every family was visited by famine and hunger. Finally, the emperor thought of a way to end his people's suffering. He ordered Hou Yi to shoot nine of the suns out of the sky. Summoning all his strength and skill, the archer executed the task to the letter, leaving only one sun in the sky. As his reward, the Queen Mother of the West summoned Hou Yi to her palace in the distant Kunlun Mountains and there she presented him with the pill of immortality. The gift came, however, with a warning. To demonstrate his worthiness, he had to pray and fast for twelve months before taking it. This Hou Yi was prepared to do, and he immediately settled into the regimen, but not before hiding the pill in his house. Unfortunately, when her husband was away in battle, Chang E noticed a faint light and a pleasing odor emanating from where he had concealed it. Being a curious woman — what woman worth her salt isn't? — and being Chinese, Chang E couldn't resist having a taste. However, she swallowed the pill and as soon as she did, gravity no longer had any power over her. Up she rose into the air and flew halfway to the moon. Hou Yi, returning home just then, gave chase across the sky, but

144

all the magic in all his arrows was powerless to halt Chang E's flight or return her to him. She flew all the way to the moon, her new domicile, while her husband took up residence on the sun. From their separation, the concepts of yin — female, moon, receptive — and yang — male, sun, active — came into being, the duality which governs the universe."

I looked at my bracelet of silver pears that symbolize my surname and bespeak separation — the state which the Chinese fear most but what, in large doses and in the form of voluntary and essential solitude, sustains me. Then I glanced at the round moon cakes, the round fruits, the round moon, all of which proclaim unity and family harmony. Oh, yes. There she was, shining bright and beautiful, clear as day.

"Of course, their separation isn't absolute," the ethnologist continued.

"Isn't it? And why 'of course'?"

"Husband and wife meet on the fifteenth day of every month, when the moon is completely round, like it is tonight. One day out of every twenty-eight" — she smiled, I thought, rather slyly — "often enough to sustain a committed relationship, and seldom enough to maintain a sense of the other's incomparable worth."

My parents, separated for nearly twenty years, saw each other once a month or thereabouts. Their separation, instigated by my mother, had been neither mutual nor amicable and resulted in an estrangement which might have lasted forever — "I never wanted to see your father again" — had I not, in turn, become estranged from my father.

I had been living in Paris, an expatriation which proved beyond a shadow of a doubt, in my father's eyes, that I had rejected my paternal heritage, my Chinese blood and upbringing. During that time, a period of four years which were neatly coterminous with my parents' estrangement and during which I longed to have a child but not a husband, I bore a son, Anton. It was also a time when I was consumed by idealistic desires, impossible dreams, and magnificent obsessions, when the lure of "a chance encounter sparked by an obscure hunger, a neat coincidence, and a fatal attraction for the defective," as the writer Judith Thurman described such passions — all of which described my rationale for choosing Heinz, the man who would be Anton's father — was more than I could resist.

"You know, you don't have to have the baby," my mother said soon after I'd returned to America a month and a half pregnant.

I didn't know how I was going to break the news to her, but she had made it easy, not knowing that the father of my child was Austrian, by taking me to dinner at Wienerwald, a Viennese restaurant on lower Fifth Avenue, where I broke down and cried into my schnitzel. I knew what she meant: an abortion (in more progressive Paris) or giving up the baby for adoption.

"But I want this child," I snuffled.

"Do you know how hard it is to raise a child? Hard enough with two parents. But with one, it will be . . . " She caught herself. "You can have other children, by another man, one who will—"

I sat up. "I want *this* child," I interrupted her, "by *this* man."

I had never been so sure of anything in my life, nor have I been since. My sudden composure and calm determination prevented my mother from trying any further to dissuade me. As for ultimatums, she knew better — better than Heinz, who had offered me the choice: "The baby or me" — to employ that tactic. Instead she told me that we — the baby and I — could live with her. She would help me raise him. She would get a larger apartment. In the meantime, we could have the sole bedroom and she would be fine on the sofabed in the living room. She had already begun buying a layette when I told her that I — we — were going back to Europe. The expression on her face! But she didn't contradict me. She didn't try to deter me or change my mind. She simply nodded and lowered her eyes so that I wouldn't see her pain and disappointment. How could I tell her that everything I had lived and learned in Paris and Sicily was at stake, would go up in smoke if I allowed myself and my child to live under her roof, according to her rules, when I was just beginning to formulate my own? So I told her that I couldn't live in the United States. I wanted to return to Europe, where I had been happy.

"That's all I want for you," my mother said throatily. "I just want you to be happy."

At those words, my composure crumbled and my tears flowed anew. "I don't want to be happy. I want to be whole."

Improbably, Anton possessed the nondominant characteristics, the blond hair and green eyes of his father, which seemed to my father to be a second slap in the face. When I returned to the United States with Anton, we stayed with my mother in her New York apartment. My father had sold our house in Riverdale and was living in

Westchester. The most recent letter I had written him, as short and infrequent as the others I'd sent him, had been mailed weeks prior from Europe.

"Have you told him?"

"That I'm back in the United States? About Anton? Not yet."

"Will you tell him?

"Why? I know what he's going to say."

"He has a right to know. He's your father, after all."

My mother had not seen my father since I'd left for Europe; she had only spoken with him over the phone, and then regarding legal matters. More communication than that she didn't want and strictly avoided. She was thriving, both personally and professionally, and she didn't want to be drawn into the vortex of the past. I did write to my father, a brief explanatory letter posted in New York. My father wrote back that "what you have done" was unforgivable, that my life was essentially over, and that he would henceforth consider me dead. I wasn't surprised by my father's words, both their bluntness and their censorious lack of specificity, and to prove I wasn't, I read them aloud to my mother. Moreover, his letter — longer and more descriptive than mine — let me know where I stood, gave me ground under my feet, the foundation I needed to build my new life, back in New York with a new son. When I looked up from the letter at my mother, I saw in her eyes a melting softness, a deep sadness, but her mouth was set in grim determination.

"Well, that's that, I suppose," she said, with a nod of resignation.

Resignation? Quite the contrary. That minimal gesture foretold steely resolve and quiet defiance, as I would learn, and within two weeks.

"Do you have any plans for tomorrow?" By my mother's tone of voice, whose range was symphonic, I knew this wasn't a question but the overture to a request.

"Not really. Nothing special," I said, warily. "Why?"

"Do you think you could be home before three o'clock tomorrow?"

"I suppose I could." I continued to look at her, waiting for an explanation. "Why three?"

"Daddy's coming over," she bit off, like crow. The admission caused the muscles around my mother's mouth to tighten but the rest of her face to slacken slightly, her skin losing some of its unusually youthful suppleness, her eyes to crackle with both "fire and ice," as Jean Cocteau had once described the eyes of Michele Morgan, whose likeness — a blond version — to my mother more than one friend or family member had remarked upon. The fire of incipient resentment, the ice of latent sorrow, the two of which met and dissolved into a mist of melancholy forbearance.

I didn't have to ask her why my father was coming, why she had asked him to come. She had arranged this meeting — God knows how much pride she had to swallow to pick up the telephone and call him (knowing I would not), what craftiness or cajolery she used (knowing that I lacked those skills or was unseasoned in them) to persuade him to disinter me and accept my present reincarnation as a single mother by choice, how much personal peace and happiness she was willing to sacrifice to permit him back into her life — for my, or, more precisely, for Anton's sake.

My father arrived punctually, at three. If my parents had once been bitterly estranged, one would never have known it now, except for a few brief but not terribly uncomfortable lapses of conversation — hardly pregnant pauses — as between well-behaved and -intentioned people who find that they have little in common and so ask polite questions and recite charming anecdotes to maintain propriety and protocol and make the time pass. Or perhaps I misread the situation. Perhaps there was much more going on under the bland surface of social rectitude than met the eye. But both my parents were maritally savvy enough and separated long enough, or knew that there was too much at stake to blow it, to let any underlying emotional current from the past produce a ripple in the present. When Anton awoke from his nap and I brought him out to meet "company," my father had already steeled himself with an unconvincing, toothy smile, but his eyes were spontaneously quizzical: Who is this most un-Chinese-looking toddler staring at me? How could such a child be my grandson? My father deflected his puzzlement by producing a Tonka truck from inside the plastic bag at his side (no doubt he had asked my mother's advice, since Tonka toys were Anton's favorite), just as he had defused a potentially poignant welcome by thrusting a box of Chinese pastries — coconut tartlets, steamed sponge cakes, egg custard tartlets — at my mother the moment she opened the door. Both peace offering and piece of armor, the pastries permitted my mother to make some tea around which we sat, well-behaved comme-il-faut adults, chatting about nothing and touching upon everything, while Anton played at our feet. After a diplomatic two cups, my father took his leave, but not before over-smiling at Anton with still-disbelieving eyes and suggesting to me and my mother that he drop by again, perhaps in a few weeks — often enough to sustain a committed relationship, seldom enough to maintain a sense of the other's incomparable worth — since he came into the city regularly to consult with his stockbroker. There was (or did I imagine it then? do I imagine it now?) a barely perceptible hesitation on my mother's part — that minimal interstice of time in which she figured that future happiness would be hers if she declined, Anton's and mine if she accepted — before she nodded and said with telling gravitas, "That would be nice."

After she had seen my father to the door, my mother glanced at me. If it weren't for you, said her eyes of fire and ice. If it weren't for me, she would never have had to see my father again, and her life would have been uncomplicated, happy, free of painful memories? Or, if it weren't for me, we would never have seen my father again, and life would have lacked a dimension, a dynamic, a wholeness, however imperfect, that is family? Both, probably. Family is rarely one thing or the other, but both, alternating at varying and unpredictable intervals. Yin and yang, the concept goes, evolved and continues to evolve the world as we know it through a dynamic interrelationship of opposites, a continuous interplay of extremes. Sun and moon. Man and woman. Union and separation.

"There are no men at our gathering," I noted.

"The moon is yin, the feminine force," the ethnologist replied, pouring me and herself another cup of tea. "No men allowed. Or, more diplomatically, as the proverb states, 'Men do not worship the moon; women do not makes sacrifices to the kitchen god.' Look."

She indicated first the full moon, now at its zenith in the sky, then our teacups upon whose brimming surface it had cast a perfect, silver circle.

"Now is the perfect moment to drink our tea."

And so we drank.

Steamed Sponge "Moon Cake"

5 extra large eggs, room temperature
1 tablespoon water
1 cup sugar
1 cup rice flour (or Swansdown cake flour)
1¼ tablespoons melted butter

If you live near a Chinatown, it's easier to buy a tin of moon cakes than it is to make them from scratch. I've solved the problem through adaptation: as long as a sweet, baked dessert is round, such as the steamed sponge cake here, it is a moon cake. In addition, I prefer the firm but springy texture of this not-too-sweet dessert over that of "official" heavy, sugary moon cakes, whatever their filling.

Beat eggs, water, and sugar for 10 minutes in a mixer at high speed, or for 20 minutes by hand, till thick and creamy. Fold in flour, then melted butter. Line bottom of a 9-inch round cake pan with parchment paper. Pour batter into pan.

Fill bottom of wok with water. Bring water to rolling boil. Set pan on steaming rack and cover. Turn heat down to medium. Steam for 20 minutes. Cake is done if toothpick inserted in it comes out clean. Turn out cake and peel off parchment. Serve warm or at room temperature.

Serves 6–8.

11

SEATED ON A STONE

I have almost always lived on islands. Islands rising out of rivers, such as Manhattan, my current part-time address, and Paris's Ile de la Cité, my postgraduate home. Or islands in the sea that are big in size, like Sicily, where I decamped after Paris; or in population density, like Hong Kong, where I resided as a child. But never have I been to, let alone lived on, a tiny uninhabited island.

Not until two years after I visited Nai-nai in Guilin, that is, where my monthlong stay instigated a writing jag that had petered out, interrupted too long and too often by paid work and family obligations, to an unbudging halt. It was then that Mirja, who I'd met years ago in Paris, where we both were attending the Alliance Française, invited me to spend a month with her and her family in the Finnish lake district. What if I spent a week of it in a rented cottage on an island with a population of one — me? Some twelve hundred islands comprise the archipelago of Turku in the Baltic Sea. Surely one of them would meet my simple but stringent requirements: sea and solitude.

Infected by my enthusiasm at first, Mirja grew tentative upon second thought. She imagined I'd be prey to *tanukis* ("Raccoon dogs that are wild. Keep your door shut."), vipers ("Venomous. Wear shoes outdoors."), and sea snakes ("Don't worry. They may be large but they're innocuous."). Her admonitions were well taken but not a deterrent. Frighten me she might, but prevent me from inhabiting my parcel of privacy in the sea she was powerless to do. She did, however, make one last-ditch attempt to deflect me from my course by suggesting, perkily, "How about an island in the middle of a lake?"

My pelagic home — a one-room log cabin with attached sauna — stood in a clearing that overlooked a swath of islet-studded sea. It had electricity but no running water or plumbing. Those conveniences were supplied by a hand pump some fifty yards behind the cabin and an outhouse about fifteen yards downwind. Twenty paces in front of my porch was a big flat lichen-encrusted slab of granite — my centering rock, I called it — where I ate my meals and spent many hours sitting, looking, being, and, eventually, writing. My island, like my cottage, was very small but it was large enough to deserve a name, Kustavi, which, translated from Finnish, means "fireweed" — the long, conical, lavender-pink flower that grows with abandon all over southern Finland. Disappointingly, Kustavi wasn't a true island. A bridge, wide enough for a compact car, connected it to Kustavi Central, its mother island and the main one in this part of the archipelago. The owner of my cottage, Mr. Karjalainen, fearing that I might come down with cabin fever, had tied red ribbons around the trunks of several trees growing in strategic bends and forks in the dirt path to show me the way to civilization and back. A big, craggy man in his fifties, he had met me at the small port in Kustavi Central and, before taking me to my cabin, driven me to a small grocery store where I stocked up on a week's worth of food: eggs, cheese, potatoes, sausages, onions, milk, bread, strawberries, jam, butter, canned tuna, curly red lettuce, carrots, tomatoes, lemons, olive oil. I was set. Not a care or concern to disturb or distract me. I could hunker down and write to my heart's content.

Kustavi Tangential, as I dubbed my exclusive island, was austere but in no way was it deprived. The antithesis of an island paradise oozing with nature's bounty, my northern retreat was all dull gray granite and twisted scrub pine. Isolated by a sea whose color was that crayon-box shade, Prussian blue — militant, opaque — my temporary address was a mere dot, a spit of land burnt clean of any luxuriance and every excess. What was left was the absolutely essential, the strictly fundamental. Just like my life there would be.

A pared-to-the-bone island isn't just a place to experience solitude, a key ingredient in the writing life; it is a metaphor for solitude. Alone on an island, you run the risk of self-discovery. But that is precisely its lure and challenge: by getting away from it all, you come face-to-face with yourself. Having led a somewhat peripatetic existence, I'd prided myself on having a rather adventurous spirit, even on being a trailblazer of sorts. That delusion evaporated on my very first trip to the water pump. Blinded by a surfeit of lightheartedness, and oblivious to the fact that three other paths radiated out from it, I chose the wrong trail home and found myself lost in the woods.

As darkness descended, I had a panic attack with all the fixings — the flight of logic, the labored breathing, the thud of heartbeat against breastbone. Finally, after anticipating attacks by *tanukis*, vipers, and sea snakes, I regained enough presence of mind to follow the path back to the pump, where the second trail I took led me safely home. "If anything can teach you humility," wrote the Finnish author and longtime lover of islands, Tove Jansson, "it is living with the sea close at hand."

So could the expectation that I'd get cracking immediately on Nai-nai's biography-in-progress now that I'd carved out a week of silence and solitude in which I would do nothing but write. I didn't take into account that it might take me the better part of that week just to get my bearings. One source of disorientation was the paradox of simplicity. Making do with little, I discovered, was more than an exercise in self-sufficiency, it was a source of self-enrichment. What little there was was more than enough. The loaves and the fishes that I'd bought at the grocery store seemed to multiply the more that I consumed them. My simple meals tasted like regal banquets for all the effort and preparation they required (Therein lay the paradox. Simple did not mean easy. Simple meant time-consuming. Time-consuming meant time away from resuming work on my grandmother's biography): water from the pump to boil the potatoes and sausages, to wash the vegetables, not to mention the dishes afterwards and, later, myself. A cup of coffee, for all the displacements (and thus time lost to writing) I underwent to obtain it, was transformed into high tea. Taking a sauna bath was a major production: two trips to the water pump with a bucket in each hand both times, tearing and crumpling the sheets of newsprint, lighting it along with the kindling, placing the logs just so to create an updraft, waiting a good twenty minutes before they burned like blazes, by which time I was more than ready to come clean in this baptism by fire.

Which is precisely the point. Everything that I did, as simple and basic as it was, took time, the one thing my secluded island (though not I, considering my purpose) had plenty of. And because it took time, which required patience, everything was imbued with a presence — a present-tenseness — that lent to the act a spiritual significance, the grace of a ritual (and the imposition of guilt that I was not doing what I'd come to do). In fact, after my panic attack disabused me of the notion that I possessed the faintest spark of an Alexandra David-Neel or a Freya Stark, I planted myself on my centering rock facing out to sea, exerting a passive resistance against the centrifugal pull of another life-threatening episode of high adventure or of mere restlessness. My renunciation rewarded me most amply. Like Mohammed's mountain, my island came to me. Above me, a seagull hovered on white boomerang wings, its Brancusian form held in place by the steady breeze: a perfect tension between matter and energy. Before me, the glacial erratic — geological émigré deposited by the Ice Age on the granite islet across from me — basked in the sunlight serene as a sphinx. Rock upon rock, it reminded me of Old Man Hill in Guilin, which was a hill atop a larger hill. The Old Man sat facing out to sea with his knees pulled up to his chest, much the way I now sat on my centering rock surrounded by remnants of my half-eaten breakfast, my untouched notebook, my capped pen.

Just then, a stately schooner, sails bellied with the wind, slid like some ghost ship out from behind the alien boulder and into heart-stopping view. I didn't wave. Neither did the sailors on her spanking deck. Exhibitionism has its place, but not on my austere stationary island nor on their majestic mobile one. I picked up and uncapped my pen, set my opened notebook on my knees, and, perhaps because I was in present tense, far from the heat and noise of human interaction and in the process of digesting my Western breakfast of black coffee, scrambled eggs, and buttered toast with strawberry jam, I began to write their polar opposite: the *renao-* and Chinese-food-filled Spring Festival as Nai-nai celebrated it in the past. The year was 1933. The place, Canton. The time, the beginning of the two-week period of shopping, socializing, and feasting that constituted Chinese New Years of old, so different from the pale, truncated version we celebrated in Riverdale when I was a child. I wrote:

During Spring Festival, my grandmother was faced with the near-heroic task of settling the household accounts. She had to pay merchants what moneys she owed them and receive what moneys were owed her before Lunar New Year, for by dawn of that day, no one could demand payment until the next Lunar New Year a full year away. Already, the city was ablaze with lights. Some of the illumination was provided by lenders, lantern in hand, out searching for borrowers who had not repaid their loan. Often the lantern-bearers headed for the temples, where the debtors in question hid among the merrymakers mesmerized by troupes of actors and acrobats.

Seated at her desk, Nai-nai was studying her ledger

while Dashao moved the cedar chests and closets away from the walls and urged the manservant Liu-wu to help her.

"Old Aunt, why do you sweep each room with inward strokes of the broom?" he asked.

"Not to sweep the family's wealth out the door," Dashao replied. "I'll never forget my mother encouraging me each and every New Year, 'Be careful to sweep each inch of the room, my daughter. The speck of dust you miss might fly into your eyes and blind you.' There!" she announced with pride. "The house is spotless. The coming year will be better than the last. Now you can start repainting the red gates, whitewashing the outer walls, and repapering the windows. And be quick about it. Everything must be finished within a fortnight."

"Do you want me to be as crooked and bent as old Wenti when I'm just a quarter of his age?" the manservant replied. "Have some pity on me!"

"And what of me?" Dashao set her hands on her broad hips. "I must prepare enough food to satisfy the appetites of both man and god for more than two weeks, and I must do it all on the first few days of Spring Festival, since no knife or cleaver may be used until the festival is over. Do you think I want to be accused of cutting into the family's wealth by wielding a sharp instrument?"

"What you're asking me to do in the time you're asking me to do it would take three men at least," Liu-wu said, sulking.

"A single diligent man would do," she replied. "And while you're at it, console yourself by thinking about my obligations. Making the sweet, steamed glutinous pudding, *nian gao*. Stuffing the rice-flour skins with chopped pork, shredded scallions, and slivered ginger to make *jiaozi*. And for a few of the dumplings, filling them with peanuts for long life; dates or chestnuts for the imminent arrival of a son; gold or silver coins so that one might never lack for money; or perhaps a nugget of jade to bring good fortune to whoever finds it in his bowl." She said this with a wink, suggesting that he might be the lucky recipient. Then she gave Liu-wu a playful shove. "Start with the outer gates. Then Li Tai-tai can buy pictures of the door gods to protect us against evil spirits. Next, whitewash the walls so she can hang the red paper couplets along the doorways. The sooner you begin, the earlier you'll be done."

As soon as Liu-wu shuffled out the door, Nai-nai closed her ledger and, together with Dashao, went to see the wispy-bearded old man who had studied under a master calligrapher in Peking. He now owned a shop in the center of Canton that sold the finest-quality rice paper, sable brushes, and inkstones. From him my grandmother bought pictures of the two heavenly guardians to paste on both sides of the main entrance of her house, and couplets printed on strips of red paper which read: "Ten thousand generations," "May all your wishes be fulfilled," "Happiness, high position, and long life." Because she was a country girl at heart and wished to be reminded of home, Nai-nai also bought paper streamers that bore the inscriptions: "Clear water ripples over the rocks" and "How beautiful are our rivers and mountains!"

When they returned home, Dashao reminded her mistress: "Li Tai-tai, in two days, the mat sheds go up in the center of the city, and the flower vendors will set up their wares. Why not ask our landlady, Sze Tai-tai, to accompany you to buy flowers? And don't bother asking Yifu if she wants to go along. If it involves spending money, she'll be the first in line."

"It will give Liu-wu an opportunity to drive the car and dress up in his chauffeur's uniform," Nai-nai said. "Hwang Tai-tai might like to join us. We'll make a party of it. We'll go the day after tomorrow."

The twelfth month of the Chinese lunar calendar is known as the bitter month, but on the day that my grandmother chose to visit the flower market, Canton was filled with bright sunshine. A mild breeze blew through the city, perfuming every street and corner with the fragrance of fresh blooms and ripe fruits. Happy and excited, Nai-nai, Hwang Tai-tai, Sze Tai-tai, and Yifu piled into the roadster. With Liu-wu at the wheel, they headed for the center of town. But the closer they got to their destination, the thicker the crowds, until the car was barely able to move.

"Oh, this is impossible!" Yifu said, throwing up her hands in frustration. "Let's get out and walk!"

Since they were mere blocks away from the flower market, her companions agreed. Directing Liu-wu to stay where he was so they might find him again, the four women hooked arms, then waded out into the raging sea of pushing and shoving shoppers. The cries and noises of various tradespeople filled the air. Each was hawking his own ware or service, and each had a specific call or sound to distinguish himself from the rest. The barber struck his tuning fork with a short steel rod. The hat seller shook a harness of bells. The puppeteer proclaimed the start of his show with a crash of cymbals and a thunder of gongs. The toy seller shook toys strung from the top of a long stick.

"Buy, little man!" he sang to a reluctant child. "They're lifelike! They have eyes and arms!"

"Green-glazed beauties! Old jars for new!" another merchant cried.

And another: "Try my confection of sugar, oil, and flour! It's plaited like a horse's tail decked out for New Year's Day!"

The jar and the horse-blossom sellers triggered the voices of the crab-apple vendor, the soup and the turnip vendors. Everywhere there was the cacophony of *renao*, the heat and noise of human relationship and enterprise.

"Only two strings left! Crab apples red and shiny as rubies!"

"Sour prune soup! Just one bowl will satisfy you!"

"Turnip roots that taste as sweet as pears!"

And amid all this, troupes of actors, Cantonese opera singers, and rubber-limbed acrobats demonstrated their skills and vied for attention with the city's beggars, who, like their competition, considered theirs a profession like any other. After all, didn't beggars adhere to strict rules and regulations, protocol, and hierarchy? Hadn't they learned how to appraise a potential benefactor on the spot, to address him with the title "Great Master" or "Your Ladyship," as Nai-nai was addressed at that very moment by a very old and stooped beggar, whom she rewarded with one *kuai*.

"Turtle, crawl to your door," he sang, "your wealth will soon soar."

"Madam took pity on me," intoned another, to whom Sze Tai-tai had given one *kuai*. "Sons and grandsons you'll soon have."

Beggar women and children surrounded them weeping at a certain pitch and rhythm, as befitting a Chinese opera singer. When Yifu ignored their pleas, one woman shouted in her face, "Don't give me money? I don't care. Save it for your coffin!"

The male beggars shouted wildly and demonstrated their sores and deformities, competing to see who might outdo the other in eliciting sympathy or evoking horror. Nai-nai and her companions linked arms and managed to push past the wailing crowd that had gathered. Every street was claimed by a certain category of beggar, each known by a distinct, highly descriptive name: Sword Slappers, who hit their chests with the flat sides of two long swords until the flesh there was a series of red welts; Nail Headers, who used a brick to tap nails into their skulls when a chosen patron refused to part with a few coins; One-Eyed Dragons, who pretended total blindness when in fact they had the use of at least one eye; Rollers, whose hands and feet were completely deformed and who would howl pitifully and thrash about in the mud; Moving Carts, paralyzed beggars who lay on carts pulled along by an ambulatory colleague; and Rock Carriers, male beggars who carried female invalids on their backs.

Arms still linked, necks straining to catch glimpses of their destination as well as the activities swirling around them, the four women both pressed on and were swept toward the mat sheds of the flower market.

"Chrysanthemums!" Sze Tai-tai sighed, overcome by

their beauty and relieved by her deliverance from the chaotic street scene.

"You're showing your age!" teased Hwang Tai-tai. The chrysanthemum was the floral symbol for the autumn of one's life, longevity, and a life spent in quiet retirement.

"You've done the right thing in coming here," said the chrysanthemum vendor, who was anything but retiring. "Come in, come in! Look at my darlings from all angles! Appreciate their beauty, rarity, symbolism — and buy!" He extended his arm and swung it in a wide arc before the creamy white, yellow, and purple blossoms. "I love my flowers, and I'm an expert in their every secret and idio- syncrasy. Just think! All there is to know about the one hun- dred and thirty-three varieties of chrysanthemum — and I know it all!

"Madam," he said, noting where my grandmother's eyes had strayed and seeing where they now settled, "you are clearly a connoisseur of floral beauty, and so I will show you only the rarest, only the loveliest, of my chrysanthe- mums. Look here — Honey-Linked Bracelets. And here — Purple Tiger Whiskers. And there — Eyebrows of the Old Ruler, the Old Ruler being none other than the vener- able Lao Tzu."

"Really?" Nai-nai said, her interest caught as much by the name of the flower as by its beauty. She nodded at the flower vendor's assistant, indicating that she would like a pot of those.

"And there next to Old Eyebrows — Evening Sun on a Duck's Back. And here — Yellow Orioles in the Green Willow. Over there — Golden Phoenix Holding a Pearl in Its Mouth."

The three other women, having wandered into other stalls, gazed upon branches of white plum blossom, pine, and bamboo — the "three friends of winter," since all of them bloomed in the darkest months. There were also sprays of pale-green-tinged peach blossoms, fragrant vellum-like magnolias, waxen-petaled camellias, and dense, velvety cockscomb. But my grandmother's very favorites were the peonies, *fu gui hua*, the "flower of wealth and honor." While some were full, feathery blooms of pure white or delicate pink, she chose to decorate her house for New Year's with an earthenware pot of deep scarlet ones. She also bought branches of plum blossoms for their calm and simple beauty; a narcissus plant in the hopes that it would open on New Year's Day; a kumquat tree heavy with fruit, for kumquats symbolized children; and a bellflower tree since red was the color of good fortune and happiness.

In contrast to the majestic schooner's single apparition, the sole event that brought humankind near my door, a pedestrian tugboat put in daily appearances, chugging its way to and from the fish hatchery about a hundred yards offshore. I gauged the time of day by its comings and goings, since I refused to wear a watch and since the maverick summer sun in these latitudes refused to abandon the sky, dipping below the horizon for only an hour or two before bobbing back up in a new day. I rarely turned on a lamp, seldom consulted a clock. And, after two hefty bouts of writing both morning and afternoon, I could read from my book of essays (novels are for tropical islands) by sunlight till nearly eleven at night. That Charles Lamb's "The Superannuated Man" was among them was providential, even synchronous, as this line makes evident: "For that is the only true Time which man can properly call his own, that which he has all to himself; the rest, though in some sense he may be said to live it, is other people's time, not his." With the unparalleled gift of true Time, the truth of which didn't prevent it from fleeing — which perhaps made it fleeter — I lit a candle and wrote the ending to Nai-nai's prophetic Chinese New Year of 1933 in the darkest hours of an early morning in 1988:

Satisfied with their purchases from the flower market, the women started to make their way back to the spot where they had left Liu-wu. Distracted by a blind palmist playing a flute, Yifu stopped and tugged on Nai-nai's arm. "Ninth Sister-in-Law, can't we stop a minute? I want to have my fortune told."

Before my grandmother could answer, Sze Tai-tai intervened. "It's so noisy and crowded here. I'll show you a much better place — one away from the flower market where the reader both tells you your past and predicts your future. That way you know whether or not you're getting an honest reading."

"Let's all get our fortunes told," Hwang Tai-tai suggested. She looked at the dwarf mandarin orange tree she had just bought at the market. "I wouldn't mind knowing if certain investments I made recently will bear fruit."

Liu-wu had fallen asleep at the wheel, but he quickly righted his cap over his eyes and drove his passengers to Tian Wangliao, the Temple of the Heavenly Gods. When my grandmother saw the "Temple," she was visibly disappointed. It was nothing but a shopping mall, full of stores and business offices. Sze Tai-tai persisted: "The worst-looking restaurants often serve the tastiest food, do they not? I assure you, you'll get your money's worth."

They entered the building only to face a second disappointment: a long line of people waited in the reception area. "This will take forever! Let's all go in together," Hwang Tai-tai suggested. "After all, we're good friends. What do we have to hide from each other?"

When their turn came, the four women entered a small, well-lit room, unfurnished except for a small desk, two chairs, and a simple wooden bookcase with scores of well-thumbed volumes crowding its shelves. Pasted on one wall was a large drawing of a face covered with dots and Chinese characters. Next to it was a large diagram of the palm of a human hand scored with various lines and marked with Chinese characters. On the opposite wall hung a brush-and-ink scroll of Mount T'ai, one of China's five sacred mountains.

Seated in one of the two chairs, the fortune-teller rose as soon as the four women entered, and bowed gracefully from the waist. He was probably in his late seventies, but his body was straight though his hair was as white as the camellia blossoms Nai-nai had just bought. His complexion was smooth and supple, pulled tight over the planes and angles of his face. But what was particularly arresting about him were his eyes; they had the youth, sparkle, and curiosity of a child's.

"We've come together to save time," Hwang Tai-tai explained, "since there are so many people waiting to see you. We don't mind standing and, being friends, we have nothing to hide from each other."

The physiognomist nodded and extended his hand,

indicating that one of the four women should sit down in the chair opposite him.

"You go first," Yifu whispered to Sze Tai-tai with a nudge, "since you brought us here. I want to hear what he says about your past as well as your future, so I know whether or not he's honest."

Sze Tai-tai sat down. Her three friends gathered protectively behind her chair while the fortune-teller scrutinized her face and examined her palms. "You have no difficulties or hardships in your life," he told her. "You have plenty of the four basics of life: food, shelter, clothing, and travel. You had a good beginning, and you will have a good end. Though your fortune is not bad, it's not particularly propitious, for though you possess money, you lack position."

Sze Tai-tai, satisfied with her fortune, rose from the chair, which Hwang Tai-tai immediately occupied. The fortune-teller looked at her face, her hands, and her general demeanor. Her "lines of destiny," as he called them. "You are a conscientious and diligent helpmate to your husband," he said. "Also, a devoted mother to your son, a loyal friend to those you like, and a fearsome adversary to those you do not. You are astute in money matters and know how to choose your friends, depending on their influence and prestige. You have had some suffering in your life which has been caused by your husband and the loss of a beloved family member, but you have been able to turn your suffering to your advantage. For the rest of your life, you may expect good luck and material comfort."

Hwang Tai-tai rose from the chair with a nod of appreciation toward Sze Tai-tai.

"Which one of you remaining ladies would like her fortune told next?" the old man asked when neither Nainai nor Yifu approached the chair before him.

My grandmother glanced at her sister-in-law, but the girl shook her head vigorously and motioned for her to be seated instead. Before Nai-nai could acquiesce, the physiognomist rose from his chair, pressed his palms together at his forehead, and bowed low from the waist.

"Madam," he said in a husky voice, "without looking at your face for more than a few seconds and without looking at your palms at all, I can tell you that your fortune is the most propitious that I have seen in my long life. You are one among millions. You possess love, fortune, position, and long life — the best of what there is to be had on earth."

My grandmother grasped the back of the chair and eased herself into it.

"Your husband will stand head and shoulders above the crowd. He will occupy the highest position in the land, save one. Had you been born a man, you would have occupied the place I have predicted for your husband. You would have been the number two, perhaps even the number one, leader in the country."

Seeing the confusion and disbelief on her face, he commented upon her features that indicated the life he foretold. "You have long eyebrows, the kind called Clear and Beautiful. You have long earlobes, thick, fat, and glossy, the kind called Shoulder-Touching Ears. These are very rare and are usually found on a rich and powerful man, an emperor, or a king. Your nose is long, too, strong and well formed with a rounded tip, a Deer Nose, which means that you are kind by nature, keep your promises, and possess wealth and long life. You also have Elephant Eyes, long and narrow with wrinkles above and below, which signifies kindness, friendliness, and wisdom. Your mouth is a Cherry Mouth, particularly fortunate in a woman. It means that you are clever and wise and possess a gentle nature, that you will always be wealthy, and that you will know a highly respected person who will help you in times of difficulty."

His clear eyes then dimmed somewhat. "There is, however, a bit of grief in your life. You and your husband do not live under the same roof. You and your husband will never live under the same roof."

"Oh, Laoshi," Sze Tai-tai blurted out, "if you only knew how accurate—"

Nai-nai placed her hand on her landlady's arm. "What you've said about my life is very interesting," she told the fortune-teller, "but it is also not at all true. In fact, you have misread all three fortunes. The husbands of the two ladies whose fortunes you told before mine occupy very high positions in the government. My husband is their subordinate and takes his orders from them."

The physiognomist smiled. "People say that fortune-tellers make up fortunes at will and at random, without any knowledge of or regard for truth and facts. I have studied books of augury all my life, madam: *The Ma-i* of the Sung dynasty, *The Pa P'u Tzu* of the Ming dynasty, *The Golden Scissors* of the Qing dynasty. What I say is based on my understanding of these venerable books. If what I have said turns out to be true, return and pay me more than what I now charge you. If it is false, come back and recover your fee." He looked into Nai-nai's eyes. "Fortune decides half your fate. Your efforts decide the other half. Even a woman born under auspicious stars must have a good heart and perform good deeds. Madam, for telling your fortune, I will charge you ten times the usual price, since you can anticipate a tenfold increase in your fortunes."

"What about me?" Yifu cried, tapping my grandmother on the shoulder and gesturing for her to relinquish the chair. "You haven't told my fortune yet."

The fortune-teller stared at the girl and drew his brows together. "Let me see one of your palms." He studied it for several seconds, then put it down on the table. "I'm very sorry to have to tell you, young miss, but your fortune is not at all propitious."

Before he could continue, Yifu jumped up from the chair, knocking it over, and began berating the man. "Liar! Charlatan! You don't know anything!" Then she turned to the three women, her face flushed, her hands clenched into tight fists. "We should never have come to this place . . . to see this . . . imposter! It's all your fault!" she shrieked, pointing to Sze Tai-tai. "You're the one who brought us here to this . . . this fake!"

"The lines of destiny that I have seen in your face and hand is based on my knowledge of the great books of physiognomy that have been passed down through the centuries. What I say are not my words but the words of the books, and the words are true. In your face and hand, I have gazed upon your future."

Yifu's anger dissolved, and she clasped her hands together prayerfully. "Will I marry?"

"You will," the fortune-teller answered. "But your husband will die young. As for you, you are comfortable now because of the goodness of others, but you will have a bad and painful end. I advise you to be kind to others and to perform good deeds, and you may alter your fortune for the better. Use the knowledge of your fortune which I have just told you to improve your lot. As for my fee, I charge you nothing."

Yifu's face had turned white with fear. "Do you think I'd pay you one cash for hearing a bunch of lies? You're nothing but an imposter! I'll report you to the authorities. My brother is very powerful. One word from him and he'll put you out of business!" She turned and stomped out of the room.

"I've read all of your fortunes," the old man told the three remaining women. "Whether or not they are accurate, you will find out in due course. I charge both of you" — he looked at Hwang Tai-tai, then at Sze Tai-tai — "one *kuai*. As for you" — he looked into my grandmother's face with a calm gravity in his eyes that had been absent with the others — "I charge you ten *kuai*. And I hope that you will come back and tell me whether or not the destiny I've predicted for you has come to pass."

On my second-to-last day on Kustavi Tangential, my all-to-myself time was beginning to weigh a bit (as were the number of filled pages in my notebook). I felt I could, I should, succumb to the urge to trade my islomanic seclusion for a glimpse of society on Kustavi Central just a bridge away. As I walked toward my destination, the forest of tortured pines gave way to deciduous trees and pliant ferns. The ground, once dappled with more shade than sun, grew brighter, more verdant. As the sun rose higher in the sky, my heart rose to my throat in anticipation of every-thing I lacked: people, stores, cafés, *renao*. When I arrived at the foot of the bridge, two cars on the other side of it, one fast upon the other and precursors of what I thought I craved, whizzed around the bend heading, surely, for the port on Kustavi Central. I did not follow their lead. I did not cross the bridge. I did not advance upon civilization. Not I. Not yet. I would be faithful to true Time, grounded in proper Place. And I knew just the spot. I turned around and walked back to my centering rock.

My centering rock, though actually in Finland, grounded me in China. My centering rock, though in the present, connected me with my heritage and Nai-nai's past — parts of which I personally witnessed, parts of which I only heard about secondhand, and parts (the lion's share, most likely) which I didn't know at all and never would. In order to make a unified whole of her life in words — in sum, a story — these last parts had to be plau-sible, based on or consonant with what I knew about Nai-nai firsthand or was told by someone else. In sum, parts which, as far as I knew, did not happen but which could have happened. That is, credible parts (credible being the operative word) which I would have to invent. There I was sitting on my centering rock, having turned my back on a dollop of civilization a bridge span away when the ques-tion struck and took hold: Why was I trying to write Nai-nai's biography, where too many parts were missing, when the manuscript obviously wanted to be a novel, whose missing parts I could make up?

I'd spent the last five years, when I wasn't working in an office or raising my family, writing abortive biographies.

The first — a complete draft of some six hundred double-spaced typewritten pages — was a biography of my grandfather. It didn't work, quite. I then wrote a second complete draft of a joint biography of my grandparents. That didn't quite work either, but I was getting close. To what I wasn't sure, but I kept the faith — faith, according to Ivan Illich, being "the readiness for a surprise." I then deleted my grandfather in good part and was about two-thirds of the way through a third incarnation — this time, a biography of my grandmother — which was what I'd come to Kustavi to resume only to discover that her biography wanted to be a novel.

That's what I'd do, I told myself, rapping my knuckles against my centering rock for lack of wood. For something better than wood. I would fill in the empty or unknown areas of my story with my imagination. I would build the bridge of my story with whatever stones — factual or fictional — lay in my path that best fit the curve of its arch.

On my last day on Kustavi Tangential, I was sitting cross-legged on my centering rock waiting for Mr. Karjalainen to come and drive me to the bus depot on Kustavi Central. I was mulling over empty areas of my novel-to-be. First, I would change Nai-nai's name — from Xiuwen to Xuewen, which means "studies literature" — so that I could "see" the novel's protagonist and not my grandmother. For additional emotional distance, I'd devise a nickname for her, I told myself, one based on her beginnings, which would be similar to my grandmother's. As she was the fourth unwanted daughter of poor Chinese peasants, it was her fate to be drowned or smothered at birth.

But her mother, who could not bring herself to kill the newborn, tricked her husband into believing she had just borne him a son, whom he proudly named Tian, or Sweet, based on such sweet news. When his wife unswaddled the child before him days later and tearfully explained that her gender mistake was caused by her temporary possession by an evil spirit, her husband fell on the dirt floor, beating it with his fists.

"What I named Tian will now be called Ku. What I called Sweet will now be known as Bitter, when bitter is all I feel to be cheated out of a son, when bitterness is all yet another daughter will bring into our lives."

His wife said: "In life we are told that we must bear the bitter and the sweet. The sweet is easy to bear. We don't question it. The bitter we say we cannot bear, yet when it comes, we bear it." She looked down at the infant dozing on her breast. "We will call her Bittersweet."

I had the appropriate nickname and the humble beginnings of my heroine — generous parting gifts from my centering rock — when Mr. Karjalainen arrived, accompanied by his ten-year-old daughter, Hannele. Since it was too early to take me to the bus in town, Hannele stripped to her birthday suit, clambered to the top of a high boulder not far from my centering rock, and hurled herself headlong into the sea.

"But what about the sea snakes?" I asked her father.

He looked at me, a baffled expression on his weather-beaten face. No snakes. Years ago, but not now. No *tanukis* or vipers either.

With more than a little envy, as well as humility

gendered by having lived with the sea close at hand, I watched Hannele turn somersault after rapturous somersault in the Prussian-blue, serpentless sea.

12

Juk Sing

$\mathcal{T}$he soggy square of cardboard wedged between the two crates read: 5 for $2 (45¢ each). Tangelos are my favorite fruit. Half tangerine, half pomelo. Half sweet, half sour. The grizzled vendor noticed, actually anticipated, where my wandering eyes settled, peeled a pink plastic bag, thin as a membrane, from the thick stack hanging from the meat hook overhead, and with a practiced snap of his wrist ballooned it full of air right over the hybrid globes.

I pointed to the buckling cardboard sign. "That's the price for the tangelos, right? Not for the mandarin oranges."

There it was. Again. The slight, turtle-like retraction of the head, the momentary hardening of the irises, the truculent grunt rather than a comprehensible reply to my question. A grunt that said perhaps yes, perhaps no, depends on who's asking. Just as I was about to turn away and find a more civil greengrocer, or one who spoke some English, or at least admitted to understanding it, he nodded, just perceptibly. I held up one hand, five fingers outspread.

Next stop, a curio shop. I chose the one — of many, all indistinguishable in merchandise and decor — right across the street. The cramped space was presided over by a chain-smoking elder. I wandered the narrow aisles and stopped in front of a pile of bamboo flutes. I was in the throes of redecorating my apartment feng shui–style: moving my furniture around for maximum harmony with the natural order and maximum energy and profit in the New Year, which was about to begin. The Chinese, or Lunar, New Year, that is. A good time to institute change. The bamboo flutes cost me 99¢ apiece. Within my redecorating budget and worth every penny, I decided, since a beam bisected the living room of my Greenwich Village apartment. According to feng shui, the beam produced "psychic compression" in the resident unfortunate enough to be living under it, thwarting both business acumen and personal development. Placed on the oppressive beam, the flutes pumped *chi,* or vital energy, around the room, obviating the beam's ill effect.

"*Juk sing.*"

I looked up into the bemused face of the chain-smoker to whom I had just handed two dollars.

"I beg your pardon?" What I meant was: Are you speaking to me? Not: What is *juk sing?*

"You *juk sing,*" he replied. "Same as them." He looked at the two flutes. "Bamboo with nothing inside. Chinese who no speak Chinese. Chinese who look Chinese no act Chinese. No culture inside. You like them." He took the two bamboo flutes in his nicotine-stained hands and dropped them into a paper bag.

I thought of asking for my money back. Instead I

threw the flutes in with the tangelos and, aware that the man's derogatory eyes were still upon me, stood in the open doorway, fingering a pair of crimson tassels shimmying in the breeze. As I crossed the threshold out onto Mott Street, I gave them a final, dismissive flick of my fingers, in answer to his disparaging comment.

I was early, and it was cold. I ducked inside the bank at the corner of Mott and Canal with its glass front and warm vestibule, a perfect waiting room and vantage point. People entered and exited, their sights set directly and unswervingly — like the straight line Chinese evil spirits are restricted to travel — on their purpose and therefore oblivious of me, while I shifted back and forth to accommodate their comings and goings. Despite the freezing temperature, the sun was out in full force and flashed its reflection off the frequently opening and closing outer doors directly into my eyes. I squinted and moved out of the way of a depositor- or borrower-to-be. Was I seeing correctly? I glanced at my watch. There they were, at precisely the appointed hour. He, holding her elbow as he chivalrously guided her across the busy street. She, in her black Persian lamb toque tilted saucily to one side. If they were younger, they could have been the proverbial young lovers; if they were older, the proverbial old partners, a "whole" couple to whom destiny had been kind, blessing them with many sons. As it was, they were separated, the parents of four daughters.

I waved. They didn't acknowledge me. I waved again, with the same results. I set my shoulder to the thick glass door and pushed. As it swung closed, I swiveled my head, in case a person might be right behind me, and saw that the bright sun striking its transparent surface turned it into a mirror: my parents were not able to see me wave, only their own reflection.

My father slipped a long mailing tube into my pink plastic bag. What's this? my eyes asked. The corners of his mouth turned down, his shoulders rose up, and he shook his head, all just minimally — a triumvirate of gestures that signified, Nothing important. The three of us walked along Mott Street. My bag of tangelos, flutes, and now, a mailing tube thumped clumsily against my shin and occupied so much space on the narrow sidewalk that I was constrained to fall a few steps behind my parents. The proverbial dutiful daughter.

My father looked over his shoulder. "I have so many. I thought I should get rid of one."

Inside the doorway of the restaurant he'd chosen — always a flight down or a flight up, never on street level — stood a man with his hands clasped behind his back, rocking on the balls of his feet as though he'd been waiting quite some time. I estimated he was about my father's age. His face was oval, the color of old ivory and just as smooth, until it crinkled in recognition and pleasure.

"This is my friend. A high school classmate from China," my father informed my mother and me in English. "And this is my wife and my daughter," he said, this time in Chinese, to his obviously non-English-speaking friend, who looked at my mother and me with solicitous interest, bobbed his head, and smiled in acknowledgment.

I looked at my mother, the wan smile of first introduction still on my lips. No names. Merely our relationship to the speaker. Friend. Wife. Daughter. Typical. As was my father's inviting someone else to lunch without telling us. What was atypical was the fact that my parents were eating dim sum together in Chinatown for the first time since their separation almost twenty years prior.

My paternal grandmother had no name either — merely a number denoting her rank in the family hierarchy, thus her duties and responsibilities to her immediate and extended family — until she married my grandfather. It was he who gave her her name. It was marriage which bestowed upon her personhood, along with a fresh set of duties and responsibilities to a second set of people, her husband's immediate and extended family.

All the banquettes and chairs in the restaurant were occupied. We'd have to wait. I rummaged in my shoulder bag and pulled out the travel section of the Sunday *Times,* an advance copy. There smack-dab on the front page and on three pages within was my very first published article. It concerned Guilin. I'd brought the entire travel section. I wanted my parents to see the place of honor and the number of pages my article occupied.

My father, however, was otherwise engaged. He was saying, now in Mandarin (some of which I understood), now in jangling, jarring Cantonese (all of which was incomprehensible), something to his friend, who responded in the same Mandarin-Cantonese mix, then, with a quick nod to my mother and me, fled down the flight of stairs. Astonished, my mother and I looked at each other, then at my father.

"He went to find an emptier restaurant," my father explained.

Just then, four Occidentals stood up, the legs of their

chairs groaning against the floor in tandem with their moans of overindulgence and sighs of satiation. A harried young woman clutching a teapot screeched at us and held up four fingers of her free hand. My mother and I cast each other a weary, knowing glance. Musical dim sum, our eyes said simultaneously. We should have expected this. Missing our fourth and resigned to mishap and mayhem, my mother and I hung back, but my father darted forward toward the waitress. After they exchanged a few words and nods and glanced at my mother and me, my father gestured us toward the liberated table before any potential usurpers, a number of whom stood behind us, could wrest it away. Once my mother and I were seated, my father yelled over the cacophony of voices, the clatter of dishes, "I'll go find him and bring him back." Then he leaned toward me, as though he had a secret for my ears alone. "Do you know? My friend has a daughter who's a professor at MIT, in biochemistry."

After he threaded his way through the tables and disappeared down the stairs, I turned to my mother. "It's amazing how proud Daddy is of the accomplishments of other people's children, as if it underscores the failures of his own."

My mother responded by smiling benignly and asking a passing waiter to bring a pot of jasmine tea.

When I was a junior at Bronx Science, my father decided that I would be a physicist. At the end of my sophomore year at the University of Michigan, also my father's choice for me (based on the fact that it was that American icon, a Big Ten college, and that many Chinese were enrolled there), I decided, by attrition more than anything else, to major in that very nebulous area of study, American and English literature, which was bad enough. But when in my junior year, after taking a single art course, I decided to transfer from Liberal Arts to Art and Design, my father put his foot down. He told me that if I carried out my insidious plan (he assumed it would be behind his back), I could pay for my schooling as well as for my living expenses. A physicist made good money and was respected. A teacher of English, which is what I would be if I majored in English, wouldn't make much money but at least I wouldn't be disparaged. But an artist! An artist led a dissolute life and was hounded by the CIA. After a few tearful and angry scenes — the tears were mine, the anger my father's — I renounced my intention to switch schools and resigned myself to remaining where I was. I'm sure it cost my father considerable face to surrender his dream for me, as well as to stop boasting to his friends in that effusively modest, self-abnegating way unique to proud Chinese parents, that I was going to be a physicist, an astrophysicist no less, to conceal the fact that I was fated to become an English teacher, perhaps a librarian (what else did one do with a degree of that sort?), something safe if dull and therefore consonant with women's work.

"I found him!"

My father and his long-lost schoolmate settled themselves into the two other chairs while my mother, expressionless, poured them some tea.

I ruffled the travel section of the Sunday *Times.* "Look how nicely—"

My father's incipient interest was distracted by the approaching trolley, whose conductor droned in indifferent nasal syllables: *"Har gow. Lo bak go. Siu mai. Char siu bao."*

It's said that Chinese food ranks as the world's most refined cuisine and that among Chinese the act of eating is also one of intense yet subtle nonverbal communication. But the eloquence of such a language escapes me. I slid the newspaper back into my shoulder bag and consumed my dim sum in a silence punctuated every so often by a discreet burp or two, or a wild burst of rapid-fire Cantonese or more mellifluous Mandarin exchanged between my father and his friend. My mother, understanding neither, and I, understanding some, retreated into a wordless world of spearing dumplings with our chopsticks and balancing the lid of the teapot between spout and rim, a signal to whichever waiter happened to be passing by that a fresh brew was needed.

My father pointed at his friend with his chopsticks, an impropriety which caused my mother to purse her lips. "Did you know? My friend's four daughters support him and his wife."

As if on cue, my mother and I raised our eyebrows, signifying that we were favorably impressed, and nodded, once, twice, proof that we appreciated the information, that it met with our approval. My mother was one of five daughters, four of whom were working by the time they were four years old, singing in four-part harmony and tap-dancing in kiddie revues. Of the quartet my mother was the sole acrobat, performer of backbends and splits, deformer of her body parts into curlicues and pretzel shapes. With what they earned — and as children, no less — they supported not only their two parents but their baby brother and sister as well. Dutiful daughters if ever dutiful daughters existed. And they weren't even wholly Chinese. But did my mother say anything? Did I?

Unlike my mother's, my own formative years were parochial to the extreme. College summers I worked at my father's office on Broad Street or at Saks Fifth Avenue, where my mother was lingerie buyer. After college I moved to Boston to attend graduate school. I walked in the door of Boston University only to walk out (I didn't even make it into the lobby), and soon landed a job in public relations at the Boston Museum of Fine Arts. After nine months I was bored, restless, and frustrated. Not knowing a soul or what I would do there and caring even less, I absconded to Paris. Four weeks, I told my parents and believed myself. Four weeks in Paris became four years in Europe. My father blamed my mother for my decision to forgo further education and instead live like a gypsy in a foreign land: "That (meaning the willingness to exhibit oneself) comes from your side of the family." After all, he continued, hadn't I displayed myself by modeling at the *Mademoiselle* fall fashion show? And again at her store where I'd been selected for the Saks Fifth Avenue College Board fashion show? After all, he had never been a Kim Loo Sister. He had never been paraded onstage before an anonymous, ogling public.

A telling remark, since my father's initial attraction to my mother was not because she had brains (which he would soon discover, and in generous supply) but because she was — and still is — beautiful and, even more, suffused with that elusive, unquantifiable virtue, charm. He was fresh off the boat, a foreign student at the University of Chicago, when he first saw my mother performing in George White's Scandals. There she was, up onstage singing, dancing, and turning cartwheels. And there he was, ogling her from the first row, literally at her feet. His marrying her — a *guailou,* and a performer to boot — had enraged his rigid Confucianist patriarch of a father to the point of relegating his firstborn son to the land beyond Dog Mountain. Not until my mother gave him his first grandchild did my grandfather forgive my father's dereliction of duty by recalling him to the land of the living, by no longer considering him dead. "You don't know your father well enough to speak that way. You don't know what it cost your father, a Chinese man, to defy his father by marrying me." This my mother told me once, when I was complaining about him, castigating him, certain that she would see my point of view and side with me. "You just don't know."

But then my mother had always served as go-between for my father and me: the interpreter of my father's feelings and my own, the smoother of ruffled feathers, the blunter of sharp words. It was she who had arranged my first encounter with him after my four "wasted" years in France and Italy — a meeting which took place over an assortment of pastries and a starvation diet of meaningful dialogue. She had been present on that occasion as she was on this: arbitrator and referee. Both times, we ate snacks from Chinatown, drank tea, spoke in platitudes, and, when we weren't speaking or eating, maintained a strained silence.

The ways my father and I saw life, the ways we lived our lives, were as different as our mother tongues. Between us lay a chasm of miscommunication and incomprehension that my mother tried valiantly to bridge with the language of wisdom, compassion, and mostly well-timed silences. When I first told him, proudly, that I was a free-lance writer, yoked to no company, he insinuated that free-lancing was tantamount to being unemployed and asked why I didn't find work at a reputable firm where work was regular and whose name everyone knew. He couldn't understand how I could live the way I did, how I managed to support both myself and Anton. As for my pleasures, he scoffed at the dancing and ice-skating lessons I delighted in. Sheer frivolousness! Again, to my mother: "That's from your side of the family." And just before I took refuge in Finland, he teased me mercilessly: "Why not go back to Langtoucun, our ancestral village? There's no plumbing or electricity there, either." (As it so happened, I would, and in his company.) When his sardonic laughter subsided, I failed to see, until this writing, the real impetus behind his raillery. I failed to see that the shake of his head at my strange views and ways and his mocking eyes, ready to dart away from me, concealed anxiety. When I thought of my father, it was this expression — of uncomprehending concern — and these feelings — of shame for his failure to have taught me what I should know; of helpless love for an almost and therefore failed son, a hapless if not wayward child — that most often came to mind. When I tried to summon an image of my father's father, whom I barely knew, it was the same vision: Grampa shaking his head sadly and brooding over his firstborn son who had failed to follow in his overwhelming footsteps.

What the Chinese fear most is to be alone in life. They love their families and friends. They want them around for the *renao* they bring, the heat and noise of human relationships. Second to the lack of human warmth, they fear physical cold. My father must have thought: What kind of woman is this daughter of mine who longs for solitude and life in a log cabin in freezing Finland? She should stay put, get married, give me a son-in-law and her son a father. She should get a real job. She should think of her happiness in the present and her security in her old age. A woman needs to have her family and her people around her. It is the proper way to live. Each generation is a link in the great chain of life. No one can drop out without breaking it.

A big platter of sesame–peanut sauce noodles was set before us — the culinary announcement to the end of our meal. My father's friend, with a glance at his watch, rose, apologized to have to leave, and excused himself from the table. My mother and I bobbed our heads, our faces imitating the expression on his but to a lesser degree. When he had disappeared, my father explained that his friend had to return home to accompany his wife, who needed to be fitted with a hearing aid. My father looked suddenly and starkly smaller, now that his friend was no longer sitting beside him. Smaller, and touchingly vulnerable. He reached across the table and began to mix the noodles so that the tofu, broccoli, and onions would be evenly distributed. He gestured, first to my mother, then to me, that we hold out our bowls so that he might fill them. Noodles mean long life. Long life, prosperity, many sons. These three blessings are what the Chinese dream of, the heaven on earth that occurs only in the land of the living, the happiness that humans experience only in the here and now.

"Daddy."

The word broke the vacuum of our silence, broke through the clatterings and buzzings of the omnipresent restaurant noise. My father looked up from his bowl of noodles. I pulled the travel section out of my shoulder bag.

"What do you think of my first article for the *New York Times*?"

I passed it to him across the table. It was about Guilin, the birthplace of both his parents. My mother pretended to be absorbed in her noodles.

"Four pages," I said. "Turn one more page. There. They told me they liked the article so much that they didn't want to cut any of it, so they inserted an additional page. Do you know what an extra page in the *Times* costs?"

He read several paragraphs with a scrutiny closer than I would have liked while my mother and I ate several mouthfuls of noodles with more propriety than usual.

"You write very well." Unspoken subtext even more gratifying than text: Do you know how much it cost me in face to say that?

"You really think so?"

He nodded, then extended his hand, the one holding the travel section.

My mother pursed her lips. "Take it, Li. She's giving it to you."

My father looked at her, his mouth slightly ajar, his eyes clueless. He closed his mouth; his eyes regained their former consciousness. He retracted his arm. "Thank you."

"My pleasure." My words were drowned out in the scraping of our chair legs against the floor as we rose to leave.

We walked to Mulberry Street, my parents legally separated but physically side by side, my mother hobbling, almost imperceptibly, my father's hand gently cupping her elbow, and me behind and between them, my left hand curled around my father's arm, my right hand about my mother's — not so much three links in the chain of life as a human triangle. The triangle, I learned at Bronx Science, is the most stable of geometric shapes. The eternal triangle, I realized, wasn't the romantic configuration but the familial one.

I left my parents on Mulberry Street, having kissed them both on the cheek, a non-Chinese practice which I had long ago repudiated and now, at this stage of my life, and theirs, without forethought, resumed.

Back in my apartment I put four of the tangelos in the refrigerator. I made tassels from a spool of red silk string and tied them around the two bamboo flutes, which I hung at angles to each other from the center of the beam in my living room, where they would free up blocked *chi,* bring me prosperity, and increase my personal development. That concluded, I opened the cardboard tube my father had slipped into the pink plastic bag. Inside was a Chinese hanging scroll: not a brush-and-ink painting but a rubbing.

I once saw, in Guilin, a man paint a picture onto a prepared, smooth area of mountainside, then carefully and patiently chisel both the rock and the paint away. With a roller, he applied a thin coat of thick black ink, pressed a large sheet of rice paper to the surface, tamped the paper with a soft mallet, then peeled the paper away. Voilà! The mirror image of the painting/rock carving, the third generation, so to speak, of the original image.

The subject of the rubbing I held in my hands was a pliant bamboo sapling growing on, gripping, really, the edge of a cliff or rocky ledge. The white, inkless sapling was delineated and defined by its black, inked background. I remembered reading in an art history book that Chinese artists leave large areas of their paintings empty not only to permit the viewer to complete the work in his imagination but also because the idea of completion is totally alien to the Chinese mind. I went to my bookshelves, located the book *Arts of China* by Michael Sullivan, and found the passage.

"The Chinese painter deliberately avoids a complete statement because he knows that we can never know everything, that what we can describe, or 'complete,' cannot be true except in a very limited sense. All he can do is to liberate the imagination and set it wandering. . . . His landscape is not a final statement, but a starting point. Not an end, but the opening of a door."

I peeled the tangelo I'd left out on the kitchen counter the way my father peeled the mandarin oranges he preferred: so that the orange remained whole and connected to its source — the stem — while the peel formed both the petals of a flower and a little cupped dish to cradle the exposed fruit. I ate each segment slowly, savoring the half-sweet, half-sour taste while I gazed at the scroll. I found my eyes more drawn to the fullness of its blackness, the depth of its emptiness that offered both substance and support to the pliant subject, than to the sapling itself.

Juk sing, I thought. The silken tassels shimmered in the fading daylight and the soft breeze blowing through the open window. The hollow bamboos from which they were suspended I'd placed at equal and opposite angles to each other, as prescribed. At cross purposes to each other. In counterbalance of each other. *Juk sing.* Nothing in them but song.

"Healthy" Sesame–Peanut Sauce Noodles
(Hot or Cold)

2 teaspoons salt
4 quarts water
½ pound fresh noodles
½ cup cold water
2¾ tablespoons peanut oil
1½ cups fresh broccoli, cut in small florets
1 small onion, cut in large dice
½ pound tofu, firm, cut into ½-inch cubes

Sauce:

1–1½ teaspoons Guilin *la-jiao* (chili sauce)
1 teaspoon sugar
2½ tablespoons creamy peanut butter
2½ tablespoons black soy sauce
1 tablespoon Chinese red vinegar or cider vinegar
1½ tablespoons sesame oil

Add salt to 4 quarts water. Bring to rapid boil over medium heat. Add fresh noodles. Immediately stir to separate strands. Continue cooking and stirring 15 seconds. Pour in ½ cup cold water.

For cold noodles, pour noodles into colander and run cold tap water over them, tossing thoroughly to stop cooking. When noodles are cool to the touch, shake in colander to shed excess water. Add 2 tablespoons oil, toss to coat evenly. Spread noodles out on serving platter.

For hot noodles, pour noodles into colander. Shake to drain off excess water. Add 2 tablespoons oil, toss to coat thoroughly. Because the noodles will cook in their own heat, use them as soon as possible, or delay cooking the noodles until just before you need them.

Steam broccoli florets in boiling water 2–3 minutes, so they are still crunchy. Run cold water over florets so they stop cooking. Set aside. Heat wok to medium-high. Add ¾ tablespoon oil, heat till sizzling, turn down heat to medium, and stir-fry onion till translucent, 2 minutes. Set aside.

Put the sauce mixture in a small pot over low heat, stirring, until the peanut butter softens and dissolves into the other ingredients. Remove from heat.

Top noodles with broccoli, onion, and tofu. Pour sauce mixture on top. Toss so that all the ingredients are coated. Serve hot or cold (at room temperature).

Makes 4–6 servings.

13

CLEAR BRIGHTNESS AND HUNGRY GHOSTS

In Mexico, they do this festival [Halloween] the right way, with no disguises. Bright candy skulls, family picnics on the graves, a plate set for each individual guest, a candle for the soul. Everyone goes away happy, including the dead. We've rejected that easy flow between dimensions: we want the dead unmentionable, we refuse to feed them. Our dead as a result are thinner, grayer, harder to bear, and hungrier.

—from *Cat's Eye* by Margaret Atwood

Ours, he [Malraux] said, is a civilization that has proved unable to replace what it destroys or leaves behind. And this, he added, is revealed to the very fact that Western civilization has lost the capacity to remember and relive death. "Where are the tombs and temples of the twentieth century?" he asked. He knew that death had been forgotten in order to forget pain. But this is not possible. Death exiled is pain multiplied.

—from *Meetings with Malraux* by Carlos Fuentes

*U*nlike my first solitary visit to China, which coincided with the Moon Festival, my second, taken in the company of my father four years later, fell between two major holidays, one for the living and one for the dead. The Pure Brightness Festival, or the Grave Sweeping Festival as it is also called, belongs to the latter category. An anomaly among Chinese holidays, it is based on the Gregorian calendar and therefore celebrated on a fixed date, April 4. The Dragon Boat Festival, on the other hand, celebrates the living and obeys the laws of the lunar calendar. It is observed on the fifth day of the fifth month, around June 21, the summer solstice.

As its name strongly suggests, the Grave Sweeping Festival is precisely that: after a long winter's dormancy, a spring day is set aside for families to pay their respects to the spirits of their ancestors by tidying up their graves and making offerings of food, drink, and spirit money. You will notice that I said spirits, not memory, of their ancestors. In China, the line dividing the living from the dead is somewhat permeable and the idea of "festivals of the living" as opposed to "festivals of the dead" is too severe a distinction. To the Chinese, the rationale behind ancestor worship lies in the belief that the spirit survives the body after death and remains in the grave, where it keeps tabs on the conduct of those family members left behind. Since spirits possess powers greater than those of the living (though less than those of gods), it behooves their descendants to appease them and keep them happy. This is accomplished by cleaning and repairing their homes and plying them with comestibles and other gifts on a day dedicated strictly to them. In return, the satisfied spirits reward kith and kin with health, wealth, and happiness.

The Dragon Boat Festival is also a day of propitiation

— in this case, of the river god, who possesses the body of a snake, the head, mane, and tail of a horse, the horns of a deer, the paws of a dog, the scales and whiskers of a fish, and the wings of a bird. In other words, a dragon. The ancient Chinese adopted this composite creature and cultural totem in the belief that he controlled the rivers as well as the rainfall. To invoke his munificence, they devised elaborate rites and sacrifices, including and most notably a human one. Violent racing contests were conducted in dragon-shaped boats, where at least one vessel had to capsize and one person must drown. This small, compensatory dose of death and destruction was a pittance when compared to the catastrophe of drought or flood the river god might unleash if his honor was neglected and his wrath went unassuaged.

My father and I arrived in China during a holiday black hole whose event horizon, while it precluded any popular festivities, nevertheless encompassed a personally momentous one: Nai-nai's hundredth birthday was on May 18, and we would be there that day and a dozen days before and after to help her celebrate.

At around the time that my father and I were heading east, Anton, a college freshman, was preparing to head west, to the Wind River Wilderness in Wyoming, to participate in a monthlong course on living in nature and making the least impact on the natural environment. A city boy, he would either love it or hate it. He loved it: getting caught in a blizzard, wading through deep snowdrifts with a seventy-pound pack on his back, cooking deep-dish yeast-crust pizza in a pan over a twiggy fire, even being mistaken, more than once, for being part Native American, what with his porcupine-quill-thick ponytail, his Slavic broad-planed and Chinese high-cheekboned face. After the experience, his "report card" mentioned, among other things, his real knack for cooking and his off-the-wall humor. Anton would return to the West: on an *On the Road*–type road trip to Colorado one summer where he canvassed door-to-door for an environmental nonprofit; then for a *Desert Solitaire* year to Arizona to work as head tour guide for a bat cave, where his off-the-wall humor was put to professional use. After high mountains and low desert, the open sea beckoned. For six months, he signed on as first mate on a twenty-eight-foot sailboat that plied the Intracoastal Waterway, from Newport to Savannah and back, a young-man-and-the-sea adventure. As with me at that age, China was nowhere on Anton's internal map. The world was flat and ended with the Western world, which included France, Italy, and Finland, countries where I had friends and where I had taken him on his twelfth summer so he might reconnect with his European half by both birthplace and blood, certain that, as with most pre-adolescents, he would want little to do with his mother — traveling together least of all — once he reached his teens, which time proved all too correct.

As pleased as I was about my second trip to China and its purpose, I made the mistake, fortuitous as it turned out, of mentioning to my father what a pity it was that we had missed the Pure Brightness Festival and would miss the Dragon Boat Festival, both by a few weeks. He, offhandedly and apologetically, conveyed my remark to Tanmin ("My daughter wouldn't have said such a thing if she thought the Chinese way"), who knit her brows and donned her thinking cap. I had witnessed these same gestures on my previous trip to China. Their meanings were unmistakable. Knitting her brows was Tanmin's way of smiling with her forehead. Donning her thinking cap was her version of ecstatic visions, personal transcendence, a steady barrage of alpha waves. If anyone could analyze a problem, devise a strategy to overcome it, and set in motion a well-conceived plan of action, it was Tanmin.

"*Meiyou banfa*. No problem," she said with a grin glinting much gold. "Leave it to me."

As if we had a choice. My father and I were kept in the dark, or at least in deep shadow, regarding what exactly our itinerary would be, usually until the moment it was sprung on us. That way, we had no say in the matter and so would pose no interference to the ready-made plans of those who did, namely Tanmin. While our days in Guilin unfurled languorously, pleasurably, often based on wishes I had so "Westernly" divulged — an ineptitude my father politely claimed to deplore while enjoying its results — they were a whirlwind of behind-the-scenes activity for her. No phone call went unmade, no potentially useful personage escaped unflattered, no stone was left unturned. Automobiles, even air-conditioned vans, turned up at our doorstep, like Cinderella's pumpkin-turned-coach, complete with driver and English-speaking guide. Keys slipped noisily into the locks of doors of private residences, art museums after hours, and offices of unreachable VIPs. Throughout, Tanmin inhabited the eye of the storm, and there she thrived, directing its course and velocity.

One morning several days after our arrival, two air-conditioned sedans pulled up in front of Nai-nai's compound to take us to the village of Langtoucun and my grandfather's house, now a museum. My grandfather had had the *siheyuan* — a family compound of rooms constructed around a courtyard or courtyards — built for his mother when he attained the rank of general in the Nationalist Army at the age of thirty. Later, he built another *siheyuan* on the shores of Guilin's Fir Lake, this time for his own use, as a refuge from the pressures and problems of the vice presidency. His life of public service, however, and the advancing Red Army kept him close to Beijing — similar to how the road we were traveling, or what there was of it, was keeping us close to Guilin. Hundreds of men and women armed with sledgehammers lined our route, pounding substantial rocks into tiny pebbles and paving a stretch of road just in time for us to drive over it. An hour or so later, having passed the last of the construction crews, we stopped on a dirt road in the middle of nowhere. The only other sign of life was a wiry man leading a soporific water buffalo on a rope, who ambled into view, gave us a dismissive glance, then picked his way down an embankment into a flooded rice paddy.

"Have we run out of gas?" I asked my father.

"We're here."

"Here?" I looked around me. "Where?"

"Langtoucun."

Jiaqiu, Nannan, and Lizi were climbing out of the second sedan, scythes, hoes, and twig brooms in their hands. Tanmin, who rode with us, pointed to a grassy hill in the near distance.

"The feng shui graves of your great-grandmother and her family. *Li Zongren de jiali ren.*" She made a sweeping gesture, literally, with both her arms. "*Qing Ming.*"

Qing Ming. Pure Brightness. Tanmin had struck again. We were celebrating the Grave Sweeping Festival today, lunar and Gregorian calendars be damned. Nannan handed the three of us walking sticks and broad-brimmed straw hats. The hill wasn't tall, but its gradient was steep and, at eleven o'clock, the sun was high in the sky, sucking up water from the rice paddies and redistributing it as a topography-embracing, steamy haze. Jiaqiu and Lizi, besides wielding the farm implements, hefted a substantial cloth-tied bundle apiece, as did Nannan. My father and I had just ourselves and our walking sticks to handle, which was plenty, as we made our way up the vertiginous walking path, then stopped some twenty feet short of the top. We had arrived at our destination, also constructed by my grandfather — the "wind and water" graves of three ancestors, each one fronted by a stone "door" upon whose jambs writhing dragons in haut-relief frolicked in stylized waves.

The Li family plot fulfilled the classic feng shui tenets for good placement and therefore ensured maximum harmony with the natural order. It sat on the south side of a Tortoise Mountain facing the Li River, and it was embraced on the east by a green Dragon Mountain, on the west by a lower white Tiger Hill, and on the south by an even lower vermilion Bird. It was the ideal "armchair" or "dragon protecting pearl" site. It was also high up enough on the hill to have good drainage, yet low enough to avoid the ravages of strong winds and foul weather. The grave plot itself was square — the best shape — with a narrow inner chamber and a wide entrance.

"Whose graves are these?"

"The one in the middle is Grampa's mother," my father told me.

The two graves flanking hers were those of Grampa's father and grandfather, he further explained. Jiaqiu and Lizi had put down their bundles and were hard at work digging up or cutting away weeds and grasses that had worked their way through the cracks in the stone flooring around the stone incense holders in front of the graves and the low stone sacrificial tables a few feet away. Nannan had opened the bundle that contained joss sticks, red candles, strings of red firecrackers, and sheets of gold and silver paper. Seated on opposite ends of one stone table, she and Tanmin were now folding the sheets into "ingots" of spirit money.

"I thought only male members of the family — the ones who carry on the family name — could be buried in the family plot."

My father considered my query for a moment, wagged his head, then said, "Grampa loved his mother very much."

"He broke tradition," I murmured, letting the fact sink in. "He went against precedent. And hers is the one in the center. The place of honor."

My father considered this, and again he shook his head, this time his sole reply. Jiaqiu and Lizi, having completed the first round of cleanup, now attacked the burial ground floor with the twig brooms, while Tanmin and Nannan set candles and joss sticks in the incense pots and placed on the sacrificial-altar tables the contents of the other bundles: platters supporting a plucked chicken, a slab of fatty pork, a whole fish, a plucked duck. All the animals were semi-cooked, a condition predicated on the belief that gods require live fish, whole pigs, and raw fowl, humans their fully cooked versions, and spirits residing in or around gravesites their partially processed counterparts devoid of appetizing condiments. To complete the table setting: four oranges, a bottle of mao-tai, and four glasses.

"Why always four?"

"It's an even number," my father said. "A yin number. An even number of food offerings is proper for spirits. An odd number of sacrifices, a yang number, is made only to gods." He shook his head. "Chinese superstitions," he murmured, in approval or in dismissal, I couldn't tell which.

Tanmin beckoned to my father and whispered something to him, after which he lit several joss sticks and placed half of them in my hand. "You hold them like this" — he pressed the remaining joss between his two palms, prayer-like — "and you bend at the waist," he demonstrated, "and bow. Try it."

I did. Awkwardly. Stiffly. Because it was the first time, and because another precedent was being broken and once again I would be the one to break it. This time, however, my father was giving me the go-ahead.

Traditionally, only male family members were permitted to propitiate the spirits of their ancestors by offering sacrifices to them. A female member was not only barred from participating in that practice, she was also constrained to keep her maiden name after marriage (a practice, ironically, that Western feminists fought against tradition to achieve) in the belief that she was only an honorary member of her in-law's family, full membership being conferred only upon her death. In life, she was treated essentially like a servant, as handmaiden to her parents-in-law. Woe betide the young wife whose mother-in-law was especially demanding! The incidents in which a married woman committed suicide by hanging herself or jumping down a well are legion. An intractable patriarchy that devalued women (and played them off against each other: see the film *Raise the Red Lantern,* directed by Zhang Yimou) could easily conceive of the *Book of Poems,* a sort of Chinese Bill of Rights, which recommended that a baby boy be given a piece of precious jade to play with, a baby girl, a tile of fired clay. Later, the words of Confucius — "Teach sons, not daughters" — bolstered the official view of women as established by Han Feizi, a third-century-B.C. prince whose governing principles were followed until the downfall of China's last dynasty in 1912. According to Han, women were useful in three ways: (1) as spies to infiltrate enemy nations (the Dragon Lady prototype); (2) as playthings for rulers and warriors (the Suzie Wong prototype); (3) or as the seedbed for future soldiers (the Submissive Spouse/Dutiful Daughter-in-Law/Earth Mother prototype).

The perfect woman was obedient, served her male master, and learned to get along amicably with as many other wives or concubines as her husband wanted or could afford to take on. Whether wife or concubine, she led a prescribed and, under Chinese law, powerless existence. A daughter was less entitled to her father's estate than an illegitimate son. If she was so fortunate as to inherit his estate, she could do so only in her husband's name. If she became a widow, her inheritance depended upon her chastity: should she remarry, she was expelled from her first husband's family, lost any rights to his estate, and forfeited her children. If, on the other hand, she preceded her husband to the grave, he retained the right to her property. In addition, he was expected to remarry. As for his second wife, she was welcomed into his deceased wife's family as their stepdaughter.

Confucian ideas regarding women were readily embraced by the Ming dynasty scholar and essayist Hsieh Chao Chi, who expatiated: "As a rule, women possess such undesirable qualities as jealousy, stinginess, obduracy, sloth, ineptitude, foolishness, cruelty, short temper, suspicion, gullibility, attachment to trivia, displeasure, worship of heretical religions, and infatuation." He concluded by saying, "The wit and intelligence of women are hardly worth mentioning." It's no wonder that under Confucian codes a man could cancel a marriage for any of seven reasons, including a wife's excessive talking or her failure to bear a son, while a wife's adultery was punishable by death (again, see the film *Raise the Red Lantern*). For proof of the latter, I needed go back only to 1989, the year that a Chinese man hammered his wife to death because he suspected her of having a love affair. The judge sentenced the man to five months' probation. He said that his ruling was based on the gravity of the (supposed) infidelity (on the woman's part) in Chinese culture, and that the ensuing shame compelled the man to commit the unfortunate deed. What made the case and its outcome unusual was that it wasn't tried in China but in Chinatown, New York City, with an American judge presiding.

"How many times do I bow? An even number?"

"It doesn't matter. Just do what I do."

Tanmin, Jiaqiu, Lizi, and Nannan had lit all the candles and incense in the incense pots. Starting from the left, my father and I stood before each grave, shook our joss sticks, and bowed in unison several times, while Jiaqiu and Lizi set off the strings of firecrackers to scare off any uninvited "hungry ghosts" — the wandering spirits of men and women unfortunate enough to have lost their lives through murder, suicide, or in childhood, or to have perished far from their homes and families, or to have had no male descendants to look after them in life and, now, in death.

What I was engaged in, I imagined, was an initiation rite besides a funerary offering. I was being inducted as an honorary male. First the flower, then the fruit. First the girl I was; then the boy I was meant to be. An almost boy. A defective boy. A defective boy who, more defectively, and unforgivably, cried.

As a child, I cried a great deal. Almost anything could get me going. A glance I thought unfriendly. A hand-me-down dress from my older sister. A wrong answer in class. A word I'd flubbed in a spelling bee. My father calling us "Filipinas" and, even worse, "Puerto Ricans" when my sisters and I grew tan in the summer. My mother tried to explain that I was sensitive. My father assured her that I was weak. Whenever I started to cry, he would laugh and point at me. Of course, that only made me cry all the harder, my mouth trembling and wavery at first then, finally, wide open and bawling. Which provided more fuel for my father's ridicule.

"You . . . look just . . . like Joe E. . . . Brown!" he would manage to emit in breathless gusts between wheezes of laughter. "Joe E. Brown!" The rubber-faced comedian with a malleable mouth he could stretch as wide as a dinner plate. I would bawl all the louder, my mouth jaw-wrenchingly and hugely open, proving my father right.

Sometimes, my father actually instigated the tears, like when he made fun of the way I walked. "Like a duck." He would get up from the table or interrupt whatever he was doing — at least one other family member present to witness his cleverness and my shame — to demonstrate. He would shuffle his feet forward, turned out in first position.

"No. Like Charlie Chaplin!" With that, he would burst into laughter and take such malicious pleasure in denigrating me that I would burst into equally spontaneous tears. "Char . . . lie . . . Chaplin!" he would wheeze and demonstrate, pointing at me. "Charlie . . . Chaplin!"

My face would flush and contort with shame and rage; my eyes would blur with tears; my mouth would twist and emit snuffling, gulping, squashed-accordion sounds. My father still laughing, his mouth as jaw-breakingly open as mine, his arms crossed and clamped over his heaving, humor-wracked chest. "Charlie . . . Chap . . . lin!" he would gasp, pointing accusingly and shuffling in place.

I never thought of escaping such torment but withstood it. It wasn't just that I was nailed to the spot with shame. I must have realized that taking flight would only have given him more ammunition — my duck feet making their quick getaway — to cut me off at the pass, to cut me off at the knees. When did I no longer bawl at his provocations? When or why did he no longer make them? When, eventually, I gave up tears in response to his mockery, those I later shed because of him and those I shed for him did not come easily. Not easily at all.

Joe E. Brown. Charlie Chaplin. Why men? Why not women? Why not Fanny Brice? Or Martha Raye? Or Carol

Burnett? They each had equally wide mouths. And why not Maria Tallchief, Suzanne Farrell, or any ballerina? They all walked with the exaggerated turnout that came with their profession, with the territory. My territory, ceded to me reluctantly but emphatically by my father, my poor thwarted father, was the bleak wilderness of the absent, the almost, the honorary, son. The Joe E. Brown lookalike. The Charlie Chaplin clone.

My father took up the bottle of mao-tai, poured some of the liquid into one of the four shot glasses on the sacrificial altars, then handed the bottle to me so that I might replicate his action with the second shot glass. He moistened the third glass, I the fourth and final one. All the while, firecrackers fizzed and popped and kept up an irritating racket. Again, we shook our joss-filled palms, bent at the waist, bowed our heads in unison before each grave, and prayed for beneficence and good fortune for the present and future generations. Then the racket and the ritual were over. Back into the cloth-tied bundles went the food and drink, platters, cups, mao-tai, candles, and unlit joss. Back down the snaking hillside path we sidled to enter the near-oven-temperature cars and start the motors and the air-con. We had fulfilled our familial duty. We had filled the stomachs of the spirits of the dead with the essence of food and drink. As for the living, we were hot and hungry. Luckily, Grampa's *siheyuan*, where Tanmin assured us a picnic lunch awaited, was a short ride away.

Even from a distance, it was an imposing structure, a fortress, protected as it was by a thick whitewashed wall some four stories high. No buildings cast their shadows upon it, which, according to feng shui, oppresses a shorter building's *chi,* or vital energy, thereby hindering the occupants' personal and financial development. It rose out of the river plain, the tallest structure, the fiefdom castle around which peasant cottages nestled for protection, open to the sun and sky and the beneficent currents of the earth's energy. We drove up to the massive red door, which the gatekeeper, a gnarly old peasant who hobbled out to greet us, unlocked with a proportionately gargantuan key. The building had recently been turned into a museum, but those hardy souls who made the pilgrimage had to put their request in writing well in advance.

"They're mainly Japanese," my father told me, "who come to pay their respects." For the Japanese, Li Zongren was a great military strategist, the hero general of Taierzhuang, the single major battle of the Sino-Japanese War won by the Chinese. To me, Li Zongren had always been just Grampa, the Deng Xiaoping–sized man who pinched my childhood cheeks bloodless till tears rolled out of my eyes. To my father, he was an icon whose towering stature cast him in its abundant shadow, minimized him, while America marginalized him. We had come to pay our respects, to acknowledge our awe, to feel the weight of his legacy.

The gatekeeper pushed open the heavy front door, which was good and wide, allowing not only our bedraggled little band to enter but also a healthy stream of *chi.* At least, that's how it felt to cross the threshold: a subtle yet noticeable influx of energy, an incremental boost to my sagging spirits. Feng shui masters, or Masters of Wind and Water, often liken a house to a living, breathing person, a human being with his own unique metabolism. *Chi* is analogous to blood and must flow evenly from room to room. Windows and doors are the building's noses and mouths, inhaling and exhaling *chi* from space to space. The building's occupants are, metaphorically, the organs of the body, functioning at their best when they are nourished by a sustained and balanced flow of vital energy — not too strong, not too weak. Which is how I felt upon entering the first of the four courtyards: like Goldilocks sitting in Baby Bear's chair, eating from Baby Bear's bowl, sleeping in Baby Bear's bed. Just right.

If the single, unusual palm tree, which bore fruit once every one hundred years, was only ovulating, the plants in the remaining three courtyards were profuse, budding, or almost ripe decades after Nai-nai's mother-in-law, Da Mama, or "Big Mama," had built these gardens. Built, not planted. According to the Chinese conception, a garden must possess four components in pleasing proportions and configurations for maximum self-cultivation and reflection — rocks, water, buildings, and plants. And in that order. Rocks and water symbolize the duality of the cosmos, the harmonious interplay of yang and yin. Architecture represents man's contribution to the planet where he dwells, while plants are nature's gift to it. In her gardens Da Mama had planted several fruit trees, including a litchi, the lowest branches of which we immediately denuded of fruit, whose leathery red integuments yielded up, disappointingly, a large stone hidden by a thin pearlized film of sour unripe flesh. She had also dredged a pond in the last courtyard, bordered it with rocks — the more grotesque and tortured in shape the better — and stocked it with her favorite fish, that symbol of scholarly aptitude, carp. Between the third and fourth courtyards, she had also dug three deep stone wells: one each for washing clothes, dishes, and vegetables.

"My grandmother had a good sense of humor," my father told me. "'How can I not be kind and fair?' she used to say. 'With three sons, I have that many daughters-in-law. If I mistreat even one of them, she has her choice of three wells to jump into to take her revenge on me! If I should mistreat all three, each has a well in which to punish me!'" Small chance of that. My father told me that Da Mama was the antithesis of any Chinese daughter-in-law's worst nightmare: how she broke the unspoken taboo that a woman must give birth alone by being present at Nai-nai's side and helping her deliver her firstborn son; how, again deviating from precedent and common practice, she insisted that Nai-nai not only confront her husband — Da Mama's own son — after he had taken a concubine but also move in with the couple, forgoing her "proper" place under her in-laws' roof and duty to them as their handmaiden.

It was in the third courtyard where we lingered longest. Extended family members and invited guests had lived in the colonnaded rooms surrounding the other courtyards, but Nai-nai and Grampa had lived here, as had my father when he returned home every summer from boarding school in Canton, encouraged by his father to stay in rural Langtoucun rather than urban Guilin so he might see how hard the peasants worked for their daily bowl of rice. Most of the rooms were minimally furnished, or not at all, but in the room that had been my grandmother's there was a four-poster and dressing table not all that different from her bedroom furniture in suburban New York.

It was time to eat our midday bowl of rice, and we repaired to the shade under the fruit trees framing the pond. A large square bamboo mat, the kind I'd seen used in China to build rudimentary roofing or entire sheds, had been set down for us to sit on, and the promised picnic lunch — one requiring no rice bowls, in fact, no implements at all — sat in the middle: a mound of pyramidal packets each covered in large blackish-green leaves and tied up with strings.

"*Zongzi,*" my father said when I asked. "Dragon Boat Festival food."

After some prodding, the recalcitrant strings around his food packet loosened, and he exhumed from the artfully folded banana-leaf wrapper (which now served as generous plate-cum-napkin) a pyramid of glutinous rice anointed with sesame oil and soy sauce and studded with chopped dates, peanuts, water chestnuts, and spring onions. It looked delicious, and I trusted that it would taste that way, if ever I succeeded in opening mine.

"Here, give it to me," offered Tanmin, who had already finished her second *zongzi*. "And while you're eating it, I'll tell you the legend of Qu Yuan, and why *zongzi* are tied up with strings. There. Enjoy, and listen."

The legend she told us was essentially this: Qu Yuan, a trusted counselor to King Huai of Chu, one of seven contentious kingdoms vying for predominance during the Warring States Period, advised the king to form an alliance with three of the less belligerent kingdoms to combat the most hostile one. But the monarch rejected the plan, and Qu Yuan was banished. Even in exile, he remained loyal to his sovereign and became a wandering wordsmith of patri-

214

otic poems. News that Chu was losing many battles and much territory to its foes grieved him deeply. But when Qu Yuan learned that his king had been captured and had died in prison, he despaired. He weighted himself with a rock and threw himself into the river. Onlookers raced out in their rowboats to save him, or at least to find his body, but to no avail. Because of his lifelong loyalty to his king, they filled segments of bamboo with rice and cast them into the river so that his spirit would not go hungry. However, they had packaged the food offerings improperly, and the wily river god — not Qu Yuan's spirit, who appeared before them to tell them so — was devouring all the rice. The right way, he told them, was to wrap the rice in lily or palm leaves so that it formed a pyramid, which they should then tie up with five silk threads, each a different color. The mighty dragon would be unable to get at the rice inside the delicate packages, what with his monstrous claws, while Qu Yuan's spirit would unravel the strings with ease, and he would no longer go hungry.

"And that's why they're called *zongzi*," Tanmin concluded, waving yet another empty banana leaf at her son, Lizi, who took it, then started to fold it. "*Zong* means 'palm,' the kind of leaf the glutinous rice is often wrapped in. So now you know why we eat *zongzi* during the Dragon Boat Festival."

I thanked Tanmin for the story about *zongzi*, the delicious *zongzi* themselves, and her assistance in unwrapping them. When I thanked her for killing two birds with one stone — celebrating two major festivals on a single day on which neither of them fell: the Grave Sweeping Festival and the Dragon Boat Festival — the smile on her face buckled then drooped into a wistful frown. (Had I said the wrong thing? Had I failed to express sufficient gratitude? Had she broken some celebratory regulation to which I inadvertently alluded that should have remained unmentioned? Why, oh, why was I so Western?!)

"Ahh," she sighed. "It's unfortunate that I was unable to arrange a dragon boat race for you and your father. That, ah, no."

She shook her head, a gesture that expressed not so much disappointment as disbelief that she had failed to come through in such a trifling matter as an aquatic extravaganza. Her lively eyes, however, were undimmed. They actually seemed to grow brighter. I turned to see what it was that she was looking at, that made them twinkle with undisguised pleasure. There on Da Mama's lake floated miniature dragon boats — the recycled, reconfigured banana leaves — which Lizi sent out, one after the other, onto its placid surface with a gentle push of his hand.

Dragon Boat Festival Savory *Zongzi*

3½ cups long-grain, glutinous rice
2 tablespoons dried shrimp, soaked 1 hour
12 ounces pork belly or bacon
4 dried black mushrooms, soaked 30 minutes
2 hard-boiled egg yolks (optional)
⅓ cup peanut oil
24 bamboo leaves, soaked in water
string

Seasoning #1:

1 teaspoon salt
¼ teaspoon sugar
¼ teaspoon black pepper
1 teaspoon rice wine or sherry
¼ cup light soy sauce
½ stalk spring onion (or scallion), finely chopped

Seasoning #2:

¾ teaspoon salt
2 teaspoons dark soy sauce

Soak rice 2 hours. Drain. Change water and soak an additional 30 minutes. Drain. Drain shrimp. Dice pork. Drain and stem mushrooms; dice the caps. Chop egg yolks. Set aside.

Heat wok, add oil, and fry the shrimp, pork, and mushrooms 1½ minutes. Add seasoning #1 and heat through. Set aside.

Fry rice in oil for 2 minutes. Add seasoning #2 and mix thoroughly.

Drain bamboo leaves and wipe dry. Brush one side with peanut oil. Place two leaves side by side. Fold the two bottoms over together to form a triangular pouch. Place some rice, chopped egg yolk, shrimp, pork, and mushroom mixture in the pouch. Top with more rice. Fold the leaves over the top and around the pouch to make a plump, triangular packet. Wrap string securely around the packet. Repeat with the remaining bamboo leaves.

Place all two dozen packets side by side in a large saucepan. Fill with cold water and bring to a boil. Reduce heat and simmer 1 hour. If water has not been completely absorbed, drain the excess. Unwrap and serve.

Makes 12 servings.

14

THE VILLAGE WITH NO NAME

The more one was lost in unfamiliar quarters of distant cities, the more one understood the other cities he had crossed to arrive there; and he retraced the stages of his journeys, and he came to know the port from which he had set sail . . . what he sought was always something lying ahead, and even if it was a matter of the past it was a past that changed gradually as he advanced on his journey, because the traveler's past changes according to the route he has followed. . . . the foreignness of what you no longer are or no longer possess lies in wait for you in foreign, unpossessed places.

—from *Invisible Cities* by Italo Calvino

Writing fiction involves observing people suffer and, usually later, finding some meaning in that suffering. Writing memoir involves observing people making you suffer and, usually much later, discovering what it is they've suffered that makes them insist that you suffer too. In other words, writing memoir involves, even requires, compassion for both the sufferer and the sufferee, compassion which if you don't have at the outset of your project you will by the time you complete it.

I was composing my thoughts and writing them down in my journal when my father opened the door (without knocking) and entered my room (without my permission). My journal served double duty: into it went descriptions of my sleeping-dream experiences, my waking-life experiences, and whatever fell in between, which most people term daydreaming or a waking dream. I call it mulling or musing, often the most interesting of the three because mulling has to do with meaning, the discovery of which is difficult enough that very few of the pages in my journal are devoted to it. So it was especially annoying that my father should unwittingly arrest potentially meaningful words which I might have written by barging in unannounced. It was also understandable, since my father is Chinese (no matter that he has lived more than twice as many years in the United States as he has lived in China) and we were in Nai-nai's house, where privacy doesn't count, in China, where the very word doesn't even exist.

That's not quite accurate. We were actually in my parents' house. It was the house Nai-nai had built for my parents, her wedding present to them. But the Sino-Japanese War intervened, forcing my parents to remain in the United States and my grandmother to be an Indian giver. Offensive term and misnomer, Indian giver, but correct in one way: the United States government reneged on what it gave to the Native Americans to keep — treaties, land, basic human rights, even the reservations onto which they were herded. Watching westerns on TV, my father always rooted for the Indians — "They belong to the Mongoloid race, like me" — even though they were doomed from the start. They fought with bows and arrows, while the white man had pistols, rifles, cannons. "The Chinese peasant fought the Japanese war machine with shovels and pitchforks, and still we won." But the red man on the television screen always lost. Years later, when my father learned that the desolate outposts where the indigenous Americans had been confined were oil- and uranium-rich, lucrative, legalized gambling havens, he felt vindicated. I could see the self-righteousness, the just deserts, the personal victory fighting to write themselves into the features of his hermetic face, struggling to express themselves via his restrained, boyish body and relieve it of steadily accumulated, successfully withheld rage.

"Daddy." A pause. "Sister Ellen wants me to talk to you." Another pause. "And to Mommy, too."

"About what." A statement.

A long pause. "She wants you and Mommy to get married."

A short pause during which there was a shallow intake of breath. "Your mother and I are already married."

An immediate answer: "I know. But Mommy told her that you both got married outside of the Church." A pause. "At the parent-teacher conference she told her. So Sister Ellen thinks you and Mom should get married inside of the Church."

A question proffered as a statement: "What for."

"For your immortal souls. She says . . . Sister Ellen says . . . that if you don't get married in the Church, then your soul and Mom's will . . ." Blurted out, "Will be dammed to everlasting hellfire."

The swift inhalation of breath. The cessation of breath. The reddening face. The bulging eyes. The pursed lips. The flaring nostrils.

"You tell that nun . . ." the voice raspy with rage and heart-woundedness, "you tell her that I'm a Buddhist. I'm a Buddhist. You tell her that."

"Hurry up," my father told me. "Get dressed and eat your breakfast. They're sending a car for us. It'll be here in half an hour." He exited the bedroom without shutting the door.

I got out of bed where I had been writing in my journal and closed the door. And I did as I was told. I said nothing about my right to privacy. I said nothing about kindly knocking on my door before entering. I was in China, in Nai-nai's house. And when you are in someone else's house, the Chinese saying goes, you must bow your head. I put away my journal, interrupted. I dressed quickly. I ate my breakfast of *mi-fen.* The car arrived, and it took us back to Langtoucun, where I had asked to return: I wanted to walk in my grandparents' footsteps. I wanted to retrace their wedding march, Chinese version, from Grampa's house in Langtoucun to Nai-nai's home in Cuntoucun, or "Village Village," too small and too insignificant to warrant a real name. I had told my father of my wish, and he had relayed it to Tanmin, who had arranged it. I had not, however, told anyone why I wanted to do this, the purpose it would serve.

The driver stopped where the gravel-paved road did, at the edge of Langtoucun. Hovering in the sun-hazed distance was Cuntoucun. To get there I needed to make my way over a very irregular path (wide enough for bullock carts, as it was strewn with the beasts' generous droppings) of flagstones, each a good foot or so distant from each other. I stepped out of the car, careful of where I set my feet. Jiaqiu, who was a member of our small party (Tanmin was attending to matters at home), motioned me back into the car.

"It's hot and Cuntoucun is far. Why don't we all simply drive to your grandmother's village?"

My father seconded Jiaqiu's suggestion, but when I insisted upon walking, my father said he would accompany me. Our journey was more like an extra-challenging game of hopscotch, jumping from one rock to the next, all the while trying to avoid the dung and mud. Jiaqiu and the driver followed behind, bumpily.

"Have you ever walked this route before?"

"No. This is the first time," my father answered.

We heard a whirring of tires, a groan of gears, and smelled the pungent stink of burning rubber. The car had stalled and listed helplessly, its front half up on a rock, the rest on the muddy plain. With a firm toehold and our full body weight behind it, we managed to push the foundering vehicle, our beast become burden, back onto all four tires and on course. It advanced, huffing and groaning, more slowly than my father and I on foot. We arrived at Cuntoucun's village gate hot, tired, and later than if we had been unencumbered by the erstwhile wheels of progress.

The village was enclosed, strangled really, by a high stone wall which blocked out not only the sun's debilitating heat but also its life-giving light. Within this tight embrace, each lane — flanked by the outer stone walls of the two-story houses themselves — was narrow and labyrinthine, its flagstones smeared with animal dung. Lanes led, torturously, to different family compounds, all in a sad state of disrepair and disuse. I peered inside the various gates at the wooden houses and open courtyards. Clucking hens wandered in and out of the rooms. A dirty, half-naked child played with a plastic rice bowl and a knotted piece of rope. A woman appeared in one doorway and stared at me with undisguised suspicion, then disappeared inside. A man in a stained tunic, smoking a pipe, studied me with grave indifference and held his ground.

Jiaqiu had left our little band to reconnoiter farther ahead. He was looking for Nai-nai's childhood home, which he had visited so long ago that he had forgotten the way. The flagstones within Village Village were set closer together than those on the rocky road we'd traversed from Langtoucun but they were just as difficult to navigate: uneven, slippery, many covered with fresh turds. There was no electricity, no plumbing here, not even an open sewer to flush away waste. It was hard to imagine Nai-nai spending a happy childhood here, that she didn't want to leave it for married life and Langtoucun.

Jiaqiu finally reappeared from behind a corner building, a smile on his face. How much he resembled Nai-nai, his aunt! The high, wide cheekbones, the elongated eyes that crinkled at the corners. He'd found her childhood home. He shouted and beckoned us forward before disappearing around the corner. Compared to us, he moved like a mountain goat on these scatological stones. My father, the driver, and I trundled on, clumsily, cautiously. When we caught up with him, he was standing by an entryway chatting with someone just within — a woman who peered out, laughed, and said something to Jiaqiu, who smiled, nodded, and waved us on. The woman, who was distantly related to Nai-nai and was of indeterminate age and, almost, gender, invited us into the courtyard. It was less filthy than the others, but still I was appalled by the poverty, the squalid living conditions. With a nasal cry, the woman summoned the other members out of the house: a few women of different ages, one holding a child, a solemn little girl. (A matriarchy? Perhaps the men were away working in the paddies.) The women smiled unabashedly, pleased to have visitors who were not only Nai-nai's close family but who'd also come from the Beautiful Country, *Meiguo,* America, so very far away.

"Your daughter?" one of them asked my father.

"The second one," he replied. "Four daughters." He held up four fingers, laughed, and wagged his head.

"We came by car," Jiaqiu informed them, gesturing toward the driver. "They both walked from Langtoucun." He was barely able to contain his amusement, camouflaging his laughter behind a polite hand and simulated coughing fit.

"From Langtoucun!" the spokeswoman repeated. "That's quite a trek at this time of day!" She looked into my face, then took my arm, felt it, and nodded approvingly. "You're young and strong, though."

She invited us in for a glass of tea, which my father declined for all of us. He apologized that we'd come unannounced and asked if we might take a brief tour of their house, since — he glanced at me — "my daughter has always wanted to see where her grandmother lived as a girl."

The women were almost giddy with the pleasure of leading us from room to room, pointing out the purpose of each. Nai-nai's parents' bedroom, the kitchen where she learned to cook, her brother and his wife Sao-sao's room.

"Your grandmother's room," the spokeswoman said, almost reverently. "This bed," she told me, "is the very one where your Nai-nai was born."

There was a young girl in it, sleeping, her back to us. The spokeswoman reached through the filmy curtain and roused her before I could stop her. The girl turned and looked up at us over her shoulder. She was an adolescent, her face flushed from sleep (or fever?), her eyes unfocused, glassy. She stood up when the spokeswoman told her to find another bed for her nap and bashfully left the room. The vacated bed was all straight lines, made of heavy dark wood. Instead of a mattress, there was a sheet of woven grass matting. Semi-sheer white cotton panels hung from the canopy and enclosed it like a cocoon.

The spokeswoman urged, "Go ahead. Take a photograph."

I pointed my camera at the tousled bed, the sausage-roll pillow filled with rice husks, the incongruous pink-and-white-plaid comforter, and snapped. But what I saw in my mind's eye, what Nai-nai's birth bed evoked for me, was entirely different.

The bed was not where Nai-nai was born, but where she had given birth to my father. She was alone because, in China, in those days, a good woman gave birth alone. A *better* woman gave birth both alone and in the fields, severed the umbilical cord with her teeth, stuffed some of the rice sheaves she was harvesting between her legs, then got on with her stoop work while suckling the newborn at her breast. But, seen clearly in my mind's eye, Da Mama broke the hard-and-fast rule of a hard and lonely birth for her daughter-in-law by being at her bedside. During her final contractions, Da Mama encouraged, "What's this? A shock of black hair thick as porcupine quills. Let's see more. That's it. Push harder. Harder. Ah, a high forehead. That means intelligence. Again. Push. Broad shoulders. Good for the fields. Push. Push! Only one more and the baby will slither out like a wet fish. Such a voice! Like a terrified goose." Da Mama clapped her hands together, threw back her head, and proclaimed in a jubilant voice, "We have a grandson! The Lis of Langtoucun finally have a grandson, with hair as thick and stiff as porcupine quills!"

Again we apologized for the intrusion. Again the woman insisted that it was a pleasure, an honor indeed. And again we made our way over the treacherous flagstones back to the car whose trunk concealed a broom, garden shears, candles, joss, a half-empty bottle of mao-tai, a few glasses, some oranges, one boiled chicken, and one dried fish. We drove the short distance just outside Village Village to the burial plot inhabited by the spirits of Nai-nai's ancestors. The flat plain was a far less propitious site than the hillside graves where Grampa's ancestors were buried, the gravesite itself proportionately simpler, as were our offerings. No dragons writhed along the doorjambs of the grave chambers; the sacrificial altars were mere slabs of concrete. But the occasion itself was no less. I took my place beside my father, shook the joss sticks, bent at the waist before each gravestone, poured the mao-tai, invoked the spirits' munificence, closed my eyes, and saw.

It was the last time I saw Nai-nai in the United States, just before she returned to China after fifteen years of living in New York. I had just returned from four years of living in Europe. Her luggage surrounded the armchair where she sat. My father, who would drive her to the airport to catch her flight, was present. Anton, almost two years old, entered the room precipitously, a few steps before I did. It was the first time — it would also be the last — that Nai-nai saw her first great-grandson. The moment she caught sight of him, her creased and puckered face released its manifold wrinkles. Her whole body collapsed, then shook uncontrollably in gurgling, giggling, girlish laughter. She managed to point at me, still cackling with laughter. *"Meiyou tofa! Meiyou tofa!"* No hair. I had no hair as a baby. Bald as a billiard ball I was, even into toddlerhood. She held out both her arms to Anton, her spasms of laughter no less kinetic, her delight in him equally extreme. *"Huangde tofa! Huangde tofa!"* Yellow hair. Yellow hair.

15

CENTENARY

But did not his uncertainty begin with the very fact that she [his mother] acknowledged him? I am not disinclined to believe that the strength of his transformation lay in his no longer being anybody's son. (This, in the end, is the strength of all young people who have gone away.) The people which desired him without picturing anyone in particular, made him only more free and more unbounded in his possibilities.

—from *Malte Laurids Brigge* by Rainer Maria Rilke

Even though I did not agree with my father, despised him for having been emasculated, I knew soon he would be one of the ancestors, so that the discords of our life would not matter any more.

—from *Chirundu* by Es'kia Mphahlele

I had bronchitis. I didn't need a doctor's diagnosis. I knew the symptoms all too well: the low energy, the high temperature, the glassy eyes, the rib cage constrained by taut if invisible iron bands. When I presented myself at breakfast much later than usual, after everyone else, but for my father, had eaten and set off to meet the day, he saw that I was not well. He put down the newspaper, his face immobile, his stare apprehensive.

"Is it possible to see a doctor? Just to get a prescription for amoxicillin, for bronchitis."

"We'll go over to the hospital right away."

Hospital. I must have looked worse than I felt.

Nai-nai's house at No. 1 Folded Brocade Road was less than two blocks from Guilin City Hospital, where she had resided for the past two years. At nearly a century, she was frail, a wisp, requiring daily medical attention, as well as Tanmin in frequent attendance. It was Tanmin (or, less often, Jiunyang) who trotted off to the hospital three times a day bearing home-cooked meals for Nai-nai — Chinese hospitals do not feed their patients — the reason she couldn't join my father and me on some of our excursions in and around the city. When I'd asked to accompany her to the hospital, she'd smiled and patted my arm patronizingly. You have other things to do, she told me. It was a circumlocuitous and diplomatic way of avoiding the fact that, besides being very delicate in physical health, my grandmother had senile dementia: my presence or absence was all the same to her. In fact, I had seen Nai-nai just once since our arrival and then only briefly, at the very beginning of our stay. My father had visited her several times — occasions when I'd been taken (purposely, I realized) somewhere else. Nai-nai's condition was something we were both aware of but didn't talk about, the two words describing it unspoken, not even alluded to. Nevertheless I wanted to visit her.

"We'll see," my father said.

Those same two words, the manner in which he said them, reminded me of another request I had made, by telephone, several years ago.

"Hello. Daddy?"

"Leslie?"

"Yes. How are you?"

"Fine. We should meet this week in Chinatown. I want to give you the microscope I want you to take to Guilin."

"Yes, of course. But I'm calling about something else. Do you remember, when we were little, the four of us, you showed us a big brocade-covered box?"

Pause. "A box."

"A box containing a lot of carved seals. Chops. Grampa's chops. Seals carved with his name. You showed them to us, once, a long time ago."

I could see it. The box, red and gold, embroidered with stylized chrysanthemums, the floral symbol of the autumn of one's life, a life spent in quiet retirement and leisurely contemplation. My sisters and I waited breathlessly while Daddy unfastened the bamboo clasps and raised the lid. Animals lived inside. Little stone animals. Dangerous-looking, improbable animals that didn't exist in America, each one atop its own stone column and nestled in its own silken cradle. Griffins, dragons, apoplectic lions.

"Can we take them out?"

A reticent nod. "Be careful. They're very precious."

"Are they made of rubies and emeralds? And topazes?"

Some of the animals were indeed flecked with red, the ones of carnelian. Or swirled with green, the ones of jadeite. Or graham-cracker brown, the ones of soapstone.

"They're precious for another reason. They carry Grampa's name." Daddy upended the animals and showed us the undersides of their pedestals. "That's Grampa's name in Chinese. Each chop was designed by a different artist. Famous artists. Whenever Grampa signed a document, he stamped it with one of these chops. That made the document official."

Pause. "What about them?"

Longer pause. "I was hoping you might consider giving them to Anton . . ."

A "toc," like the receiver on the other end had been dropped or hit. I realized it had, by a sharp, indignant exhalation of my father's breath. I had been presumptuous.

"Not now, of course. I was hoping that you might save them for him. For later, for when he's grown."

Another "toc." A puff of wind, harder, more heated this time. "Why should I?"

"Because he carries Grampa's name."

My father was holding his breath. I knew. That kind of silence, a withholding, made that kind of noiselessness: the obverse of sound, not just its absence. He was holding an exhalation. I knew, because I was doing the same. Holding it so tight, my sucked-out lungs were ready to implode.

"He's the only one of your grandsons who does," I rasped, knowing I'd gone too far. "He's the only male to carry the family name. To carry it on. Well, that's all I wanted to say." I shut my eyes at my impertinence.

My sisters and I set up the tiny stone animals in pairs, like Noah's Ark. In single file, to see how far they'd stretch across the liv-

ing room carpet. In rows, like a classroom. In a circle, facing the center, like guests seated around a banquet table.

"You'd better put them back now. I just wanted to show them to you."

I slipped one of the animals into my pocket. But when the stone menagerie was put back to sleep in their little cradles, I slipped it out again and, aching with reluctance, set it back in its perfectly molded niche, the last one to be filled. I burned in bed that night, berating myself for being too chicken to have filched it while I had the chance.

Pause. No "toc." "We'll see."

At the hospital, I was treated immediately. The moment my father told the nurse on duty that I was ill, she took me to a doctor who, after examining me, proclaimed what I'd known all along. He didn't prescribe antibiotics, he gave them to me, after an injection of gamma globulin, to start the ball rolling. Two small bottles, each a week's worth, just in case of a relapse.

"You don't want to be sick for your grandmother's hundredth birthday," he said as a way of concluding the visit.

When I tried to pay for the pills and the shot, the cashier waved my money away, then tittered into her rejecting hand, as if I was being naive, stupid. I looked at my father, who shook his head, signifying: What can you do? I insisted no further. Double the dose and double the indebtedness. *Guanxi.* Connections were both blessing and burden, a double-edged sword.

"Since we're here, let's go see Nai-nai."

My suggestion caused my father to frown.

"Don't worry. I won't step into her room. I'll stay well outside, in the corridor."

Still looking doubtful, even anxious, he accompanied me up the stairs and down a hallway leading to her room. We passed a few groups of people — family members carrying away empty food containers, lunch baskets, bamboo steamers. A gaunt, middle-aged man wearing a robe that was too big for him and smoking a cigarette glanced at us, then looked out the window. As we approached Nai-nai's room, I heard a crooning voice in the process of pleading, encouraging, cajoling, praising what must have been a recalcitrant child.

"Just a few more spoonfuls, and we're done. Eat it all up before it gets cold. *Juk* just the way you like it. Jiunyang made it. Open. Wider. Ahhh. There. Isn't it delicious? Yes, I'll give you more, but first you have to eat what's in your mouth. You're dribbling. Close your mouth. Swallow. *Hao. Hen hao.* Good. Very good. Now open again."

I peered into the open doorway. Tanmin was seated in a chair pulled up to Nai-nai's bedside. She was feeding *juk* to my grandmother, who was propped up on her side and faced away from the door. I could see the clear outline of her fetal-shaped body under the thin white sheet. It was child-sized, curled into itself like a nautilus shell, lost in the large hospital bed in the huge private suite. Tanmin recoiled slightly upon seeing me and my father, who entered the room and stood behind her, his arms down by his sides, his hands loosely clenched.

"Ma," my father whispered, bending over Tanmin's shoulder. "Ma."

"Yau Luen has come to see you for a second time this morning," Tanmin trumpeted into Nai-nai's exposed ear. "Your son, Yau Luen."

"Shei ya?" Nai-nai replied in a feeble voice. Who?

"Ma," my father repeated in a thick voice. He smiled, or tried to, but the result was a grimace, abject, leaden, weighing down the lower half of his face. "It's me. Your son, Yau Luen."

"Yau Luen," Tanmin shouted into her ear. "Your son. He's brought Lei shi with him. Your granddaughter." To my father: "She can't hear you. You have to yell. YAU LUEN. YAU LUEN."

"Yau Luen," Nai-nai mimicked dully. "Yau Luen."

Two doctors entered from the adjacent room, greeted my father cordially, then in low tones said something to Tanmin.

"It's time for your medicine," Tanmin yelled, getting up from her chair. "We're going now . . ."

Nai-nai's head moved a few scant degrees on the pillow. *"Bu. Bu yao. Bu yao."*

"You must take your medicine. It's good for you. You'll feel better after you do."

"Bu yao," Nai-nai moaned.

My father and Tanmin stood aside to permit one of the men to pass. He scooped up Nai-nai — weightless, resistanceless — in his arms and whisked her off into the adjacent room. Her torso was so shrunken, her lolling head so disproportionately large, that her thin, gangling arms and legs looked grotesquely long, pendulous, spider monkey-like. Tanmin and my father joined me in the corridor, where we immediately engaged in small talk: my bronchitis, the medication I'd just received, Nai-nai's centenary in three days. A low wail startled me, nailed me wordless in place. I stared at my father, at Tanmin. They too had been

235

stunned into silence, but theirs was complicitous, edgy. Their eyes sought the floor, the window, anywhere but mine. The wailed words were repeated, this time in a rising shriek: *"Shou buliao! Wo shou bu liao!"* I can't bear it. I can't bear it anymore.

Tanmin, repossessed of her brisk equanimity, laughed and patted my arm. "Don't look so worried. It's nothing," she assured me. "Your grandmother's a little excited, that's all. She'll calm down once her medication takes effect."

"Shou buliao. Wo shou buliao. Wo yao si." I want to die.

Tanmin laughed harder. I glanced, horrified, at my father, whose breath had stopped, jammed deep inside him and locked up tight.

"Tanmin! Tanmin! *Lai! Lai!*" Come. Come.

His torso shuddered, his face imploded, his mouth twisted open and sucked at the air, sharp and short: a reverse sob, an inward cough. This sudden seizure lasted only a second, the physical manifestation of the emotionally registered fact: Nai-nai had called out another's name.

"Lai le. Lai le." I'm coming. I'm coming.

Tanmin excused herself and scurried, almost joyfully, back into Nai-nai's room, liberated by a quotidian event, a perfunctory obligation. Trapped in our company, she would have had to deny the obvious, invent palatable explanations, diverge ever farther from the truth. In the empty corridor, which seemed to amplify sound, I could hear her consoling, cosseting, gently shaming Nai-nai, as she would an unhappy child. Gradually, Nai-nai's screaming abated. She wept with infantile abandon. The sobs and moans I heard bespoke not suffering and torment but deliverance and relief: for Tanmin's essential presence, to her personal ministrations. Superfluous, my father had begun to shrink. He was becoming an absence, a forgotten ghost.

"What were they doing to her? Why was she scream-ing like that?" I shouldn't have asked these questions, but I wanted him to stop dissolving, to return from wherever he had started to go.

"Transfusion."

I barely heard his reply. "Blood transfusion? How of-ten must she get it?"

"Every day."

"Every day!"

Nai-nai was moaning again, *"Shou buliao,"* and Tanmin was crooning comfort to her. I stood in the corridor still petrified in place; my father deliquesced with each *shou buliao,* became less and less substantial.

"What if they stopped. Stopped the transfusions."

My father looked at me, finally. "They can't. She would die."

"She wants to die. Keeping her alive is only prolong-ing the pain, and it's intolerable. Can't you stop them? Stop the transfusions. Let her die in peace."

I awaited the wag of the head I had witnessed all my life — the one that communicated more than the words he sometimes used in its stead, or in tandem. "What can you do," stated, not as a question but as its own answer. Or al-ternatively, "What's the use." Also rhetorical.

Me, whining: "Daddy, Lonny and Brucie McManus are play-ing in the Blue Eagle Club. That's my clubhouse. I don't want them playing in it. They're going to wreck it."

My father: "What can you do."

Me, resentful: "The chocolate cake that Mommy and I made

and decorated with gumdrops and colored sprinkles for the raffle? Sister Theodocia said that it wouldn't bring in more than a dollar, so she said she'd buy it for a dollar. She didn't even let it be raffled off, and everyone brought money with them to try to win it. It was the prettiest cake of all. I should have told her she couldn't have it for a dollar. Not for a dollar fifty, even."

My father: "What's the use."

Me, incredulous: "Kevin Cantwell didn't know his arithmetic today. Sister Ellen made him take off his shoes and socks and count on his toes. In front of the whole class."

My father: "What can you do."

Me, sobbing, as are all my sisters: "Bert's been run over by a car! Mom says he's dying! I'd like to run over the stupid idiot who did it!"

My father: "What can you do."

Me, incensed: "Phoebe Wong is going around telling everyone that I turned my back on her. That's an outright lie! Someone interrupted me when I was talking with her, that's all. The next thing I knew, when I turned back to continue our conversation, she was gone. I should tell her to quit spreading lies about me."

My father: "What's the use."

Me, exasperated, self-pitying: "Anton's hair is to the middle of his back. Everywhere he goes, people say: 'Yes, miss?' In bars, too. Especially there. He's actually considering dreadlocks. Slathering raw egg and honey in his hair and coiling it into snakes, Medusa-style."

My father: "What can you do."

But that wasn't what he said, or did. He turned toward me, or rather on me, growing more opaque, less diminished in the process. "How American you are! What do you know? What do you know? They're keeping her alive because they have to. Do you ever think about what some people have to do?"

My father softened to see what must have been the stunned and stupefied look on my face, but he continued to solidify, not to seep away.

"Nai-nai's one hundredth birthday. It's not just family and friends who will be celebrating it. The governor of Guangxi, government officials, newspaper and television reporters — they're coming from all over the country, all the way from Beijing!"

Still, I was not elliptical enough, I was too American, too occluded to understand "the Chinese way." The Chinese way that he had always insisted I be but never explained when I'd asked him just what that was. Instead, that infuriating wag of the head.

"Leslie . . ." He shook his head sorrowfully: That I was so uncomprehending? That harsh reality was what it was and that nothing we could do would change it? That he was forced to be explicit, and therefore traitorous, so un-Chinese? "It's good propaganda. Why do you think the government invited her back to Guilin, gave her back her house, restored it — five families had been living in it, five! — sent for Jiaqiu and Tanmin to look after her? The government wanted to show the world how far China had come after the Cultural Revolution. And so soon. So fast!" Another wag of the head. "They wanted ABCs (American-born Chinese) to come back to visit. They wanted recognition from the West and to be part of the world community again."

"And they used Nai-nai to do it," I said, amazed, amused, disbelieving. Nai-nai. My grandmother. All seventy-odd senile pounds of her.

"Yes, they're using Nai-nai. For every privilege, there is responsibility. For every responsibility, there is privilege. And still you don't understand."

"No, Daddy, I don't."

"Mao invited Grampa back to China. Zhou Enlai, the premier himself, met Grampa at the airport. The following year, the Cultural Revolution broke out. At the height of it, Grampa died, just a few years after he returned home. The diagnosis was gastroenteritis. But some people think he was allowed to die, deprived of the medication that would have saved him, because he had lived in America, and because he had served in Chiang Kai-shek's Nationalist government. All Westerners were considered foreign devils at that time. And Chiang was the devil himself. Even Zhou Enlai was powerless to save Grampa."

My father was fully formed now, rock-solid, life-sized. Larger than life. Like when I was a little girl.

"For every responsibility, there is privilege. For every privilege, there is responsibility. Two sides of the same coin. Reciprocity. You understand? When Deng Xiaoping took power after the Cultural Revolution, the Chinese government asked Nai-nai to come home. They said they would give her back her old house ..."

"The house she had built to give to you and Mom."

"Yes. She would be cared for by live-in relatives, by doctors from the city hospital who would look in on her twice a week. When I brought Nai-nai back to China, we were met at the airport by Zhou Enlai's widow. You understand? We were taken on a tour of China to see how much it had progressed from the old days, from the Cultural Revolution, when Grampa came back to live only to be allowed to die. When I saw the house, met Tanmin and Jiaqiu and the doctors who would care for her, I knew that I had done the right thing in bringing her home. The Chinese government has kept its promise. Nai-nai has lived a long, full, and happy life."

Nai-nai was whimpering wordlessly now. Tanmin was crooning less forcefully. My father looked at me, both angry and beseeching.

"Why do you think the government has been so good to Nai-nai? Out of the goodness of their hearts? Because she is the wife of Li Zongren. Because she is good propaganda for them to send out to the rest of the world. Why do you think Jiaqiu and Tanmin are happy to be Nai-nai's servants? Do you think the cramped apartment they lived in before is anything like Nai-nai's house? Do you think they could snap their fingers and have city officials doing their bidding, or chauffeured cars appear at their door, or eat the food they eat? They keep Nai-nai alive because as long as she lives, they live like kings. The Chinese doctors keep Nai-nai alive because their jobs are at stake if they don't. The Chinese government keeps Nai-nai alive because they want overseas Chinese to come back and visit, invest, stay on. Their actions say louder than any words: See how well we treat Chinese who left China and are curious to know what China is like now. See how we welcome those of you who come back to the fold. And here is the proof: the wife of Li Zongren, Li Xiuwen, who left the United States fifteen years ago to return to her homeland, celebrates her one hundredth birthday, honored by her country and surrounded by her family and friends."

My father shifted his eyes away from mine to look out the window. By their expression, they were unseeing; rather, they were inward-looking. He was digesting what he'd just said, or the fact that he'd said it at all, that he hadn't swallowed his words along with his breath this time but let them stream out with each smooth inhalation and exhalation. Never had I heard him speak at such length. And never had I felt more at a loss for words with which to answer him, to refute him. Vanquished, I struggled with my dumbstruck silence. I wanted to be right, which I was, as an American. I wanted him to be wrong, which he was, as a Chinese. There was no answer, right or otherwise. There was only silence. Mine, my father's, Nai-nai's. Silence.

The gaunt man in the oversized robe was still smoking. He had just been joined by another man, neither a patient nor a doctor. A family member perhaps, or a friend. They began to talk in low tones. "You shouldn't," I overheard. I knew the remark concerned the cigarette dangling from the patient's mouth. Tanmin scurried out of Nai-nai's suite and over to us.

"She's quiet now," she said in a hushed voice, a hedge against Nai-nai's starting up again. "We can go."

As we passed the two men in the corridor, one of them said, loud enough for us to hear, "That's the son of Li Zongren."

I had heard those words said of my father as I'd walked at his side. As we walked through the airport when we landed in Hong Kong, again at the airport in Guilin, and often on the streets of this city.

"That's Li Zongren's son."

"There goes the son of Li Zongren."

"Do you know who that is? Li Zongren's son."

This time, in the quiet hospital corridor, the statement rang with a different sound — not one of envy or the excitement of a "celebrity" sighting but with rue, sympathy, even pity. At least, that's the way I heard it or its subtext: My father didn't even have his own name. He was a man of no name or, at best, a secondhand, hand-me-down name. Even Yau Luen, my father's given name, means "junior," son of Delin, my grandfather's sobriquet. All his life my father's name had been a double-edged sword, a blessing and a curse. It was a lofty pedestal on which he stood, granting him status, prestige, *guanxi*. It was an icon, an idol, a heavy burden he bore and could never set down, never mind that he was being crushed under the weight of not living up to it.

"Names emerge when institutions begin," according to the Tao Te Ching. "When names emerge, know likewise when to stop. To know when to stop is to be free from danger."

Grampa, too, suffered from name trouble. When Mao's Communist forces were winning one battle after another, my grandfather, then vice president, was being saddled with a faltering government and a collapsing nation. At Chiang Kai-shek's farewell address (he was off to Formosa, where he had already transferred a good amount of the Chinese treasury), my grandfather listened to the words by which he would become head of state: "In the hope that the Communists may be moved by my earnestness and that the people's suffering may be relieved, from January 21, 1949, Vice President Li will succeed the president to exercise his duties and powers in accordance with Article 49 of the Constitution which provides, 'In the event that the president is for any reason unable to perform his functions, his duties and powers shall be exercised by the vice president.'"

"But where do you mention your retirement?" my grandfather whispered, when the document was handed to him for his signature and seal. "Or even your resignation? And Article 49 states, 'in the event that the president's office becomes vacant,' and not as you read, 'in the event that the president is for any reason unable to perform his functions.' You are, after all, hardly incapacitated—"

"How can you quibble over incidentals at a time like this?" hissed Sun Fo, one of Chiang's cronies, the man he would have preferred as vice president. "Just sign the document! Where is your sense of propriety? Didn't you hear him say that you were succeeding him as president? How many guarantees do you need?"

Setting his personal concerns aside, for the national situation was critical, my grandfather signed his name to two copies of the document and pressed his personal seal to them. Only afterwards did he read what he had signed, which differed in a very fundamental way from what Chiang had read: "From January 21, 1949, Vice President Li will act for the president in exercising his duties and powers in accordance with Article 49." My grandfather had become acting president of China, not president. My grandfather was an instead-of. Like my father was a son-of.

I was no one's son — failed, almost, or otherwise. I was my father's daughter. But that did not make me who I was: an autonomous and social being who needed to be left alone and to my own devices yet at the same time to have a vital connection with others. A vital connection to my father in particular, now more than ever, for whatever reason. A reason I would not discover (nor would he) for another two years.

Two days before Nai-nai's one hundredth birthday, my father and I pedaled off on our bicycles with the mutual understanding that we would be much more helpful by our absence than our presence. Before we left, we mentioned our approximate destination to Jiunyang — who in turn would inform Tanmin, busy planning last minute details of the large-looming occasion — but not before we made our getaway, lest the Great Facilitator felt obliged to arrange some form of entertainment we would rather have avoided.

What my father and I were capable of doing we had already done: ordered four hundred porcelain bowls decorated with Guilin's famous *shan-shui* and hired a noted calligrapher to handpaint on each bowl the ideograms of Nai-nai's name together with the benediction *wan wan sui,* "May you live ten thousand years." The bowls would perform double duty: receptacle for the *mi-fen* Jiunyang would serve to each guest and take-away party favor. The house we had swathed in bunting and swags and hung with huge tasseled paper lanterns — all of them red, the color of happiness and good fortune.

Provisioned with a few steamed wheat buns stuffed with red-bean paste and a thermos of hot tea, my father and I made for the open countryside around Eagle Mountain. We'd cycled around this oversized hill noted for its excellent feng shui once before, accompanied by a phalanx of officials. This time we were blissfully on our own.

The masses living on Guilin's outskirts, I noticed, were taking Deng's dictum — to be rich is glorious — to heart. Two- and three-story cinderblock houses, roomy but graceless, flanked both sides of the road. Over their low stone walls abundant gardens burgeoned with cash crops, thanks to Deng's "responsibility system," which eschewed strictly collectivized farms and promoted small plots of land set aside for private use. No more ubiquitous and pallid cabbages, but a wide spectrum of greens: *guy-lan,* bok choy, bitter melon, winter melon, mustard greens, snow peas, string beans. And who should be tending these meticulous gardens but, most often, a tiny sun-bonneted elder, either flexibly squatting on her heels or wielding a giant anodized aluminum watering can as though it were a feather. "Remember when Nai-nai took over our childhood sandbox to plant Chinese vegetables?"

My father nodded. "She would wait for Laddie to go potty, then collect it to fertilize her garden."

Laddie, whose name had somehow morphed into Bertram, was our cocker spaniel. He had come all the way from Missouri with papers proving that he was the offspring of champions: the son of Bozo Red and Leonard Belle. Son of champions or not, with his stubby legs and outsized paws, he was without a doubt the runt of the litter. Which only made us think he was that much more beautiful. Which only made us love him that much more. Unabashedly. Our Bert.

"No!" I gave my father a horrified look. "I would never have eaten her vegetables if I'd known."

"You never ate her vegetables as it was."

I laughed, with both embarrassment and pleasure. My father chuckled, in spite of himself.

"How I'd love to eat them now. Actually, Jiunyang's cooking is just like Nai-nai's, minus Bert's night soil. When I eat Jiunyang's meals, it's like being back in Riverdale. Like time has reversed. Only this time, I'm loving bok choy instead of sneaking it to Bert under the dining room table."

We hopped off our bicycles under the generous shade of an old banyan tree near a placid tributary of the Li River. From this vantage point we had a wide-angle view of Eagle Mountain, complete with its full wingspan and tiny, scavenging head. And from this distance the single spanking-new feng shui grave at its foot — hyperbolic, white marble — was almost invisible. It loomed large on our first visit, the very reason for our "pilgrimage." The officials who took us there were eager for me, a writer, to know who was buried behind the gravestone incised with gold-leaved ideograms: Chang Ya-juo, the Guilinese mistress of Chiang Kai-shek's son, Chiang Ching-kuo, recently deceased president of the Republic of China. The woman who had borne him two sons — twins — one of whom was presently a high-ranking member of Taiwan's cabinet. Naturally, she had been persecuted during the Cultural Revolution, but both her sons had managed to escape to the ROC. Years later, not only had she been rehabilitated, her crime of concubinage to the son of Public Enemy #1 exonerated, she was actually honored as the mother of Chiang Kai-shek's twin grandsons, her remains exhumed from their humble, forgotten resting place somewhere in the Guilinese countryside and given pride of place and public attention with her very own mountain. When I visited the People's Republic of China four years prior, no one dared even whisper the same words less one: Republic of China. ROC. Taiwan. The Three Nos regarding that renegade province were still in full effect: No Contact. No Communication. No Trade. Now, clearly, the stops were being pulled out and the Three Nos were subverting, as evidenced by this brilliant piece of feng shui diplomacy, to eager but unofficial yeses.

"When we reinterred her remains here," one of the officials explained to me, "naturally we lit hundreds of firecrackers and burned a lot of joss and spirit money. Just as we finished setting fire to all of them, a huge wind came up out of nowhere — very strange, very strange — and swept the flaming offerings in front of her grave right up into the sky. Tongues of fire! Tongues of fire! She's speaking from the grave! She's calling to Chiang Kai-shek's son! She wants to be reunited with him!"

I smiled and nodded politely. So that's why they brought us out here. Someone wants reunification with someone, surely.

"We forgot to bring a blanket," I noted. The banyan's exposed roots were hard going but supplied ready-made picnic chairs. I set myself down on one of them, swiveled the cap off the thermos, and unwrapped the lukewarm steamed buns, one of which I handed to my father, who sat beside me gazing at Eagle Mountain. Clearly, he saw something else, something that saddened him.

"I gave your mother a Chinese tablecloth with lots of embroidery. Made in Shanghai. Very expensive."

"When? Recently?"

He wagged his head. "When we were first married. She

never used it. She probably gave it away. She never appreciated Chinese things."

My father's eyes were red suddenly, his mouth slack. All these years. All this time that's passed. And still the things we remember, the memories we hold on to, or that hold on to us.

"That's not true, Daddy."

Another wag of the head. An effort to fight off tears. Tears for a tablecloth, for time gone by, now time returned. The Tao Te Ching says, "Going on means going far. Going far means returning."

"That's not true. Mom used it. She still does. At Christmas, at Easter. When there's company. It's too beautiful to be used every day. She saves it for special occasions. She cherishes all the Chinese things in her apartment. But they're special. Not for everyday."

I could see our house at 5201 Fieldston Road: our living room, the fifties decor, the Danish modern, the grace notes of chartreuse and plum, the Japanese painting of crashing waves, stolid rocks, ghostly gibbous moon over the mantelpiece, the pleasure boat carved from a single piece of ivory, the languid ivory Kuanyin.

"The Chinese scrolls in the living room. They were too precious for everyday, too. You displayed them on special occasions, or simply when you wanted to look at something beautiful."

My father seemed mollified. The threat of tears had subsided; the underlying sadness and anger were in remission.

"Do you know how important those scrolls are?" he asked, rhetorically, brightening. "Very expensive. Very expensive." He bit into the steamed bun. Everything my

249

father ate looked more delicious than what I ate, even when we were eating the same thing.

"Did Grampa really disown you when you married Mom? Because she wasn't wholly Chinese?"

My father chewed like so many Chinese men: noisily, smackingly, with his mouth ajar. He talked like so many Chinese men, too: when he shouldn't, when his mouth was full of food. And when he should speak, he didn't. He answered me, but only after shaking his head, having considered my question while pretending not to, a practiced insouciance: "Your grampa loved children. After Marcy was born, it was okay."

The gesture reminded me of another incident, one where my father's insouciance was also required:

Anton (home from college): "Hi, Grampy."

My father hugged Anton — something he'd never done. It was performed awkwardly, sloppily, quickly, like a first kiss. He lurched into Anton as if he had stumbled over his own feet. Anton caught and steadied him while my father recovered his equanimity — not his equilibrium as Anton supposed — after the failed embrace. I looked at my father, my heart tender, close to aching. He didn't see me. He was looking at his grandson. He said: "You look different."

Anton (pulling on his ponytail): "Yeah."

My father: "You look . . . like a Taoist priest."

Taoist priests, unlike Buddhist monks, let their hair grow instead of shaving their heads. Like the ferocious Taipings, the nature-loving Taoists were Long Hairs, too. My father was simply stating the truth. He was also expressing his appreciation of Anton's physical transformation. Pulled away from his face, my son's long, light brown hair set his broad, high cheekbones in pronounced relief, emphasized the almond shape of his olive-green eyes. Anton looked Chinese, finally and almost. But as had happened with the thwarted, insouciant hug, so it was with my father's heartfelt, offhand compliment: Anton cut off his Taoist ponytail the very next day.

"At the University of Chicago, were you and Mom denied student housing because you were Chinese? Like the anti-Chinese anti-miscegenation laws in California prevented Uncle Tamer (who is Lebanese) and Auntie Bubbles (my mother's younger sister) from marrying in that state, so they had to cross the border into Nevada?"

"Who told you that?"

"Mom did."

A wag of the head. "Your mother took a big risk marrying me. Luckily, one of my professors liked me. A good guy. He helped us find off-campus housing, that's true. But that wasn't the reason. It was because we were married, not because I was Chinese, that I wasn't eligible for student housing. In those days, if you were an undergraduate, you couldn't be married. You were kicked out of college if you were found out." My father nodded appreciatively. "Your mother took a big risk in marrying me. She was very brave."

I frowned, which happened whenever I tried to put two and two together, a remnant of my St. Margaret's arithmetic test days. "How do you figure that?"

"What do you mean?"

"Well, it was you who would have been kicked out of college if they found out you were married. Not Mom. Like it was you your father disowned for marrying Mom. Her parents welcomed you with open arms. So, it seems to me that you were the one who took all the risks. Mom was just along for the ride. You were the brave one."

My father blinked, the expression he assumed when he put two and two together, and nodded.

"Yes, I was the brave one."

He said this, perfunctorily, not because he believed it but because he was forced to acquiesce to its infallible logic, which he would have rather refuted. He did not want to take credit for any form of bravery, to be drawn into the past. He would have rather we dropped the subject and found something more interesting and significant than the fact that he, in his modest way, twice stormed the status quo and withstood its effects. For that, he had quickly agreed with me, only to suggest: "Eat. They might save us something from lunch, but if not, this is all we'll get until dinner."

I obeyed. Dutifully, appreciatively, I ate a second red-bean bun with a small, secretive smile on my lips. Now and then, my father coughed, which he did fairly often these days. A dry, hacking cough — food that went down the wrong pipe, or my throat is dry, or Guilin's air is polluted, he would say, then add, but in Beijing it was even worse — for whose cure or at least temporary interruption I passed him a second cup of still-hot tea.

The day we had all been preparing for, anticipating (for the festivity and the fanfare), and dreading (for the festivity and the fanfare) had arrived. Over the past week or so, the house had acquired the look of a before-and-after cosmetic makeover. The final touches — a long table set against one living room wall and spread with giant sheets of red paper and ballpoint pens for the signatures of well-wishers, and a second long table set along the opposite wall

on which to repose the gifts of those same well-wishers —
had been perfectly timed and efficiently executed not to
impede the household's more mundane activities. And yet
Nai-nai's home was just a way station, the first leg of the
journey to the birthday girl herself. Nai-nai lay groomed,
sedated but awake, and swaddled in a clean pair of flannel
pajamas in a freshly made bed. Her hospital room was similarly hung with painted scrolls depicting peaches or cranes
(both symbols of longevity) or peonies (*fu gui hua,* "flower
of wealth and honor") and was a depository for the over-
flow of gifts from her house: hexagonal clear plastic boxes
containing plastic peaches, cranes, or peonies in garish,
food-coloring colors; and birthday cakes, their abundant
pink, blue, or yellow frosting sometimes of neon intensity.

Tanmin, Jiaqiu, Jiunyang, Nannan, and Lizi oversaw
the festivities at No. 1 Folded Brocade Road. My father and
I stood at the head of Nai-nai's bed thanking the officials,
poets, professors, artists, and journalists for joining us in
celebrating such a happy and auspicious occasion, the center and cause of which was entirely oblivious. By Nai-nai's
blank, unfocused stare, she was dreaming with her eyes
open. What she saw — all these people milling around her,
bending over her, moving their mouths so close to her face
in grimaces that suggested speech but revealed a vacuum, a
human black hole; people some of whom took her spidery
hand, the one that had crawled out from under the sheet,
and shook it in their fleshy two; even her own son and
granddaughter standing stolidly at her bedside — were all
insubstantial images, moving shadows with no specificity
or significance, ghosts neither hungry nor well fed, neither
to be feared nor enjoyed. Ghosts that were just there, and

then, just as quickly and meaninglessly, gone, extirpated, replaced by another amorphous image subject to the same irrevocable fate of coming-and-goingness.

My father passed me a plate of birthday cake — a small slice of a two-layer yellow cake thickly spackled with white frosting ornamented with fluted pink-frosted ribbons and rosettes — and looked at me with anticipatory, even apprehensive, eyes. He had just fed Nai-nai a forkful to the popping of flashbulbs, the click of camera lenses, the whir of camcorders. I nudged a bit of cake, complete with rosette, onto the fork which I lowered toward my grandmother. She opened her mouth, birdlike, avaricious, to receive the offering. It was the cake that was important, its taste and the pleasure it gave her that she craved. That I, her granddaughter, was at the other end of the fork was meaningless. My name, my relationship to her, had been forgotten, just as I no longer remembered the wretched taste of her bok choy which made me despise it so, even though I recalled despising it so, the antithesis of how I felt about it now. The cameras' flashes exploded, blinding me, but not Nai-nai. Their rapid starbursts were merely another form of ghost, a ghost of light rather than of darkness. *Wan wan sui*, Nai-nai, I said silently, hoping she accepted telepathically the spirit, not the letter, of this wish, since she seemed to be indifferent to the opaque ghosts of the people and things swirling around her. *Wan wan sui*. May you live ten thousand years.

I turned and looked at my father. He was nodding.

My father died when he was seventy-four, less than a year after his mother's death at the venerable age of 102. Since Nai-nai's return to China, he had made an annual visit to see her. Nineteen round trips in that many years. The year she died he made a second trip soon after the first to attend her funeral, an occasion more lavish than her centenary just two years before. Throughout the long flight to New York he was bothered by a constant dry cough that permitted him no sleep and sometimes barely allowed him to catch his breath. When he went to see a doctor, he was told he had lung cancer. My father did everything the doctors ordered ("Your father is just the best patient," a nurse told us. "A real gentleman. He does everything he's told without complaining, and he apologizes for bothering us every time he has to call on any of us for help."), but he was merely going through the motions. Not only was he resigned to an imminent death, he admitted that he had no reason to live, now that Nai-nai was gone. My father not only believed he was dying, he decided to die, and with as little fanfare as possible.

It was just before dawn that the nurse told my mother, seated at the right side of his hospital bed, and the woman who was his companion of twelve years, seated on the left, to: "Take his hands. He's going." Each woman took one hand and placed it in her lap where she held it tight, as if that might prevent or at least delay my father's spirit — Catholic for my mother, Confucian for his companion — from leaving his body, or perhaps assure safer or smoother passage. I saw (how could I have missed it all these years?) the significance of his body, supine, comatose, his arms flung out from his sides, his hands nailed to the laps of the woman he had married and the woman he was living with. The physical manifestation of the existential dilemma and unrelieved drama my father had borne all his life — in his lungs, as it turned out. The lungs, where one either holds on to grief or expels it through sobbing, keening. I was witnessing the final moments of this silent tug-of-war so perfectly expressed by the two women claiming him. A tug-of-war between, on the one hand, his American life and, on the other, his Chinese soul: between being the son of a famous father or his own individual self, whoever that might have been, between embracing cultural precedent or fulfilling his own personal desires, if indeed he believed he had a right to them or in their very existence. My father pulled right and left, East and West. My father crucified. The nurse approached the bed, took his hand from my mother and felt for his pulse. Then she left the room and returned a few minutes later with the doctor, who pronounced my father dead at 5:40 A.M. The date was April 4, 1993, Palm Sunday by the Gregorian calendar, the Grave Sweeping Festival by the lunar one.

Steamed Red-Bean Buns

1½ cups flour
2 teaspoons baking powder
pinch of salt
¼ cup sugar
1 tablespoon melted lard
¼ cup warm water
1 can (3 ounces) red-bean paste
extra sugar

Sift flour and baking powder together in a bowl. Add salt and sugar. Slowly stir in lard and water. Mix until the dough is soft and smooth. Cover with a damp cloth for at least 30 minutes.

Add sugar to the red-bean paste to taste. Thicken the paste by heating it in a small pot over a low flame and adding cornstarch or rice- or potato flour until the paste is firm and "dry" enough to form into balls.

Place the dough on a lightly floured surface and knead lightly. Divide it into six pieces and shape into rounds. Place a ball of red-bean paste in the center of each round and pull the edges of the dough up around it. Pinch the edges together to enclose the red-bean ball. Brush the seam with water and seal it with a square of paper.

Place the buns, paper side down, in a steam basket. Steam the buns in a pot of rapidly boiling water for 12–15 minutes, raising the lid of the pot several times during the steaming process so the buns don't burst.

Makes 6 servings.

Afterword
If Stones Could Speak

Marco Polo describes a bridge, stone by stone.
"But which is the stone that supports the bridge?" Kublai
Khan asks.
"The bridge is not supported by one stone or the other,"
Marco answers, "but by the line of the arch that they form."
Kublai Khan remains silent, reflecting. Then he adds: "Why
do you speak to me of stones? It is the arch that matters to me."
Polo answers: "Without stones there is no arch."

—from *Invisible Cities* by Italo Calvino

One last story remains to be told. Not by me, but by a stonemason who lived in Guilin. That is, he was a stonemason, until he became the very material he had mastered. To hear his story firsthand, I returned to Guilin.

On my previous two trips, Old Man Hill — brooding, lantern-jawed, gazing out from under a monstrous brow across the South China Sea — was not high on my to-do list. For one, he was isolated, far away from the other karst formations anthropomorphic or eidetic enough to merit their own myths and which I had visited up close: Elephant Trunk Hill, upon whose back I climbed to inspect the hilt of the sword thrust between its weary shoulders, only to discover that the protruding object is, in fact, a Buddhist dagoba, or reliquary. Folded Brocade Mountain (whose accompanying legend is a hybrid of *Cinderella* and *Rumpelstiltskin*) and Single Beauty Peak (shades of *Jack and the Beanstalk*), both of which I scaled for the spectacular views at the top. Luotuo, or Camel, Hill, a geological version of a recumbent dromedary at whose flanks lay a scraggly combination of zoo and circus, complete with very sad, barely sentient pandas.

By contrast, Old Man Hill resisted the casual visitor. He was distant, emotionally as well as physically. But I was a persistent pilgrim. I made the long, arduous journey, during which I suffered, among other ailments, a bruised ego and a guilty conscience, and finally arrived at my destination's off-putting, cold-shouldered, hunched back. I walked around to where my unwitting host could see me, which he gave no indication of doing. Perhaps he was asleep. It was hard to tell with a man of stone.

"I hope I'm not intruding . . ." I began.

A sound came from the crag. A sigh, or perhaps simply an exhalation, like wind rushing through a tunnel or a soughing through trees.

" . . . but I've come a long way, even if it is only in my imagination, which sometimes takes the longest time and makes for the farthest journey of all. I was hoping that you might tell me your story, if you have a moment, of course."

This time, what exuded from the massive rock was most definitely a sigh.

"I have nothing but time, all the time in the world. And you are interested in stories and stones, stones in stories, and stories in stones."

"Yes," I replied, surprised and pleased that I didn't have to explain my presence and purpose any further.

"Have you brought one of each with you? A story and a stone, as offerings?"

"I have. Do you want them now?" I swung my bag off my shoulder and deposited it at his feet.

"When I've finished telling you my story — and only if you're satisfied with it. Sit down. People who stand in my presence make me feel even older than the hill I am. As old as the proverbial 'since time began.' And time, as you must know, began with stories. How else could it start?"

I sat down in front of him, my legs crooked in at hip and out at knee, in a W, the obverse of the lotus position, the way I used to sit when I was a child anticipating a story, hungry for narrative, the meat of meaning. He began with a sigh, a rumble of breath in his stony lungs. The air he exhaled was cold, moist, subterranean, mineral.

"My name is Lao Shi. Not the *laoshi* that connotes 'teacher.' But the *lao shi* that means 'old stone.' I was forty years old before I married, having finally scraped together enough money to afford a wife. Two years later, she bore me a son, whom we named Xing, which means 'happiness.' A son, after all, is a big happiness."

I nodded in acknowledgment, not necessarily agreement.

"A month later, my wife died. I was left with an infant

and no idea how to care for him. Fortunately, I found sympathetic nursing mothers willing to share their milk, and so Xing was passed from one mother to the next. When he was old enough, I fed him *juk* at night when he awoke and cried. And during the day, I strapped him to my back while I worked, hacking rock out of hillsides and setting stones into walls. My friends hinted that I should remarry, but who would want to marry a poor stonemason with a small child? And why would I want a stepmother for Xing, when such women treat their stepchildren as badly as mothers-in-law treat the wives of their sons?

"Years passed, and Xing became a strong young man, while I quickly grew gnarled and withered through toil and care. When I suggested that he was old enough to work and that I would gladly teach him my trade, he hooted in disdain, 'There's no future in being a stonemason — unless you're satisfied with an empty purse and an aching back. Not I. I'm going to be rich!' When he went down to the river to swim, which he did often, I offered to buy him a bamboo raft so that he might become a fisherman. 'Fishing?' he exclaimed as if I'd gone mad. 'There's no money in that.'

"Every trade I mentioned he rejected, as though it were an insult, until one day recruiters from Hepu, a region along the coast famous for its pearl oyster beds, arrived in Guilin searching for novice divers. A good swimmer with powerful lungs, Xing decided that here was the opportunity he had been waiting for. 'If diving for pearls was so lucrative,' I asked him, 'why did the recruiters have to cast their nets as far as Guilin to collect new divers? Why didn't boys from Hepu jump at the chance to gather pearls for them? Because the South China Sea is given to sudden storms and treacherous currents,' I said, 'because the risks outweigh the rewards.' When reason failed to deter him, I pleaded with him to stay for my sake. At seventy, I was an old man who hoped my son would take care of me in my final years as I had cared for him all of his life. But Xing would not be dissuaded. I did, however, extract from him a promise: that in three years' time he would return.

"The morning of his leave-taking, again I implored: 'Remember your promise to return to Guilin in three years. That is all I ask of you.' Then I raised my walking stick and pointed to this hill where you and I now sit. 'At the end of three years you will find me there, waiting for you.' Xing fell on his knees and swore that he would return in three years' time. And so we parted."

The sun was at Lao Shi's back. I couldn't see his face, which was in shadow (the eyes had always been in shadow, beneath the ponderous brow), but I heard his labored, rhythmic breathing. With each inhalation, he gathered and ordered memory. With each exhalation, he gave memory speech.

"Will you help me tell the next part of the story?"

"Me?"

"You are a writer."

"But this is your story," I demurred. "How can I know what happened to you?"

"The next part of the story is what happened to Xing, and about that I have only clues and guesses, same as you. A myth doesn't come alive, which you have done for me, until the tale has both a teller and a listener, unless it evokes both memory and imagination. And unless it changes.

Myths survive because they evolve. They change with the teller, the listener, and the times."

"But what can I know about what happened to Xing?"

"What I've already told you about him and about me, what you know about diving for pearls and about the South China Sea, or what you can imagine. You see?" he said, chuckling, so that some loose rock dribbled down his chin. "Already you're looking out, like me, across the sea, looking for Xing. But unlike me, you see him."

I looked at Lao Shi doubtfully. "I do?" in surprise. "I do," in amazement. "I do. He's boarded a boat along with some other recruits. They've all been given a string bag for collecting oysters and a sharp knife for cutting them away from the coral seabed. The boat has reached Hepu and dropped anchor."

"Like the other divers, Xing has jumped overboard and now follows the older, experienced divers down, down to the oyster bed," Lao Shi continued, looking into the distance where my eyes had settled on the long, faint line of the horizon. "Suddenly, he feels a strong current. Through his goggles, he looks around him — where have all the other divers gone? — then above him. The huge shadow of a great shark glides by, creating a second strong current, and twitching between its jaws is one of the recruits. Panic-stricken, Xing drops his bag of oysters and follows the older divers who kick madly for the surface, where they're plucked out of the foaming water steeped in blood."

I picked up the thread of the story in the interstice of silence, which was followed by a sigh — a distant roar, then a hiss, like the bursting foam of a wave breaking upon a beach.

"The following day, Xing refuses to venture out in the boat. Instead, he practically hugs the shoreline, working the shallow beds of young oysters whose shells, once pried open, reveal pearls, if any pearls there are, no larger than a grain of sand. Week after week, he works the same shallow beds, earning barely enough to live on. When fully three years have passed . . ." I looked up at the old man, who continued:

"Xing is distraught, close to despair. The brutal wind whips his torn trousers about his knees and whistles around the corners of the flimsy hut he has built for shelter. He raises his arms above his head and cries: 'Father! Father! I have no money to keep my promise. Even if I did, how could I return to you like this, a failure?' He drags himself to a rocky ledge overlooking the sea where the surf spatters him with its chilling spray and his only thought is the simple desire to sink peacefully beneath the waves, when a blinding ball of light rises out of the sea. When Xing can open his eyes again, a beautiful woman is standing beside him and the once-furious water is smooth as glass. Stunned by the apparition and at the end of his tether, Xing pours out his heart to her: all the physical hardships he has endured and, finally, his unfulfilled promise whose deadline is that very day."

"The woman is touched by Xing's story," I said when Lao Shi paused, indicating I should continue, "particularly the sincerity with which he speaks about his about-to-be broken word. To help him keep it, she gives him a pearl the size of a litchi nut. She tells Xing that his father has grown very old since his departure and that he should set out immediately for Guilin. Then she disappears.

"Xing sells the pearl for several ounces of silver, enough for the journey home. But how can he face his father empty-handed? He must invest it, he decides, and make a profit, so that his father will be proud of him, so that all the misery of the past three years can be forgotten. With the silver, Xing buys a day's catch of fish straight off the wharf, which he takes to the city of Canton and sells. With the handsome profit he buys manufactured goods: tackle, rope, nets, canned goods, clothes. These he takes back to Hepu and sells at the marketplace, where his profits grow even greater. Great enough so that he buys himself a boat and sets himself up as a merchant selling and buying his way between Canton and Hepu. His profits continue to increase, almost exponentially and, with them, thoughts of taking a wife, one of the willowy beauties brought to his attention by several Cantonese matchmakers, who know a good catch when they see one. Thoughts of his father in far-off Guilin and his unkept promise grow fainter with every tael of silver he pockets, with every new deal he makes. Besides — and you'll excuse me for saying so, but the story requires me to say it — how can Xing possibly take his beautiful urbanite bride back to the rural home of an impoverished old stonemason?"

"An impoverished old stonemason who has hardly been idle since his son left," Lao Shi intervened authoritatively, a bit of pique flavoring his gravelly voice. "Oh, no, since Xing's departure, I worked harder than ever so I could buy a small plot of land that might root my son to Guilin, from which he would never stray again. Hacking and carving rock for this purpose was my sole hope, the one thing that kept me alive. Every tap of my hammer on my chisel

266

was one less second that I would have to wait for Xing's return, one more copper coin to purchase a piece of property to hold my son to native soil. The day you say the woman rose from the sea and appeared before Xing was the day I threw down my hammer and chisel and ran to this very hill where he would find me waiting for him. Whenever I saw a young man in the distance with a load over his shoulder, I waved and shouted, beside myself with gladness. But never were any of them Xing. And so I returned to this hill every day. And every day brought the same results. Other fathers whose sons had gone off to make their fortunes all had letters and gifts from them. I had only silence. Silence grew heavy on me. Heavy as my footsteps as I made my way up the hill to see if Xing had come home that day, then down the hill to my home knowing he had not. Until one day, having climbed the hill, I decided it would be for the last time. At sunset, instead of returning home, I sat where I am sitting now and vowed I would not budge until my son returned to me, even if it took forever. So here I sit, waiting still. I don't know when I turned to stone. Perhaps soon after my heart did."

We remained in silence for a few minutes, both of us gazing out over the South China Sea where the sun was slung low on its diurnal arc.

"Your son broke his promise to you, but it was out of an overdeveloped sense of ambition, of wanting to please you, to make you proud of him."

"Out of greed and self-importance," Lao Shi rackled, his chin set more solidly than ever.

"At least you have the pleasure of knowing that he was successful in what he chose to do," I replied.

"You say that because you feel the opposite about yourself. You displeased your father and your mother by your life choices, your familial transgressions. But just think. You gave your father the son you weren't and that your mother didn't. By not marrying, by carrying the onus of unwed mother, no small shame in Chinese society, you were able to become your father's 'son,' demonstrate your filial piety, and carry on the family name through a son of your own. You had to break an honored custom in order to fulfill a sacred duty, the foremost duty a son has toward his parents. To carry on the family name."

"I've never thought about it that way," I said, hoarsely. "I never thought about it, consciously, at all."

"And you came back to Guilin. You came back in your father's company. That meant more to him than if your novel had sold a million copies. What mattered is that you wrote it. You revealed your Chinese side. More than that, you appreciated it."

"He never read it."

"He died before he could. He read a third of it. Do you know how hard it is to read when you can't breathe? Try doing anything when you're suffocating."

"I know he read enough to tell me that I'd misspelled Nai-nai's given name."

"You spelled Nai-nai's name wrong."

My father was flipping through a copy of Bittersweet. *They were his first words regarding my book, which had just been published. They were more than a correction. They were an accusation, a reproof.*

"I deliberately changed Nai-nai's name so that I could write

about her in a fictional way, so I could write about her, and our family, at all."

"It's Xiuwen, not Xuewen."

"Stop pitying yourself. Think of it this way: that he gave your book that much attention. That he was searching for ways to say something, anything, to you that revolved around you and what mattered to you, and not him and his illness. He was not an articulate man, even in Chinese. He showed his love in other ways, maladroit though they were. It was for you to ferret them out, translate them. He hefted your novel and declared it 'solid as a rock.' Remember?'"

"I think I'd better be getting back." I stood up, opened my bag, and shoved my hand into it, feeling for paper and stone.

"We haven't finished the story yet. Please sit down."

I looked up at him, irritated, but I sat back down glumly, my legs splayed as when I was a child. I tossed a pebble on the ground in front of me, a chip off the old block. "My turn, or yours?"

"Mine, since I know how it ends. For both Xing and me. Successful, you say. Yes, more successful than you think and than I'd dreamed. The same year that I turned to stone, the Dragon King held a birthday party for himself and invited all the lesser dragons and water gods and goddesses, including the beautiful water spirit who had appeared before my son in his moment of need. As part of the celebration, the guests had to tell a story, a story that revolved around an event that had happened to them that year. A minor goddess who inhabited the Li River near Guilin chose to tell my story, of how I had turned into stone. The

Dragon King and everyone present, especially the water spirit, were appalled and incensed to learn of Xing's unfilial behavior, his broken promise and its terrible results. After the party ended, the water spirit swam to Hepu and inquired about my son's whereabouts. Told he was a rich merchant living in Canton, she swam upstream and appeared before him on his sumptuous boat, where he was busy writing up new orders. When he didn't recognize her, thought she was some groupie hoping to become part of his entourage, she spoke: 'You promised me that, with the pearl I gave you, you would leave immediately for Guilin and your father, to whom you had promised to return after three years. You broke your word not once but twice. Why didn't you return to Guilin?'

"Xing was silent, stunned by the woman's sudden apparition as well as her words, words that had to do with the past he'd rather forget and nothing to do with what was important to him now.

"'Your father has turned into stone waiting for you. And I am here to reclaim the pearl I gave you, believing that you were telling me the truth. Have you nothing to say for yourself?'

"Xing, forgetting where he had come from and remembering who he had become, finally spoke up. 'My father has turned into stone, you say? Saves me the expense of buying a casket, doesn't it? As for the pearl you gave, not lent, me, I thank you for your generosity. It's turned me into a very rich man.'

"The water spirit let out an angry, anguished howl that made the hairs on the nape of Xing's neck stand on end, then she vanished from sight. A storm blew up out of nowhere, churning the black water and frothing the dark waves that rose higher and higher over Xing's boat. A thick wall of water gathered and climbed with appalling speed, hovered over Xing's boat like a menacing ghost, then with its full force plummeted onto the deck with a thunderous roar, snapping the craft in two like a dry twig and sending it and everyone aboard to the bottom of the sea."

"My father requested that his ashes be scattered at sea," I murmured, after a while. "The moment we did, the water grew choppy. The boat pitched and yawed. We had to hold on to the railings and poles not to be thrown about, or off. The turbulence lasted for several minutes. It was a bit frightening, and somehow appropriate, as though my father were speaking, which he so rarely did. Making his presence known, now that he was absent. I'm sorry about your son."

"But satisfied with the story, I hope, though it lacks a happy ending."

"Are there endings to myths? They seem to go on and on, at least as they touch the lives of the living."

"And the dead, I assure you. Or not the dead, the mythic."

From my bag I extracted the requisite gifts, rock and paper. I felt that I had forgotten something. I should have brought an offering of food. Or had I forgotten on purpose, food propitiating both the living and the dead but not the mythic? The paper I'd brought with me was a preface, "Sucking on a Stone," the barest beginnings of a story, a tentative start, a promise, hopefully, of things to come. The rock was a stone given to me, not by my mother in the form of a story as was the preface but by Nai-nai in actual fact just before she left New York to return to Guilin. It was an oval piece of creamy-white, translucent jade the Chinese call "mutton fat" that fit snugly in the palm of my hand and caused my fingers to curl over it in a loose fist. It was carved to resemble a cicada. I extended both my hands, the one holding the rock, the other holding the paper, toward Lao Shi.

"You know, of course" — the way he said "of course" led me to believe that whatever it was I was supposed to know I didn't and that now he would tell me — "as all Chinese know, that the cicada is a symbol of regeneration and immortality. The insect sheds its skin at maturity, then sleeps underground for years before emerging into the world above. The ancient Chinese buried their dead with a piece of jade. They believed it prevented the body from decaying and that it guaranteed a fortuitous rebirth in the next life. The stone was cut and shaped to fit different parts of the body. For example, that cicada-shaped piece in your hand would be placed in the mouth of the deceased in the hope that he would speak in the hereafter. There it would become a 'tongue of jade,' an oracle or the vehicle for oracles. The best way to offer a gift is to wrap it, don't you think? A gift within and a gift without."

I looked at the objects in my hands and saw, finally, what he was alluding to. I began to fold the preface around the jade cicada to make it presentable, a present, although Lao Shi already knew what lay inside. Still, there was pleasure in revealing what is known as there was in what is unknown.

"They say that nothing is as solid as a rock, as enduring as stone. A book is only pages, thin, transient, torn, time-faded, tossed aside, or out. Pages of paper. Isn't that so?"

"Now you sound like my father." I folded the final flap and wound a few blades of long tough grasses growing at my feet around my offering, then tied them tight at the pointy top. The packet looked like a *zongzi*. I'd brought "food" after all, nourishment for the numinous.

"Then you must go back farther than your father. To your grandfather, who played finger games with you. Rock-scissors-paper, remember?"

"Yes. Scissors cuts paper," I said perfunctorily. "Rock smashes scissors. Paper enfolds rock." Then I realized: "Paper wins. Paper enfolds rock, every time."

"I accept your gifts, but I cannot take them. That is, you'll have to bring them to me to where I can use them."

"You mean I have to . . ."

"Will you? Place the cicada in my mouth? Note how jagged and squat my body is. Stepping-stones practically, and not too many of them. It shouldn't be difficult for you to climb up my back, across my chin, and crawl into my mouth."

It wasn't difficult at all. His back was gradually stepped, like a miniature Egyptian pyramid, and the sun was setting, so it was cool, with a gentle breeze blowing in from the sea. His neck and chin required a little bit of reconnaissance before I found the best route to his parted lips, where I threw a leg up, pulled my torso across, and crawled inside. Where I found myself reminded me of the kiva I once entered in the tufa cliff dwellings outside of Santa Fe — a tiny cave where members of a tribe of Amerindians long defunct purified their thoughts and meditated.

"I'm in." My voice resonated against the stone walls. "Now I know why they call it the 'mouth' of a cave," I couldn't resist saying.

"Are you afraid?" The rock floor vibrated slightly, less than a tremble, more like a buzz.

"No," I answered truthfully. "On the contrary, I like it in here. I feel safe and protected. It's like a womb, and the sea I see is the amniotic fluid. Just keep your voice low. And by all means, don't swallow."

"How about if I let you do all the talking? Read to me, will you? From the story on the paper around the stone."

"It's not a story. Only a potential story's possible beginning."

"Then begin at the beginning, if you please. Time stands still when one's being read to."

I cleared my throat. Lao Shi gathered his knees even tighter into his chest. The setting sun bathed both our faces with gold. The jade cicada was warm in my hand.

"When we were little, my mother thought of a uniquely devious way of getting my sisters and me to eat our dinner. It was usual at that time (the 1950s) for mothers of small children who were dilatory at the table to employ the classic admonition, 'Just think of the starving children in China.' Or India. Or Africa.

"My mother told us a story instead."